THE END OF RUSSIAN AMERICA

NORTH PACIFIC STUDIES

No.1

*Explorations of Kamchatka: North Pacific
Scimitar*. By Stepan P. Krasheninnikov.
Translated and edited by E.A.P. Crownhart-
Vaughan. OHS, 1972.

No.2

*Colonial Russian America: Kyrill T.
Khlebnikov's Reports, 1817-1832*. Trans-
lated and edited by Basil Dmytryshyn and
E.A.P. Crownhart-Vaughan. OHS, 1976.

No.3

*Voyages of Enlightenment: Malaspina on
the Northwest Coast. 1791/1792*. By Thomas
Vaughan, E.A.P. Crownhart-Vaughan, and
Mercedes Palau de Iglesias. OHS, 1977.

COVER:
New Arkhangel on Sitka Island, Alaskan headquarters
of the Russian American Company and of Russias's
colonial possessions in North America.
(From Duflot de Mofras,
Exploration de Territoire de L'Oregon)

THE END OF RUSSIAN AMERICA
CAPTAIN P. N. GOLOVIN'S LAST REPORT
1862

Translated
with
Introduction and Notes
by
Basil Dmytryshyn
and
E.A.P. Crownhart-Vaughan

Oregon Historical Society
Portland
1979

OBZOR RUSSKIKH KOLONII V SEVERNOI AMERIKE
[A Review of the Russian Colonies in North America]
by
Captain-Lieutenant
Pavel Nikolaevich Golovin
Published in:
MORSKOI SBORNIK, izdavaemyi pod nobliudeniem morskago
uchenago komiteta
Tom LVII
No. 2
Fevral
Sanktpeterburg
V tipografii Morskago Ministerstva
1862

LC 79-84285
ISBN 0-87595-084-1

CONTENTS

ILLUSTRATIONS

MAPS

PREFACE

In 1972 the Oregon Historical Society published the first volume in a new series entitled North Pacific Studies. The account by the young Russian explorer, Stepan P. Krasheninnikov, of a little known and important aspect of the 1741 Bering Expedition, *Explorations of Kamchatka, 1735-1741,* was a most appropriate inauguration for this series, for it embodies both aspects of providing rare and obscure source materials on the explorations of several nations in the North Pacific, and of translating foreign materials into English for the convenient access of scholars and others. The second volume, also a translation from the Russian, was Kyrill Khlebnikov's classic description, *Colonial Russian America, 1817-1832* (a companion volume of his study, prepared from the original manuscript sources, is in preparation). With the publication of the third title, the focus turned to Spanish explorations: *Voyages of Enlightenment: Malaspina on the Northwest Coast, 1791/1792.*

The present volume, the fourth, is Captain Pavel N. Golovin's official account of Russian America in 1861, on the eve of Russia's withdrawal from her American Colonies. The fifth title will be a companion to this, for it will present Golovin's unofficial view of the same mission, in the form of his personal correspondence to his mother and sister during this voyage of investigation. The intimate and highly entertaining letters in this volume, *Civil and Savage Encounters*, are unique for their revelations and observations of life, not only in Russian America, but in Europe, the eastern seaboard, Panama, Acapulco and San Francisco during 1860 and 1861. Among other manuscripts in preparation is the description and analysis of the *Logbook and Remarks* for the celebrated voyage of the American ship *Union* to the Northwest Coast, under John Boit, 1795-1797, edited by Edmund Hayes, Sr.

In all our translations our aim is to strive for absolute accuracy, yet to achieve, as best we are able, the same ease and flow of language that marks the erudite tone of the original works. For the convenience of the reader we have broken overly-long passages into paragraphs and have standardized punctuation. We use the Library of Congress system of transliteration, but omit ligatures and apostrophes. For clarity we use contemporary spellings for many place names such as Sitka, Kodiak and Alaska, rather than Sitkha, Kadiak, Aliaska. Where a place name has been changed, variants are given in a glossary.

Russian terms are explained in another glossary, which also includes equivalents of weights, measures, and a note on dates. Foreign words are underlined the first time they appear; all italics are those used by Golovin. Plurals of words retained in Russian are anglicized according to common English usage by adding "s", such as promyshlenniks and prikashchiks. All footnotes are Golovin's own, unless otherwise identified.

The success of this international editorial project is most profoundly indebted to the generous assistance and warm scholarly cooperation of many persons and institutions in North America and in the USSR. These include: The Geographical Society of the Academy of Sciences of the USSR, Leningrad: M. I. Belov and A. F. Treshnikov; Saltykov-Shchedrin State Public Library, Leningrad; Naval Museum, Leningrad: E. G. Kushnarev; Museum of Anthropology and Ethnography of the Academy of Sciences, Leningrad: R. V. Kinzhalov, E. V. Siebert, R. G. Liapunova and A. D. Dridzo; Lenin Library, Moscow: B. P. Kanevskii; Institute of Ethnography of the Academy of Sciences, Moscow; Institute of General History of the Academy of Sciences, Moscow: N. N. Bolkhovitinov; Zhdanov State University Library, Irkutsk; Far Eastern Sector of the Geographical Society, Khabarovsk. In Alaska, the Right Reverend Gregory, Russian Orthodox Bishop of Sitka and Alaska. In Canada, James R. Gibson of York University, Toronto. In Washington, D. C., Robert V. Allen of the Library of Congress. In Portland, Colonel M. J. Poniatowski-d'Ermengard. Our heartfelt thanks and gratitude go to all those persons associated with the Oregon Historical Society who have made this publication possible: Thomas Vaughan, Director and General Editor of North Pacific Studies; Priscilla Knuth and Bruce Hamilton, Editors; the Publications Committee under the chairmanship of William Swindells, Jr; Wendy Won and Louise Godfrey, manuscript and index preparators. The impetus for this entire program came from the dual cooperation of the Northwest Area Foundation of St. Paul, Minnesota, and the North Pacific [Irkutsk Archival] Research Group of the Oregon Historical Society, which has been so boldly chaired, first by John Youell, now by the Hon. Samuel S. Johnson; Jane West Youell and Elizabeth Johnson have also generously supported the production of this volume.

To all individuals and institutions mentioned, we extend our warmest thanks.

Basil Dmytryshyn
E. A. P. Crownhart-Vaughan

Portland, Oregon

INTRODUCTION

The reign of Alexander II (1855-1881) abounded in monumental developments which profoundly affected Russia's domestic and foreign policy. The most far-reaching of these domestic programs was the emancipation of the serfs in 1861, followed by the reform of the press, schools, local self-government, towns, courts and the military. These reforms ushered in a new era in Russian history. In the realm of the Tsar's foreign policy the most significant aspects were the annexation of large areas of central Asia, the Amur basin, the Maritime Province and Sakhalin Island, and the decision to sell the vast colonial possessions in North America to the United States.

In retrospect the sale of Alaska was among the most highly charged of these historical decisions. It removed Russia from the North American continent and placed the United States in firm command of the North Pacific littoral. Three basic factors influenced Russian resolve to dispose of her North American colonial possessions.

First, the colonial venture in America, while successful in its early stages, became a serious economic liability by the middle of the 19th century, thanks in part to: the inability of the bureaucratized Russian American Company to adjust to changed circumstances; the exhausted supply of fur-bearing animals; the difficulty of supplying the distant region with competent personnel and requisite provisions; and the lack of interest and support by the government for the American colonial enterprise and its increasingly expensive social welfare demands.

Second, the Crimean War (1853-1856) exposed the vulnerability of the remote Pacific region as well as Russia's inability to defend it. Much has been written about the war from the point of view of the campaigns in the Black, Baltic and White seas; the hard-pounding follies of Lord Cardigan and the dashing but ill-fated Light Brigade have been immortalized along with the vicissitudes of Balaklava and Sevastopol. However, notably few accounts deal in any depth with the campaign in the Pacific. Few historians mention the fact that a significant Anglo-French squadron, staging out of the Hawaiian Islands in two successive years, maneuvered in the Sea of Okhotsk off the east coast of Siberia and the elusive Amur River mouth. The squadron eventually bombarded

and invested the supposedly impregnable harbor of Petropavlovsk on Kamchatka
where a small Russian squadron was based, captured a vital Russian American
Company supply ship, Sitka, and briefly occupied the harbor of Aian in Siberia,
as well as the Kuril Island of Urup.

Third, the emancipation of serfs and the reforms that followed forced
Russian officials, from the Emperor down, to concentrate on urgent matters in
the European part of the Empire, rather than in distant Alaska.

The decision to sell Alaska was not sudden. As early as December 1856
the Emperor's brother, Grand Duke Constantine, head of the powerful State
Council, sent a memorandum to the Foreign Office urging that consideration be
given to the matter of liquidating Russia's interest in her American colonies.
This precipitated a full scale government review both in Alaska and in St.
Petersburg in order to identify problems, search for options, and discuss
possible solutions. The fact that the charter of the Russian American Company
was due to expire in 1862 added to the urgency of finding a solution.

The three year period from 1861 to 1864 saw the publication in Russia of
several volumes of richly informative reports on Russian America; an astonish-
ing amount of literature when compared to the total official information
published during the preceding 60 years from the time of the chartering of the
Russian American Company in 1799.

The massive and compendious two volume work by Petr A. Tikhmenev,
Istoricheskie Obozrenie Obrazovaniia Rossiisko-Amerikanskoi Kompanii [Historical
review of the founding of the Russian American Company], 1861-63, gave the
public the first detailed picture of the commercial operation of the Company
from its inception to 1860. However, because Tikhmenev was an official of the
Company, many felt his account biased. A supplement to the official journal of
the Naval Ministry, *Morskoi Sbornik* [Naval Anthology], was published in four
parts in 1861-62 as "Materialy dlia istorii russkikh zaselenii po beregam
vostochnago okeana" [Materials for the history of Russian settlements on the
shores of the Pacific Ocean]. These materials included Kyrill T. Khlebnikov's
valuable "Zapiski K. Khlebnikova, o Amerike,"* Vasilii M. Golovnin's "Zapiski
kapitana 2 ranga Golovnina o nyneshnem sostoianii Rossiisko-Amerikanskoi
companii...1818" [The report of Captain Golovnin on the present condition of
the Russian American Company...1818] and a number of important descriptions of
early voyages to Alaska and the Pacific Northwest made by Russian and other
seafarers. The present work by Captain Pavel N. Golovin was published in
Morskoi Sbornik in 1862.

Concurrently with these publications the Russian government conducted its
own thorough review of the entire colonial enterprise. In May 1860 the

---

*English translation, *Colonial Russian America: Kyrill T. Khlebnikov's Reports,
1817-1832*. Translated with introduction and notes by Basil Dmytryshyn and
E. A. P. Crownhart-Vaughan. Oregon Historical Society, Portland, 1976.

the Ministry of Finance, on instructions from the Emperor, sent Active State Councillor Sergei Kostlivtsov to Alaska on a fact-finding mission. At the request of Grand Duke (also General-Admiral) Constantine, the Naval Ministry appointed Captain Pavel N. Golovin to accompany Kostlivtsov and to provide his own independent analysis of the situation. Upon their return from Alaska in October 1861 both men submitted full and detailed reports to their respective authorities: Kostlivtsov to the Ministry of Finance and Golovin to the Naval Ministry. Golovin's report, which is presented here for the first time in English translation, was published immediately, in February 1862, in *Morskoi Sbornik.*

Pavel Nikolaevich Golovin, the author of the present work, was a career naval officer, the descendant of two old and distinguished Russian noble families, the Kholmskois and the Golovins, who had for generations served the Empire in many capacities. Golovin was born in 1823 and was educated in the Aleksandrovskii Military Academy and then in the Naval Academy, from which he graduated in 1837. He was assigned to the Baltic Fleet and cruised the Baltic, North and Mediterranean seas. His rise in rank was steady. In 1844 he was promoted to Lieutenant, in 1853 to Captain Lieutenant, and a year later was made Senior Adjutant of the Inspector's Department of the Naval Ministry. In January of 1862, having just recently returned from his arduous voyage to Alaska, Golovin was given another assignment in the frozen Baltic, in the course of which he fell ill with pneumonia. In spite of this he continued on assignment to Hamburg where his condition became critical, with liver involvement and edema complicating an already serious situation. He returned to St. Petersburg weak and beyond recovery and died three days later.

As in the case of Kyrill Khlebnikov, our subject has never been included in the *Bolshaia Sovetskaia Entsiklopediia*; coupled with the fact that he died when he was just 39, biographical information about him is fragmentary. One notable exception is a brief reminiscence by his close friend and naval colleague, Rear Admiral Voin A. Rimskii-Korsakov, elder brother of the famed composer. According to Rimskii-Korsakov, Golovin loved Navy life and was a poet and composer of songs about the sea, which he had begun to write as early as 1839. Golovin also had a great talent for writing in an enthusiastic yet realistically detailed manner. This talent is evident in the numerous biographical articles he wrote about celebrated naval officers, which appeared in *Morskoi Sbornik* in the mid 1850s. These accounts were well received in naval circles and widely read throughout Russia.

Rimskii-Korsakov also relates that Golovin was a lively, cultured, very popular individual, always a bright spark in any group. In contrast to some young officers, who were only ambitious for rank, promotion, and decorations, Golovin enjoyed all the pleasures and stimulations his many and varied assignments offered. He loved wine, song, fine food, good conversation, new experiences. Yet he was always a disciplined officer and meticulously carried out every military assignment. As a result, even as a young man, he was given many difficult and important assignments, culminated by the longest and most trying, this voyage to Alaska on behalf of the Naval Ministry.

To accelerate his journey to Alaska, Golovin opted to travel west instead of the slower land journey across Siberia. The trip to Alaska took Golovin through Germany, Belgium, France, England, across the Atlantic to Boston, New York, Philadelphia and Washington. From there he went to Panama, overland to the Pacific, and visited Acapulco and San Francisco en route to Sitka. He followed the same route for his return trip. On this journey he was accompanied by Kostlivtsov, his counterpart representing the Ministry of Finance.

From various points along the route, Golovin sent home to his widowed mother and his sister lengthy informal and highly descriptive letters detailing the progress of his trip. These letters are extremely rich since they provide beautiful descriptions of people, scenes, events and situations he encountered. The Oregon Historical Society is most fortunate to possess copies of these letters, which are currently being edited and translated and will appear in a forthcoming volume in the North Pacific Studies series.

Golovin's report consists of four sections: In the first, he considers the founding and early activity and problems of the Russian American Company; the second analyzes the climate, resources and both the subjugated and hostile native populations of the region; in the third he critically reviews the educational, religious, industrial and commercial activities of the Company within the colonies, and its trade with California and China; in the final part he offers a number of recommendations which would, if implemented, put the entire region on a sound economic and administrative basis, free of interference by the bureaucratic establishment. Some of the more interesting and significant threads which run through his entire report are his concern for the wellbeing of the native population, his awareness of the abundance of natural resources of the region and the latter's potential to supply the Asiatic portion of the Russian Empire.

When his report was published, it aroused great interest among the educated Russian public, as evidenced by the number of reviews and letters which soon appeared in such journals as *Severnaia Pchela, Russkii Mir, Kronshtadskii Vestnik, Moskovskie Vedomosti* and *Morskoi Sbornik* itself.

Although Golovin was in some ways critical of the Russian American Company, in general his was not a seriously derogatory critique of its activities. For this reason it aroused violent anger and resentment among some persons opposed to Company activities and policies. The most outspoken of these was Aleksandr F. Kashevarov, a creole (of mixed Russian and Alaskan native parentage), who had been educated in St. Petersburg at the Kronstadt Navigation College, had performed valiantly as a navigator and cartographer during his service with the Company in Alaska, and was at that time living in St. Petersburg where he was compiling an atlas of the Pacific Ocean.

Kashevarov prepared a slashing, bitterly critical reponse to Golovin's report, detailing the true picture of the Company's treatment of native Alaskans and revealing abuses which had never before been made public. But before Kashevarov's reply was set in type, Golovin suddenly died. Kashevarov, unwilling to criticize a dead man so critically, rewrote his article. But even his modified remarks incurred harsh counterreactions, some of which cast aspersions on his parentage. At this point Baron Ferdinand von Wrangell entered the debate. In a letter to *Morskoi Sbornik* he declared that as former Chief Administrator of the Russian American Company he held the Company in higher regard than Kashevarov. However, von Wrangell in all honesty conceded that the latter's accusations were founded in fact. Von Wrangell's remarks carried great weight, and in light of intense emotional reaction attendant upon the emancipation of serfs the previous year, public as well as official opinion became extremely critical of the now revealed situation.

The question of finding a solution to the problem of the future of the Russian colonies in North America was referred to a committee of 14 distinguished men, including government officials, scientists, and members of the Russian American Company itself. The committee considered the reports of Khlebnikov, Tikhmenev, Golovin and Kostlivtsov, and the opinions of former Chief Administrators of the Company, von Wrangell, Adolph Etolin and Ivan Furuhelm. The deliberations of this committee, and its report, were published as a compendious two-volume work in 1863 by the Department of Foreign Commerce. The volumes are entitled *Doklad komiteta ob ustroistve Russkikh Amerikanskikh kolonii* [Report of the committee on the organization of the Russian American colonies]. This work is being edited and translated into English for the first time, and will be published as part of the North Pacific Studies series.

All these accounts, previously unavailable in English, give a new dimension to an important period in Russian-American relations, and to a feverishly debated period in American history.

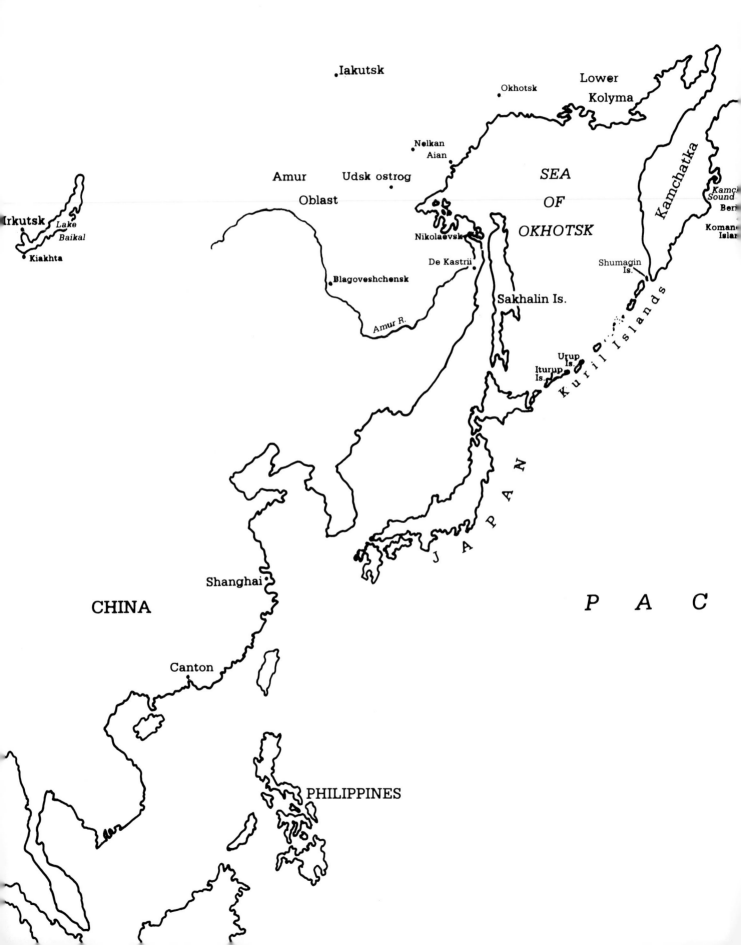

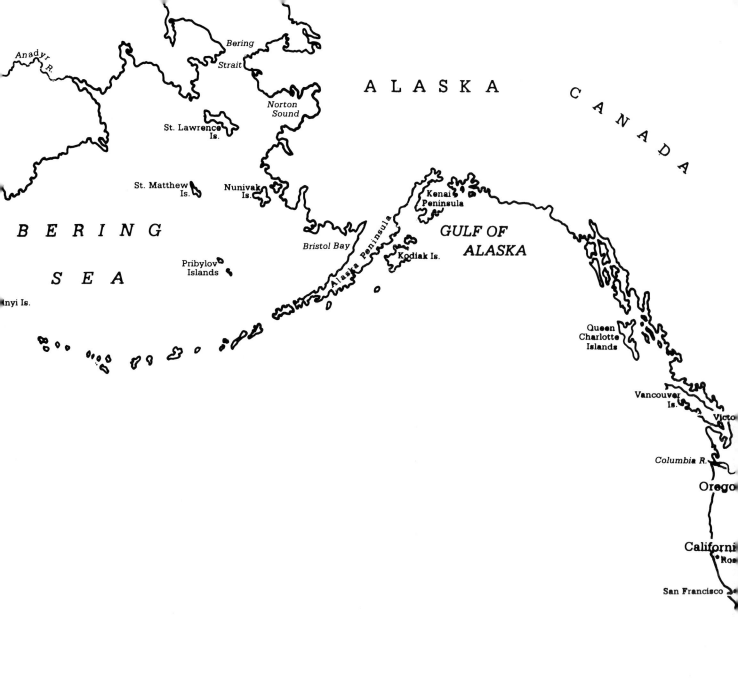

Anadyr R.

Bering
Strait

Norton
Sound

St. Lawrence
Is.

ALASKA

CANADA

St. Matthew
Is.

Nunivak
Is.

Kenai
Peninsula

GULF OF
ALASKA

B E R I N G

Bristol Bay

Kodiak Is.

S E A

Alaska Peninsula

Pribylov
Islands

Queen
Charlotte
Islands

nyi Is.

Vancouver
Is.

Victo

Columbia R.

Orego

California

Ros

San Francisco

I C   O C E A N

Sandwich
Islands

THE RUSSIAN NORTH PACIFIC

Place names are those used by P. N. Golovin in his *Report*.
For current name, where different, see Place Name Glossary. Additional places have been identified for clarity.

CC '79

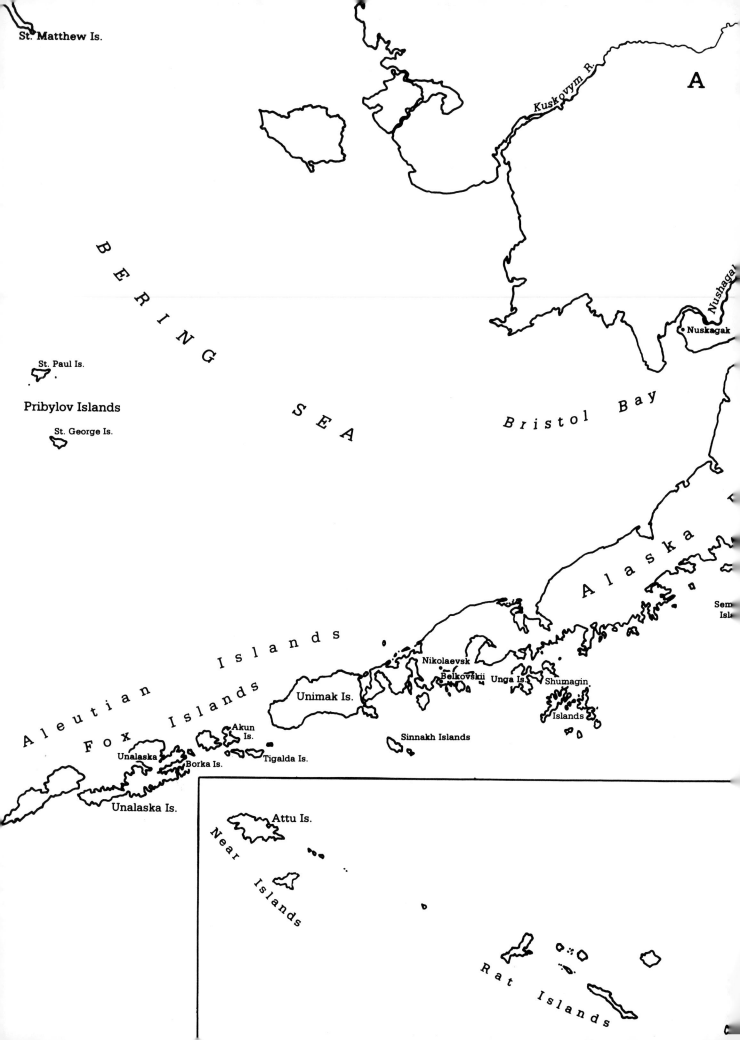

St. Matthew Is.

Kuskovym R.

A

B E R I N G

Nushagak

• Nuskagak

St. Paul Is.

Pribylov Islands

S E A

Bristol Bay

St. George Is.

Alaska

Sem
Isl

A l e u t i a n   I s l a n d s

Nikolaevsk

Belkovskii

Unga Is.

Shumagin

F o x   I s l a n d s

Unimak Is.

Islands

Akun
Is.

Sinnakh Islands

Unalaska

Tigalda Is.

Borka Is.

Unalaska Is.

Attu Is.

N e a r

I s l a n d s

R a t   I s l a n d s

A L A S K A

Susitna Glacier

Plavezhnoi Lake

Tleieshitna R.

Susitna R.

Knyk R.

Copper R.

Cook Inlet

Nikolaevsk

Kirinsk R.

Georgievsk

Kenai

Chugach Sound

Konstantin Is.

Konstantin (redoubt)

Konstantin Harbor

Simeonovsk

Peninsula

Voskresensk

Kenai Bay

Cape Saint Elias

Lake Iliamna

Coal Cove
English Bay

Aleksandrovsk

GULF OF ALASKA

sula

Strait

Katmai

Afognak Is.

Shelikhov

Elovoi (Elovka) Is.

Pavlovsk

Lesnoi Is.
Pavlovsk Harbor

Karluk

Kodiak Is.

Three Saints Bay

CC '79

amok Is.

SOUTHERN ALASKA
THE HEART OF RUSSIAN AMERICA

Place names are those used by P. N. Golovin in his *Report*.
For current name, where different, see Place Name Glossary. Additional places have been identified for clarity.

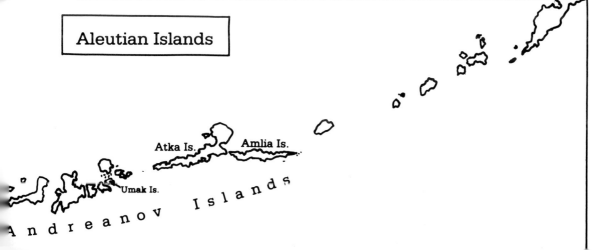

Aleutian Islands

Atka Is.

Amlia Is.

Umak Is.

Andreanov Islands

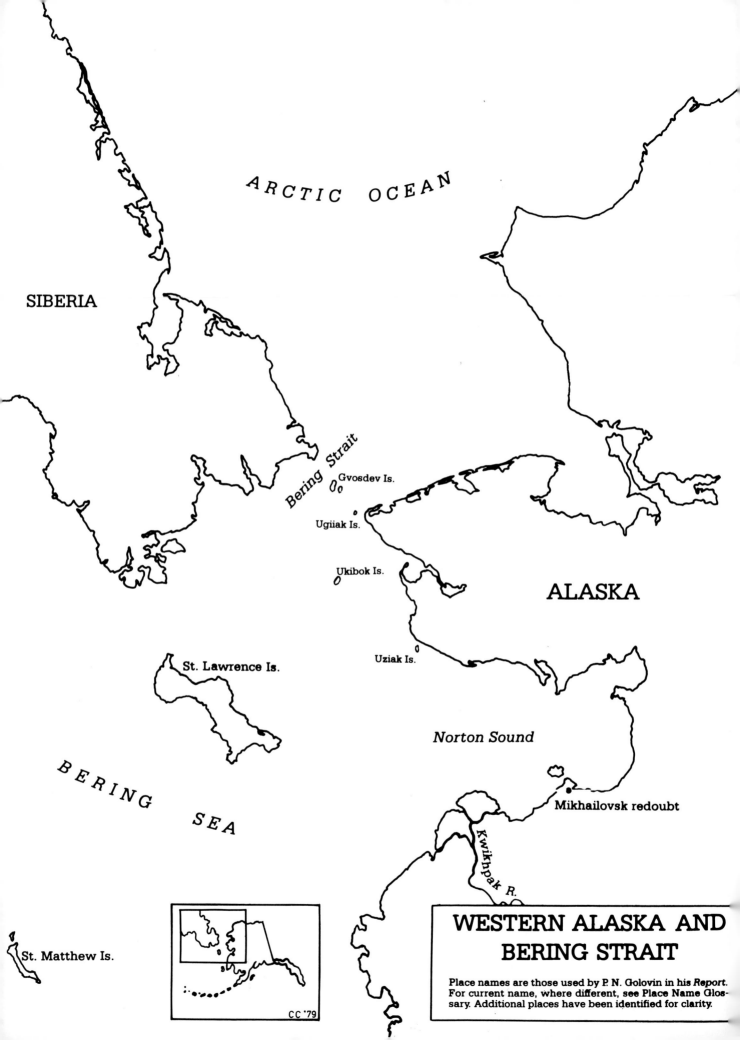

ARCTIC OCEAN

SIBERIA

Bering Strait

Gvosdev Is.

Ugiiak Is.

Ukibok Is.

ALASKA

Uziak Is.

St. Lawrence Is.

Norton Sound

B E R I N G

S E A

Mikhailovsk redoubt

Kwikhpak R.

St. Matthew Is.

CC '79

WESTERN ALASKA AND BERING STRAIT

Place names are those used by P. N. Golovin in his *Report*. For current name, where different, see Place Name Glossary. Additional places have been identified for clarity.

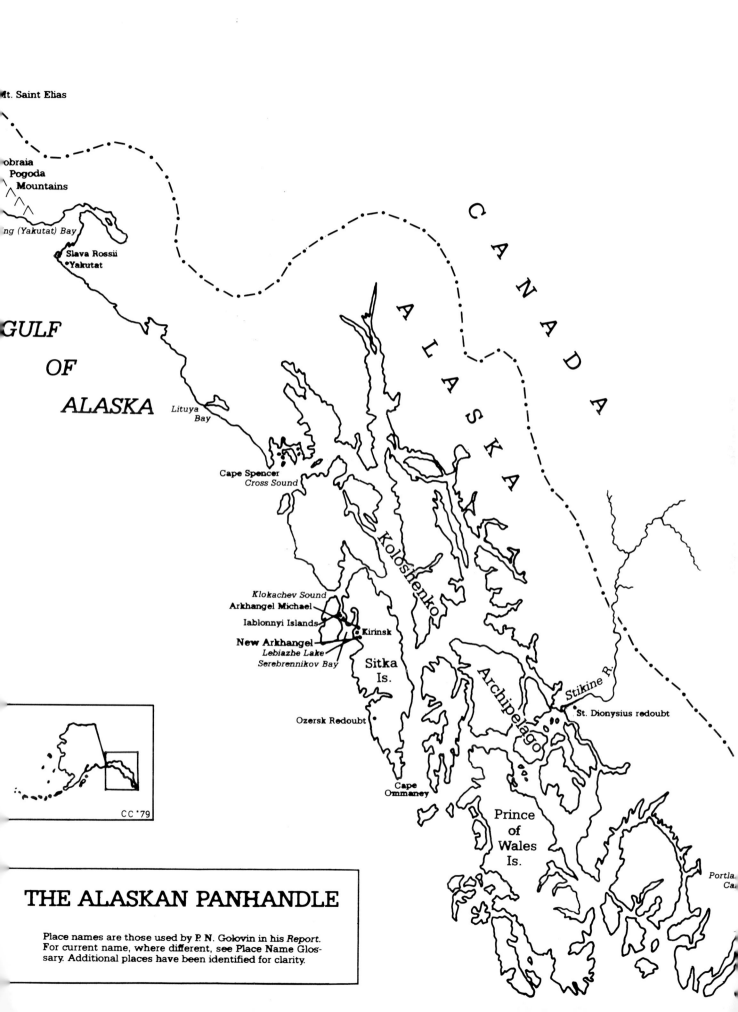

Mt. Saint Elias

obraia
Pogoda
Mountains

ng (Yakutat) Bay

Slava Rossii
•**Yakutat**

GULF

OF

ALASKA

C A N A D A

A
L
A
S
K
A

*Lituya
Bay*

Cape Spencer
Cross Sound

Koloshenko

Klokachev Sound
Arkhangel Michael
Iablonnyi Islands
•**Kirinsk**
New Arkhangel
Lebiazhe Lake
Serebrennikov Bay

**Sitka
Is.**

Archipelago

Stikine R.

•St. Dionysius redoubt

Ozersk Redoubt•

Cape
Ommaney

**Prince
of
Wales
Is.**

*Portla.
Ca.*

CC '79

THE ALASKAN PANHANDLE

Place names are those used by P. N. Golovin in his *Report*.
For current name, where different, see **Place Name Glos-**
sary. Additional places have been identified for clarity.

New Arkhangel on Sitka Island, Alaskan headquarters
of the Russian American Company and of Russia's
colonial possessions in North America.
(From Duflot de Mofras,
Exploration de Territoire de L'Œregon)

THE ARRIVAL OF THE RUSSIANS
IN THE ALEUTIAN ISLANDS

The Aleutian Islands were discovered by Captain [Vitus] Bering in 1741. At the same time Captain [Aleksei] Chirikov, who had been sent out together with Bering for purposes of exploration, became separated from the expedition, and while searching for it, sighted the Northwest Coast of America between 48° and 49° of northern latitude. Furs brought back to Russia by crew members from the ships of that expedition and accounts of newly discovered islands awakened the spirit of enterprise among many Russian merchants and service persons in Siberia. Of the latter [Emelian S.] Basov, a sergeant in the Kamchatka command, was the first to try his luck. He built a boat called a shitka [sewed]* because it was sewed together with whale whiskers, and called it Kapiton. In 1743 he undertook the first voyage to Bering Island.

Following Basov, other promyshlenniks set out for the Aleutian Islands, either outfitting ships at their own expense or organizing small companies on a share basis. In 1764 the Russian government granted the privilege of exclusive hunting and trapping rights on the Aleutian Islands to a company formed by the merchants [Emilian] Iugov and [Nikifor] Trapeznikov, on the condition that they collect iasak from the native inhabitants for the government, and that in addition they pay into the state Treasury one-tenth of their own catch. Subsequently however, in 1779 to be precise, the collection of iasak was entirely done away with.

One can understand how expeditions that were outfitted for hunting by persons who did not have adequate financial backing, and were only concerned with making a profit, did not always meet with success. Ships which were poorly fitted out and even more poorly handled were wrecked while sailing in those unknown and inhospitable waters. But in spite of this, the amount of furs taken was considerable, and this attracted bold spirits.

---

* Russian terms are underlined when first used; terms used only once are explained within brackets; terms used more than once appear in the Glossary; Russian sources for some translations are placed in brackets; some others have resisted translation.--Eds.

Grigorii Shelikhov [1747?-95], a merchant from Rylsk, was the first to realize the size of the profit it was possible to make from the newly discovered land, if one had enough means to outfit expeditions in a proper manner and to organize permanent factories, not only on the Aleutian Islands, but along the Northwest Coast of America as well. Pursuing this objective, Shelikhov, together with Captain Mikhailov and the merchant Ivan Golikov, organized their own company. In 1783 Shelikhov had three <u>galiots</u> built in Okhotsk, and set out with 190 promyshlenniks for Kodiak Island. He anchored there in a bay which he named Three Saints Bay. He began to build small forts on various sites and set up factories, first on Kodiak, Afognak and Unalaska, then in Kenai Bay and Chugach Sound. He returned to Okhotsk in 1786.

Ivan Golikov's self-serving activities were detrimental to the interest of the company, and in 1795 Shelikhov had to organize a general commercial office in Irkutsk so that the supervision of affairs could be entrusted to special administrators under the overall direction of Shelikhov himself. When Shelikhov died that same year, the affairs of the company were almost totally disrupted because of Golikov's efforts and interference. However Shelikhov's family managed to resolve the crisis, and in 1797 a new company was organized with its head office in Irkutsk, and this undertaking was successful.

Kolosh stone carving of a Russian soldier in New Arkhangel.

THE ORGANIZATION OF THE RUSSIAN AMERICAN COMPANY,
PRIVILEGES AND VARIOUS ADVANTAGES GRANTED TO IT
BY THE GOVERNMENT

Irkutsk authorities informed Emperor Paul I of the organization and activity of the new company, and in accordance with the example of foreign companies, he authorized the company to draw up permanent rules of operation and to submit them to the Commerce College for their review. In accordance with this authorization, the company, under the name of the United American Company, prepared a document in which it outlined the basic points for organization, regulations for administering the office, election of directors, the obligation of the Company to enlarge its settlements and commercial operations, to discover new lands and islands, spread the Christian faith, enter into trade relations with the inhabitants of the newly discovered lands, and to develop Russia's trade in the Pacific. Emperor Paul I approved this document and took the company under his patronage and directed regulations and privileges be drawn up for it for a twenty-year period. On July 8, 1799* he approved these privileges. From that time on the company was known as the Russian American Company; among its other privileges it was given the right to extend Russia's possessions along the Northwest Coast of America not only north of 55° latitude, but south as well, providing this seemed both advantageous and possible, and these lands were not already occupied by other nations.

An Imperial decree of October 19, 1800 ordered that the Governing Board be transferred to St. Petersburg, and that a special office be maintained in Irkutsk. Meanwhile the shares of the Company increased in value more than 200% over the original cost, and therefore, for the more convenient sale of the remaining shares, in August 1801 the Emperor permitted them to be split into shares of 500 rubles, of which 7,350 were to be issued.

In 1802 Emperor Alexander I was pleased to increase the Company's capital by 10,000 rubles when he purchased 20 of these shares to benefit the poor. His

---

* When Golovin gives a single date, it is according to the Julian calendar, which was in official use in Russia from 1700 to January 26, 1918; in the author's time the Julian calendar was 12 days behind the Gregorian calendar already in use in Europe. Golovin sometimes gives dual dates to indicate this difference.--Eds.

example was followed by the Empress and by the heir apparent. By these means,
thanks to government action, the Company's capital increased significantly in a
short time. But the government did not stop at this. In order to enable the
Company to send ships from Kronshtadt to the colonies, in August 1802 the Emperor authorized a loan bank to lend the Company 250,000 rubles for a period of
eight years at the current interest rate. In March 1803 a sum of 100,000
rubles was authorized to be issued from the ekskontnoi office; in June
1806 an additional 200,000 rubles from the same office, for the customary use
of the Company, with the usual interest deduction; the sum was to be issued upon
the request of the Governing Board of the Company. In the same year a special
flag was given to Company ships. In addition, the government authorized naval
officers and lower rank personnel to be released for service on Company ships,
on the basis of a decree of April 9, 1802. These privileges were renewed on
January 1, 1822 for a period of 20 years* and then were renewed for a second 20
years beginning January 1, 1842.**

---

* The Emperor approved these on September 13, 1821.
**The Emperor reviewed and approved these in 1844, but it was decided to consi-
der them effective as of January 1, 1842.

Kolosh warrior in battle costume,
with slat armor and wooden mask.
Drawing made from Voznesenskii
Coll. of Museum of Anthropology
and Ethnography of the Academy of
Science of the USSR, Leningrad.
(S.A. Shternberg, *Otdel Severnoi
ameriki*, Leningrad, 1929)

THE ESTABLISHMENT OF SETTLEMENTS

It is clear that in supporting the Company, the government intended to extend Russian influence in the Pacific as well as in China and Japan, and with the assistance of the colonies, to stimulate trade in distant Siberia. For its part, the Company understood very well both the intent of the government and its own special interest; using the privileges granted to it, the Company began to establish permanent settlements both on the Aleutian Islands and along the American coast. Some of these were in places where settlements had already been established by earlier promyshlenniks and companies. Some were in new areas better suited for developing trade with the natives and extending influence over them, as well as for developing agriculture and livestock breeding.

By 1819 the Company had settlements on the Komandorskie Islands, on Atka, Unalaska, St. Paul, St. George, Kodiak and Baranov or Sitka Island; on the American coast on Kenai Bay there were redoubts and odinochki at Pavlovsk, Georgievsk, Aleksandrovsk and Voskresensk; in Chugach Sound at Konstantin and Elena; in Bering Bay or Yakutat Bay at Nikolaevsk; and near Cape Saint Elias at Simeonovsk. There had been an earlier settlement called Slava Rossii in Yakutat Bay, but it had been destroyed by the Kolosh [Tlingits] in 1803 and was never rebuilt. On the island of Urup, the eighteenth of the Kurils, a settlement was destroyed by the people who lived there because of the bad management of the prikashchik whom the Company had placed there. Lastly, in 1812 the Company established the small Ross settlement in California on the shore of New Albion in 38°34" northern latitude and 122°32" western longitude, for the purpose of developing agriculture and stockbreeding, in order to assure a food supply there for colonies whose climatic conditions prevented these pursuits. It is true that at first the Ross settlement occupied only a small area, but by 1817 the Indians who held the land near Ross expressed their willingness to the administrator of the settlement, Lieutenant [Leontii] Hagemeister, to give the Company as much land as was needed. The hunt for sea and river otters along the California coast provided a substantial profit.

When the Company established the Ross settlement, they did not ask permission of the Spanish government that at that time controlled California, and the Catholic missionaries and officials of the California Presidio regarded the expanding Russian settlement with distrust. There were no quarrels, however, until Mexico and California broke off with Spain. When Mexico declared her independence, the new government claimed the Ross settlement and demanded that the Russians give it up. These importunities produced no results until the Company, receiving no support from the Russian government, realized that the Ross settlement was bringing no profit because of poor management and in 1835 decided to sell *all the property and livestock* in the Ross settlement to a Mexican subject, [John] Sutter,* for the sum of 42,857.14 silver rubles.**

---

* Sutter paid off part of that sum at various times. According to Bodisco, the Russian envoy to the United States, the Company authorized the Russian consul in San Francisco, an American named Stewart, to obtain $15,000 still outstanding from Sutter. Stewart disappeared with the money he had received from Sutter. Thus taking into account all the expenses involved in sending persons to California to try to locate the Sutter money, according to Company records the amount still owed to the Company for the sale of Ross is 37,484.45 paper rubles.

**Technically, until 1897 Russia was on the silver standard. However from the reign of Catherine II until the mid 19th century, during the reign of Alexander II, the Russians resorted to issuing paper rubles to finance their constantly growing deficit. Both fluctuated greatly at home and abroad, but generally the ratio was one to three.--Eds.

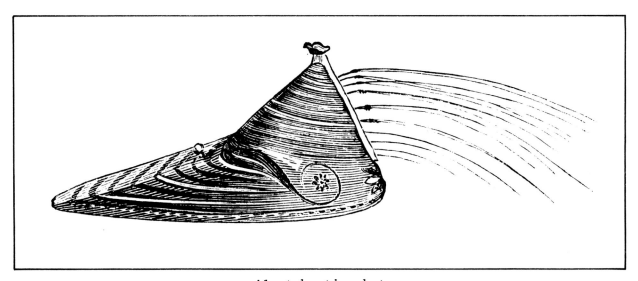

Aleut hunting hat.

DISAGREEMENTS WITH ENGLAND AND THE UNITED STATES OF AMERICA; THE FINAL DETERMINATION OF THE BOUNDARIES OF RUSSIA'S POSSESSIONS IN NORTH AMERICA

At the time when the English Hudson's Bay Company and the American Northwest Company were arguing over the boundaries of their possessions on the Columbia River and in Oregon, whaling ships of those powers and various adventurers appeared along the boundaries of our possessions, killing whales, buying furs from the natives and supplying them with liquor and firearms, to the obvious detriment and danger of our Company. The Russian American Company requested protection by the government. By an ukaz of September 4, 1821, Emperor Alexander I declared that all Russian possessions along the Northwest Coast of America from Bering Strait in 51° of northern latitude, along the Aleutian Islands, the eastern coast of Siberia, and the Kuril Islands from Bering Strait to the southern tip of the island of Urup, that is, to 45°51" northern latitude, as well as whaling, fishing and hunting rights on the islands, in the harbors, bays and throughout the extent of these possessions, were all reserved for the exclusive use of Russian subjects. At the same time the decision was made to send naval cruisers to our colonies, with instructions to remain there and seize all foreign ships that were hunting or trading within the boundaries of our colonies. Upon review by a special commission, they were to be subjected to a special monetary fine or to confiscation.

In accordance with this decree the American brig Pearl of Boston, which had sailed to Sitka to trade, was seized. The American government protested the prohibition on hunting and trading within the limits of the Russian possessions, and also the establishment of the boundaries of these possessions at the fifty-first degree of northern latitude on the American coast, basing its protest on Paragraph I of the privileges that Emperor Paul I had granted the Russian American Company, in which the boundary line of our possessions on the Northwest Coast of America had been set at 55° of northern latitude,* beyond

---

* The point on the Northwest Coast of America that had been determined by Captain Chirikov and accepted as a discovery made by the Russians was set on the map by the Academician [Gerhard F.] Müller at 55° of northern latitude; however when Chirikov sighted the American coast, he set his location at 48°. A sloop

which the Russians were not to go, having made no further discoveries at that time. Furthermore, the Americans had always taken advantage of free trade in those waters, and thus could not be restricted in this regard by any nation.

England also protested, since by setting the boundary south of the 55th parallel Russia appropriated for herself a part of the American coast that had been claimed by Hudson's Bay Company, which also had been trading with the savages who inhabited Russian possessions.

Negotiations proceeded for some time, and ended finally with the conclusion of a Convention with the United States on April 5, 1824 and with England on February 16, 1825. The first Convention delineated the boundary of Russian possessions along 54°40" north latitude. Both Russian and American subjects, for a period of ten years, were to have the right to sail freely, to fish and to trade with the natives in all areas of the Great or Pacific Ocean that were not occupied by either of the signatory powers. After the conclusion of this convention, the American ship Pearl of Boston was released.

In the convention with England the boundaries of the Russian possessions were more specifically delineated: beginning at the southernmost extremity of Prince of Wales Island, below 54°40" north latitude and between 131° amd 133° west longitude from Greenwich, the line of demarcation follows north along Portland Canal to a point on the mainland where it touches 56° north latitude. From there the line follows along the watershed of the mountains, which lie parallel to the shore, but does not extend inland more than ten leagues from the coast to the point of intersection with 141° west longitude. And finally, from that point, the 141st meridian forms the Russian boundary along the Northwest Coast of America all the way to the Arctic Ocean.* Navigation and trade rights for both nations in those regions were set forth, and in Paragraph VII, freedom of navigation and trade within our possessions and England's was given to ships of the treaty powers for a ten-year period only. On the basis of these terms, the port of New Arkhangel was open to English ships with the sole proviso that if, after a period of ten years, Russia should give a similar privilege to any other nation, then that privilege should be extended to English vessels as well. In accordance with Paragraph IX, both countries bound themselves not to sell the savages hard liquor, firearms or other weapons, powder and so forth.

---

that Chirikov sent to shore under the command of navigator Avraam Dementiev and twelve oarsmen did not return, which was also true of three men sent ashore the second day to search for Dementiev. The former Russian ambassador to Madrid, Zinovev, reported on February 26, 1789, that the ship St. Charles, under the command of Captain Goro, had found some eight [sic] settlements near San Blas [sic], between 48° and 49° of northern latitude; and that in each of the settlements there were from sixteen to twenty families, that is, 462 Russians. This is the reason that the Company maintains that the actual boundary of our possessions in America should be between 48° and 49°, and not at 55°, as erroneously stated in the privileges that Emperor Paul I granted to the Company.

* Golovin clearly delineates the boundaries of the Alaska Panhandle.--Eds.

When the ten-year period expired, the Russian government announced that free navigation for foreign ships within the limits of our possessions would henceforth cease. The American envoy in St. Petersburg requested that the terms of the convention be extended for some time, but his request was denied. He protested, but the Russian government remained firm in its decision, and the Americans were forced to yield, especially after a Hudson's Bay Company ship, which had been outfitted for the purpose of establishing a factory on the Stikine River with the intention of diverting trade with the natives into the hands of the English, was prevented by the Russians from reaching is destination.

During the time we were negotiating with the Americans, the English government found it opportune to act. Hudson's Bay Company threatened to seize the mouth of the Stikine River, located within Russia's possessions, and build a fort and factory there for the purpose of trading with the natives. Since the Stikine River flows through territory belonging to the English, and only its mouth lies within Russia's possessions, and since according to the terms of the convention with England the English had the right of free navigation on such rivers, Hudson's Bay Company hoped that the ship it had outfitted would enter the Stikine River freely and carry out its task. But news of the English intention reached New Arkhangel. Baron von Wrangell, at that time Chief Manager of the colonies, anticipated them and built a redoubt at the mouth of the river and sent a cruiser there with orders to prevent the English ship from entering the Stikine River. Thus the English attempt was frustrated. The English government protested, however, demanding compensation for losses of about 135,000 silver rubles to Hudson's Bay Company resulting from this action. In order to settle this affair peacefully, the Russian American Company agreed to lease to Hudson's Bay Company for a period of ten years beginning June 1, 1840 the St. Dionysius redoubt [near the mouth of] the Stikine River and a lisière ten leagues wide lying along the seacoast from 54°40" northwest between Cape Spencer near Cross Sound and the Dobraia Pogoda Mountains. Hudson's Bay Company agreed to pay 2,000 sea otter pelts per year. The contract was renewed in 1849 and in 1859, and is due to expire January 1, 1862.*

As a result, at the present time our colonies are delineated by the above mentioned conventions; that is, they include the Northwest Coast of America from 54°40" of north latitude up to the Arctic Ocean, all islands lying along that coast and in the Bering Sea, also the Aleutian and Kuril islands as far as the island of Iturup, which forms our boundary with Japan.

----

* I had the opportunity of reading details about the disagreements with the Americans and with the English, in addition to the evidence found in the colonial archives, in the following works: *L'Oregon et les Cotes de l'Ocean Pacifique du Nord*, by M. Felix (Paris, 1848), and *Narrative of a Voyage Round the World, Performed in Her Majesty's Ship* Sulphur, *During the Years 1836-1842*, by Captain Sir Edward Belcher, R. N. (London, 1843).

SOIL, CLIMATE AND VEGETATION

Almost all of the islands lying within Russia's possessions in America are of volcanic origin. The soil generally consists of granite and volcanic clay. On the islands that lie close to the American shore, south of the parallel of Mount Saint Elias, the littoral is covered with a deep layer of stones and fossilized shells. In some places there is a good deal of tundra and swampland, but there is everywhere a rather deep stratum of clay or decomposed vegetation. Generally speaking, the area is mountainous. There are many volcanoes, either dormant or still active, especially on the Alaska Peninsula. The peaks of most of these mountains are permanently snowcapped.

In summer the islands are thickly blanketed with green grass, but the Aleutian Islands are completely unforested. There is a small amount of forestation on Kodiak Island near Pavlovsk Harbor, and on the nearby islands of Afognak, Lesnoi and Elovoi. Opposite these islands on the mainland there is abundant forest, which is also true of the island of Sitka and others nearby. Trees grow on the mountain slopes up to an elevation of 1500 feet. On the islands the trees are mostly evergreens, fir, pine, larch and cypress; on the mainland there are also birch and aspen and other varieties that grow in that latitude. Fir and pine reach a goodly size and grow straight and symmetrical. On Sitka it is not unusual to see tree trunks 90 feet high and two and a half feet in diameter at the crown.

An attempt was made to plant trees on the Aleutian Islands; about 1805 some young fir seedlings were brought there from Kodiak, but almost nowhere did they survive, and at the present time there is not a single tree. The climate is blamed for this, but it should also be taken into account that the whole experiment was very poorly conducted because there were not enough experienced persons involved. This is the extent of experimentation.

The climate on the islands is not at all favorable. Rain and fog are almost constant, and there are very few clear days. Heavy freezes are rare, but it often rains throughout the winter. The average temperature is +3° Reaumur.* On Kodiak Island the climate is somewhat better, with a more moderate

---

* On Reaumur scale 0° is freezing point of water and 80° boiling point.--Eds.

winter. Along the shores of the mainland, especially in Kenai Bay, the weather takes on a more continental character. Summer is hot and dry, there are freezing temperatures in winter, flowers are perfumed and berries have both flavor and scent; but on all of the islands including Sitka the berries are watery and flavorless even though they are large and luscious in appearance, and the flowers have no fragrance. Potatoes and radishes grow well enough in kitchen gardens, but cabbage is not successful and attempts to grow grain crops have met with no success as yet. Apparently climate is not so much to blame as lack of experience, especially the lack of persistence and determination, and the poor choice of location to carry on agricultural experiments. I shall have more to say on this subject later, in the chapter dealing with provisioning the colonies.

There is abundant mineral wealth here. Unfortunately it has been but poorly explored, but there is no doubt it exists. Coal is found all over in large or small quantities, especially along the Kenai shore where coal veins extend for a considerable distance deep into the interior of the country. Explorations that have been made in the colonies at various times have been very superficial and have been limited to the coastal area. The interior, not only of the mainland but even of the island of Sitka, has still not been explored. Some expeditions have been sent north up several rivers which empty into the Pacific or into the Bering Sea, but these have explored only the banks of the rivers, and have not penetrated into the interior of the island and no one knows what is to be found there. It is true that it is extremely difficult to penetrate the interior reaches of the island because of the mountainous topography which is covered with virgin forest where enormous trees grow right out of those that have fallen. The trees grow close together and reach a gigantic size. But in spite of all this, even these superficial explorations have found obsidian, basalt, graphite, various kinds of clay, red chalk, ochre, various other pigments and sulphur in different places in the colonies. Large pieces of pure copper have been found along the Copper River, and gold has been found in Kenai Bay. The problem is this: is it economically feasible to mine these metals? Will the anticipated profit cover the enormous expenses? These questions cannot be resolved without careful research.

The most important rivers that flow from the mainland into the Pacific or into the Bering Sea are the Copper, Susitna, Kakhna, Kwikhpak and Kuskovym. There are also many small streams on the Aleutian Islands, and at a certain time of year they are all teeming with fish that come in from the sea to spawn. There are also lakes of considerable size, and in various places there are sulphur and mineral hot springs.

Only on the mainland and the offshore islands are there good harbors and bays. On the Aleutian Islands all the open approaches are filled with submerged and protruding rocks, which make the approach to the islands extremely hazardous, especially in summer and fall when a very dense fog prevails throughout the Aleutian chain. In winter and spring icebergs drift there from the Bering Sea.

LAND AND MARINE ANIMALS, FISH AND BIRDS

Land animals on the islands include the bear, fox, mink, polar fox (both blue and white), and marmot (a ground squirrel). On Sitka and the nearby islands there are wild chamois [iaman], and on the shore of the mainland, in addition to these, one finds the wolf, lynx, wolverine and ermine, but the latter are of poor quality. Among amphibious animals the walrus and seal are found primarily along the American coast from the Bering Sea to [the Gulf of?] Alaska, but they can also be found in other places. The sable, riverine otter and beaver are to be found only on the mainland. The sea otter is found on the Aleutian and Kuril islands, along the coast of Kamchatka, in Shelikhov Strait near the Alaskan shore, and in small numbers in Kenai Bay and farther down the American coast. Sea lions and seals are hunted nearly everywhere on the Aleutian Islands and along the mainland coast, but rarely south of Chugach Sound. Fur seals are found only on the islands of St. Paul, St. George, Bering and Mednyi. They always return to the same place to breed in spring, and leave the following autumn. No one knows where they spend the winter. Various kinds of whales can be found everywhere, but their number decreases every year thanks to the zeal of foreign whalers who do not hesitate to kill them in our bays and inlets, and now the catch of whales is very small.

There is always a great variety of fish to be caught in all parts of the colonies, particularly cod, halibut, bream, sea perch and a number of others. Periodically herring come in vast numbers. Red fish of the salmon family include the king salmon, dog salmon, humpback and the malma [Dolly Varden trout] and others. Red fish come near shore and swim in schools into the rivers and streams to spawn, at which time they are caught by the tens of thousands. Even bears come to the rivers and catch salmon with their paws.

Sea birds of various kinds are to be found in large numbers and are used by the natives for food. The Aleuts make a special type of shirt called a parka from the skins of certain birds. Migratory birds also occur here in great numbers, especially geese. Hummingbirds come to Sitka in June. In the chapter dealing with a description of trade, the vegetable, animal and mineral kingdoms will be discussed in greater detail.

THE POPULATION OF THE COLONIES

The population of the colonies comprises the following: Russians and
foreigners who come to the colonies for a period of Company service; creoles,
born of Russians and subjugated natives [tuzemtsy]; and finally, independent
natives [inorodtsy].* The indigenous population is divided into dependents:
Aleuts, Kodiaks and Kurils; semi-dependents: Kenais and Chugach; and those who
are independent: Mednovtsy, Kolchans, Malegmiuts, Kolosh or Koliush [Tlingits]
and others.

Russians who are in service in the colonies are divided according to the
responsibilities assigned to them. Thus individuals who have more responsibility for colonial administration, or who are naval or land personnel and staff
officers, or captains of ships, belong to the distinguished [pochetnyi] category;
the second group, the semi-distinguished, includes free navigators, prikashchiks
and persons who have secondary responsibilities. After these come sailors,
soldiers from Siberian line battalions and laborers. Many come to the colonies
with their families; others marry creole women; those from the lower classes
marry native women. Those who pay taxes are assigned, for the duration of their
stay in the colonies, to the category to which they belonged prior to their
departure from Russia; they retain all their legal obligations.

Although the Company tries to select capable persons of strong moral
character for top level positions in service in the colonies, no such criteria
are used in choosing individuals for the second and third categories of personnel. This is primarily due to the comparatively low level of pay, which
attracts very few volunteers to travel to a land that is far distant and for the
most part quite unknown. Industrious and moral persons can easily earn a salary
in Russia equal to that paid by the Company to persons willing to go to the
colonies. Thus volunteers who go off to the colonies are for the most part
persons who have gone through fire and water, so to speak. And when they come
to the colonies, obviously they are not transformed into better persons. It

---

* Nineteenth century Russian legal terminology distinguished between natives
subject to Russia, tuzemtsy, and those who had not been subjugated, inorodtsy,
which also implied "foreign-born."--Eds.

is true that major crimes and misdemeanors are not usual in the colonies, but drunkeness, debauchery, violence, laziness and insubordination are very, very common, especially among soldiers and laborers.

It often happens that laborers arrive in the colonies, marry indigenous women, have children, and rather than remaining just for a seven-year period they remain in service for a longer time. After this length of time it is impossible for them to return to Russia with a family, with no money, and to try to earn a living there. Thus they remain permanently in the colonies.

In 1809 the Governing Board of the Company for the first time requested the government to allow 33 Russian promyshlenniks to settle permanently in the colonies and to be reclassified as *colonial citizens*. This was granted by an Imperial ukaz, and on April 2, 1835 likewise at the request of the Governing Board, the Emperor issued a statement through the Committee of Ministers granting the Company the right to settle in suitable locations service persons who because of ill health or old age wished to remain in the colonies permanently. These persons were also classified as colonial citizens and were removed from the classes they had belonged to in Russia on the basis of the last reviziia [census of tax payers], but they were still obliged to pay taxes.

The Company's charter stipulated that colonial citizens be given land, be provided with the means to start a new life, be supplied with agricultural implements and hunting equipment, grain for planting, livestock, and all necessary provisions for one year. The Company is also obliged to see that colonial citizens do not suffer want in the future. These settlements were first organized along the Kenai shore, on Afognak and Lesnoi islands and in other places deemed suitable.

In its 1858 report the Governing Board, among other matters, speaks of colonial citizens: "Since they are provided by the Company with all needs and necessities, colonial citizens comprise a moral and industrious group of people. For those persons who come to the colonies on a short term basis, they serve as useful examples, people who have diligently and usefully completed their service with the Company. Generally speaking, this category has completely fulfilled the objective set for it."

I totally disagree with this opinion of the Governing Board, from the first word to the last.

Of course one should give full credit to the Company for the fact that in making these persons colonial citizens it not only supplies them with all necessities but also gives virtually all of them an annual pension as a reward for service. But what is the result of this? During personal interviews and conversations with colonial citizens, I heard nothing but complaints, all directed at the Company. They all said, "Of course we are satisfied and thankful to the Company, but . . . ." And then came their petitions: 1) that their pensions be increased, even though each receives from 150 to 700 paper rubles annually; 2) that their sons not be required to hunt sea otters with the Aleuts; 3) that their children be paid by the month rather than by the day, so that holidays and

days off will not be excluded from payment; 4) that they be allowed to buy with
cash anything they need, in any amount, from Company warehouses, without hindrance; finally, 5) that the Company buy from them items that they have made.
The result is that although the Company takes care of them, they are still
dissatisfied; not only do they feel in no way obligated to the Company for its
generosity, but they maintain that they create greater profit for the Company
by allowing their children to be hired for Company work, and they feel that the
Company should look after them permanently.

Do many of the settlers consent to let their children enter Company
service, even on quite generous terms? Such examples are rather unusual. On
the contrary, former service persons try very hard to keep their children at
home. They find themselves in need because they do not want to work, and
because they teach their children to remain idle day after day. Colonial citizens are obligated to sell their furs to the Company at the going price, but do
they have many to sell? They do not hunt sea otters, so their entire catch
consists of the few foxes, which they trap near their dwellings. Moreover,
colonial citizens can sell their garden produce to anyone at any price they
wish, as well as lumber, firewood, livestock, berries, fish, etc. They are
entirely free to do this, but if they sell anything to the Company, they feel
that they are doing the Company a favor. They can hardly boast of their morals,
and drunkenness would obviously be an even greater problem for them if they
could get unlimited quantities of vodka.

In a word, in my judgment colonial citizens are nothing more than moral
parasites.

Later on when I report in detail on conditions in the colonies, I shall
more than once have an opportunity to say that the shortage of labor impedes
the Company greatly. This shortage forces it to use all possible means to increase the population of the colonies with persons who could be of real use to
the Company with their work. Unfortunately the matter has not been handled as
it should have been, and measures that the Company has taken have not brought
the desired results. In these colonial citizens the Company does not have moral
and industrious citizens, but rather, useless persons, immoral, burdensome to
the Company; by their example they discourage others from being industrious and
indeed show how one can exist with no great effort, relying not on their own
resources but on outside assistance. It is strange that the Governing Board
does not realize this, since the colonial administration bears the full burden
of this abuse. It is even stranger that the Governing Board has not corrected
its misapprehension of the problem, and deliberately deceives the government by
praising things that should be criticized. Nearly 60 years have passed since
the first colonial citizens were organized in the colonies, and there is no
productivity to be seen from them or their offspring. And the Company continues
to be short of workers. This is no place for philanthropy. A commercial company that has been given some degree of governing power cannot squander its
resources, cannot remain ignorant of how to gain real profit for itself and for
the country.

The locations which have been selected for the Russians to settle in are

also unsatisfactory. By virtue of climate the islands are unsuitable for agricultural pursuits or for any other kind of endeavor whatsoever, except for
hunting sea animals and catching fish--undertakings to which the Russian settlers have an aversion. They could and should have been settled on the mainland,
for example, from Kenai Bay down to our southern boundary. It is true that at
the 60th parallel it would be difficult to carry on agriculture and livestock
breeding; but the Russians cannot penetrate the interior of the country, where
according to all evidence there is mineral wealth, until they have entrenched
themselves along the coast. Then they can gradually move up rivers such as the
Copper, Susitna, Kuskovym and Kwikhpak, and in this manner penetrate to the
sources of wealth in the center of the indigenous population, since they will
have guaranteed communication with the sea by means of these rivers. Moreover,
it is necessary to extend settlements south along the mainland. In the early
stages this was obviously very difficult because of the proximity of the Kolosh
[Tlingits] who terrified the settlers. Forts had to be built in every settlement for protection. But over a period of 60 years, it should have been possible
to cope with the Kolosh.

    In any case, I am of the opinion that under the present circumstances
colonial citizens are a totally useless class of persons who are a burden to the
Company as long as they exist and will continue to be so to the government, if
the government assumes responsibility for administering the region. If it was
hoped that by creating a class of colonial citizens the region would gradually
be settled, the goal has not been accomplished. How could anyone have supposed
that aged and infirm persons would contribute to increasing the population? It
would be another matter if they would permit young persons to marry, and give
them land for their permanent use, and if they would settle several families in
one location under the condition that they protect their own property from in-
cursions by independent natives, and that they become like American "squatters."
Of course such persons would eventually create a class of useful and industrious
settlers; they would not be afraid of the nearby Kolosh; and the Northwest Coast
would in reality belong to the Russians.

    One can see only one positive aspect in having created colonial citizens:
It was a humanitarian measure that provided a livelihood for old and disabled
persons who otherwise would have had a difficult time making a living for themselves. From this point of view one has to consider colonial citizens not as
colonists but rather as invalids who are being cared for by the Company. With
help they could settle the land and be of real use.

    At present there are the following numbers of Russians in the colonies:
529 men and 66 women, a total of 595 (See Appendix 2).

	Men	Women	Total
Colonial Citizens	54	40	94
Settlers not yet registered as colonial citizens	10	9	19
Total number of settlers	64	49	113

Creoles for the most part are descended from Russian men and Aleut women, infrequently from Russian men and Kolosh women, and very rarely from native men and Russian women. Creole children remain creoles, no matter how their blood is mixed. As a general rule it would seem that children should belong to the class to which their fathers belong. This rule has been changed in the colonies. One has only to be born a creole to become completely independent, to have no obligations, pay no taxes, and to live and work for oneself. One would think that when the special cast of creoles was created it was envisaged that this would help settle the region. In fact, if they had been put in the same class to which their fathers belonged, the creoles would have been assigned to various classes in Russia and consequently could have been recalled by these classes; however, since a special caste of completely free persons had been created, they naturally found it more to their advantage to remain in the colonies, and their fathers very rarely returned to Russia. If this was the goal, then it certainly has been attained, for the creole population increases every year and presently comprises more than one-third of the entire Aleut population and more than one-sixth of the total population of the colonies with the exception of the Russians (See Appendix 2).

One can predict that in a few decades the creole population will become dominant in the colonies and completely replace the Aleuts, whose number is gradually diminishing. It is not enough to settle the region. It is essential that the population should be useful in some way and participate in the development of the economy and enrichment of the area. But it is apparent that up to the present time the creoles have not been of any use. If they continue in this way, then nothing good can be expected of them in the future.

The first creoles were the illegitimate children of Russian promyshlenniks and Aleut women. When the Russians arrived in the colonies they readily established contact with native women, which was considered both natural and commonplace. Later the clergy began to harry these alliances that had never been legalized, and the men's paramours became their wives. But their way of life did not improve. The mothers' blood expressed itself in the children in their inclination toward hooliganism, primitivism, dishonesty and laziness. However, although creoles are all likely to be sensitive, proud, and quick to take offense, they do have good qualities, notably an aptitude in mechanical crafts. For the most part they are well-proportioned and very good looking, especially the second and third generations; but they early acquire an inclination toward a carefree life, and this has a tragic effect. They soon become weak. Between the ages of 30 and 35 nearly all suffer from a chest disorder which often develops into consumption. The result is that very few creoles live to an advanced age. Drink, especially, is their ruination.

The Russians who live in the colonies have not lost sight of the illegitimate origin of the creoles. They look at the reprehensible conduct of the creole women and the careless attitude of the men, most of whom are willing to hand over their wives to anyone in exchange for a few bottles of rum. Consequently not only [do the Russians] look on them with great contempt, but the word "creole" is used as a pejorative. Even the Aleuts have no respect for the creoles, and say that they are lower than Aleuts because their mothers were immoral women. This contempt, this constant oppression, is very destructive to the sensitive nature of the creoles. They are ashamed of being called creoles. They thus have no liking for the Russians, but they have no choice but to be on close terms with them and suffer their insults. They consider themselves men of the land and of course want to attain some stature, but they are downtrodden and forced to submit to Russian influence. This is the result of their having been assigned to a special caste. No measures the Company has instituted have been able to change this state of affairs.

Obviously there are very fine persons among the creoles, but they are the exceptions, and I am speaking about the group as a whole. Even education and rank do not always benefit their crude natures. Thanks to the efforts of the Company many creoles receive an education; some obtain the rank of noncommissioned officers; others command ships or hold various responsible positions in the colonies. But in the group as a whole, there are only a few gratifying exceptions. Under strict supervision they behave acceptably, but when left to their own devices they revert to their natural behavior and become embittered drunkards.

Creoles, as noted earlier, have no obligations, pay no taxes, and only those who have been educated at Company expense have an obligation to serve for a specified number of years after their education is completed. Those who have been educated in Russia must serve the Company for ten years; those educated in the colonies serve for fifteen years, beginning at the age of seventeen. Orphans are cared for and maintained at Company expense. Children born out of wedlock are also raised by the Company.

When creoles are in Company service they of course receive wages and living quarters and provisions, just as the Russians do, and their pay is increased according to the quality of their work. If a creole wishes to remain in Company services after his obligatory period has been completed, he then concludes an agreement with the Chief Manager which he considers satisfactory. In spite of this, very few remain in service. Most, after they have fulfilled ten or fifteen years in service, decide to settle on an island somewhere, or as they say, put on a parka and go to sleep. Nearly all receive pensions from the Company. It should be noted, however, that the period of obligatory service is too long for the creoles. If the Company wishes a reasonable return for their investment, or if it wishes to make useful persons out of them, knowing their lazy natures, it seems that five years of obligatory service should be adequate. At the end of this period the Company would then have to offer its service personnel such benefits as would entice them to remain in service. It would be even better if the government were to assume the responsibility for education in the colonies and prevent the Company from exploiting human labor and capability to the detriment of human rights. I will have the opportunity to speak of this matter later in the chapter on training facilities and schools.

Both free creoles and those who have concluded their Company service settle on the islands. Those who live on the islands of Atka, Unalaska and Bering, as well as those who live in the Belkovskii settlement on the Alaska Peninsula are engaged in hunting sea otter, and several of them are very good, alert promyshlenniks. Those who live on Sitka and on the islands near Kodiak consider it beneath their dignity to go hunting with the Aleuts. Some go out individually to hunt whales; others work at breeding livestock and planting gardens or building small sloops, cutting lumber, etc. In general they all trap animals on the islands at a certain time of year. They are quite free to sell their goods to whomever they wish, at any price they choose. They are only obliged to sell their furs to the Company at a set price. The Company buys anything else from them at the same price an outsider pays. They have complete freedom of activity, they have as much land as they wish, cut as much timber as they please, and the Company provides them with livestock, the only condition being that after a certain period they must return the animal that was given to them for breeding purposes or pay a certain amount of money. A cow, for example, is worth 40 rubles, paper. Everything they need, such as clothing and provisions they can obtain from the Company warehouses at a set price on the same basis as all Company service personnel.

In spite of all this, the creoles made almost the same complaints as the Russian colonial citizens did. They asked that their children not be forced to go out with the Aleuts to hunt sea otters, that their pensions be increased, that they be paid for voluntary labor not on a daily but rather on a monthly basis so that holidays and days off are included, and that the Company permit them to buy larger amounts of supplies from the warehouses. Their children are not forced to go out on hunting parties. The colonial administration has only suggested to them that they send their sons on such expeditions in order to train them to become promyshlenniks and to give them the opportunity to earn good money. But the creoles have decisively rejected this, saying that their children are not accustomed to such hunting and have enough for their needs. Some own livestock; others speculate in it. They may buy a cow for 40 rubles from the Company and sell it secretly for 60 or 70 or 80 rubles, and then ask the Company to give them another cow because the first one was killed by a bear or fell off a cliff somehow. Their gardens are not kept in good condition, and there is nothing to be said in regard to agriculture.

It is obvious from all of the conversations with them that they rely on the Company and feel that it is obliged to care for them, feed them, and provide drink. If they sell anything to the Company they feel they have done the Company a favor. Simply stated, they do not like to work in any proper manner. Meanwhile their desires increase with every year; they want tea, sugar and coffee but have no means of obtaining these. Thus they feel deprived, and of course they do not blame themselves but the Company. They lose sight of the fact that they should provide for themselves and not look to others for help. The Company bears the entire burden of babying these people and has nowhere to turn for help. The result is that the creoles have been and continue to be useless to the region, to the Company, even to themselves. At present there are 925 male creoles in the colonies and 971 females; a total of 1,896.

THE ATKHINSK, UNALASKA AND KODIAK ALEUTS

The Aleuts belong to two different tribal groups: one includes the Atkhinsk and Unalaska Aleuts who live on the Fox, Andreanov and Rat islands, and other islands of the Alaska Peninsula; the others, the Kodiaks or Koniags, live on Kodiak Island and the nearby islands. The languages of the two tribes are completely different, but their way of life, habits and customs are almost identical, so that everything said about the Kodiaks may apply equally to the Unalaska and Atkhinsk group.

Some time ago both tribes, who are quite populous and are of a warlike disposition, were almost constantly battling one another. Disputes over hunting and fishing were the causes of the discord, and such disputes were usually set- tled by force. We know from accounts that these battles destroyed a large part of the population of the Aleutian Islands, although there was still quite a large population when the first Russian promyshlenniks appeared on these islands. At that time there were nearly 10,000 persons.* With the arrival of the Russians the number of Aleuts began to decrease rapidly. Aside from a smallpox epidemic which broke out in 1836, the major cause of the decrease was the killing of Aleuts by Russians. Then too venereal disease (which was spread by the Russian promyshlenniks), the need to settle Aleuts in other places in the colonies, and finally to a degree the change in their way of life, their diet and customs that resulted from contact with the Russians--all of this contributed further to the decrease in the Aleut population. It is an incontro- vertible fact that when savage people come into contact with civilized people they gradually die out. Wherever white men go the native population rapidly decreases. There is no doubt that the change in life style and customs, diseases brought by the newcomers and the debauchery which whites spread among the natives has an immediate and tragic effect on these innocents of Nature. The natives become weak, downtrodden, and soon die. But all of these detrimental influences in time lose much of their effect, and the second and third generation are less affected than the first. Thus in time the native population should stop decreasing, even if it does not begin to increase again.

The Indians are disappearing in America because they are being killed,

---

* According to the census made on order of Councilor [Nikolai P.] Rezanov in 1806, there were 5,234 Aleuts of both sexes, including 1,509 children.

just as the Aleuts decreased in number because they were killed by merciless Russians. The names of Glotov, Solovev, Natrubin and their companions strike fear in the Aleuts even to the present time. Thousands of persons were victims of the cruelty of these unbridled criminals who destroyed whole settlements with sword and fire. Even afterward, although the killings were halted, for a long time they did not think of an Aleut as a human being, but only as an animal. We know that [Aleksandr A.] Baranov, the first Chief Manager of the colonies, regarded the life of an Aleut as nothing. Many of them died during the unprecedented transfers by baidarka from Kodiak to Sitka. Having killed off a large part of the Aleut population, the Russians destroyed the rest of them morally, by introducing them to debauchery that had never before existed among them. No one considered improving their way of life, or their welfare. It is true that the Aleuts accepted Christianity and tried to go to church and diligently attempted to fulfill their religious obligations, but they scarcely have a genuine conception of the benefits of the Christian religion. Persons who have a good understanding of the Aleuts feel that they would become ardent Mohammedans tomorrow, if the government ordered them to do so. The deeds of the first Russian promyshlenniks forced the Aleuts into total submission, and not one of them thinks of disobeying any Russian.

The Aleuts have many good qualities: they are peaceful, good, hospitable, willing to help those close to them, and honest. There is no thievery among them, and one never hears of major crimes. But at the same time they are very lazy, heedless and given to gluttony. As far as debauchery is concerned, its decrease is due in large part to the fact that Aleut women are not wives but sexual companions [samki], and feel no shame when they satisfy their natural desires. Aleuts are very sensitive; harsh or rude words hurt them deeply, and physical punishment is condered such a degradation that to punish an Aleut means in essence to force him to commit suicide. Consequently any punishment for minor infractions is usually simply a reprimand.

The Aleut diet consists of dried fish (iukola), whale meat, and that of sea lions, seals and other marine animals; roots, sea cabbage, various shellfish and marine birds. All of these are prepared with whale and seal blubber, without which they cannot properly exist. They also like bread, tea, sugar, treacle and rice, but they can only obtain these products by paying cash for them at Company warehouses; the Company, using the excuse that they should not accustom the Aleuts to luxury, supplies them with these items in very small amounts. The Aleuts themselves told me that they would willingly eat bread if they were given enough. "But you ask and ask, and they do not give it to you. They say there is none! And sometimes you cry, and then you go home." There is some feeling that it would be harmful to accustom the Aleuts to eating bread, but I suppose that in this case there is more likely a commercial consideration since the Company finds it unprofitable to bring any great amount of grain into the colonies. In the chapter on provisioning the colonies, I will attempt to explain that in this instance the Company's concern is unfounded, and that the Aleuts suffer, without any benefit to the Company. Also, as a result of our inquiry based on petitions from the Aleuts, the present Chief Manager [Ivan Furuhelm] has already issued an order aimed at supplying the islands during the current year with double the amount of last year's rations.

A great deal has been said about the Company holding the Aleuts in a condition of slavery, and about Company officials and prikashchiks oppressing the Aleuts. It has already been mentioned that the first promyshlenniks mistreated the Aleuts, and even during the first period of the Company's existence the condition of the Aleuts improved very little. Even if Baranov had wanted to protect them from oppression, he could hardly have done so, because he had to entrust the administration of the islands, offices and stores to persons under his command, and, with a few exceptions, these persons were far from moral. In the first stages they sent whatever persons they could to the colony, without exception, because they had no choice. Few would volunteer to travel to such a distant and completely unknown land. But later the situation gradually changed. Chief Managers were chosen from educated persons with a more humane outlook, and also not only humanitarianism but the interest of the Company itself forced them to understand that the activities of earlier days had no place now. Consequently prikashchiks and office administrators were selected on the basis of their proven honesty and good behavior, and they were strictly prohibited from interfering with the affairs of the Aleuts, regardless of circumstances. The responsibility of these persons, right up to the present time, is exclusively the matter of accepting pelts from the Aleuts and in exchange giving them whatever they need from the Company's stores, keeping order in the areas under their jurisdiction, and sending sea otter hunting parties off to a given rendezvous at the proper time. They have no power to pass judgment and are not allowed to settle disputes among the Aleuts; consequently the only way in which they can oppress the Aleuts is that when they receive the pelts they may arbitrarily downgrade pelts and thus pay less for them. But this is not to their advantage, only to the advantage of the Company, for when the catch is received in the main offices it is again graded, and the prikashchik must present a very strict and detailed account of all the items he issued to the Aleuts for their needs. Additionally, captains of Company ships who supply all the islands with necessary provisions and goods every year must accept every petition and complaint from the Aleuts, collect all necessary evidence right then and there, and report on this to the Chief Manager. The Chief Manager himself is required to visit one or two departments of the colony each year so that during his five-year stay he certainly manages to visit each one. He also sends a trusted official out from time to time to take a survey and to take the census in various places. Prikashchiks are very much aware of the fact that abuses will not go unpunished, and that the Company rewards good service very generously. Consequently, the motive of personal gain forces them to carry on their affairs honestly.

Regardless of all our inquiries, we did not find a single complaint about mistreatment by prikashchiks. On the contrary, we quite often heard the Aleuts praise prikashchiks, and express gratitude to them for their good conduct. The only obligations the Aleuts owe the Company are these: going out on sea otter hunting parties that are outfitted at Company expense, taking pelts during these hunts, and selling all their furs to the Company at an established price.

I shall discuss the success of the hunt in some detail in its proper place. For now, let us only consider to what degree these obligations are a burden to the Aleuts.

When Russian promyshlenniks began to voyage to the Aleutian Islands, the government instituted an obligation binding on all companies and promyshlenniks to collect iasak from the natives for the Treasury; but in 1779 by an ukaz of Empress Catherine II the collection of iasak was completely abolished because of the disorderly state of affairs among the natives. When the Russian American Company received its privileges, it was stipulated that the Aleuts were only obliged to send a certain number of baidarkas on sea otter hunting parties each year and to sell all their furs to the Company at a set price approved by the government. This obligation had good and bad aspects, but at that time it was reasonable because such obligatory work also existed in Russia.

The Aleuts are by nature so lazy and carefree that none of them would go out hunting unless they were in great need. They could live on fish during the summer without any work whatsoever, and on other edible provisions such as shellfish, which is always available at low tide. An Aleut does not think about the future. Therefore if winter is severe and ice covers the tidal flats, the Aleuts go hungry and often have to eat hide by cutting it in tiny pieces and boiling it in water. But they never think about improving their lives. It is too much to expect that they would decide to organize big sea otter hunting parties, which is the first prerequisite for a successful hunt. During the hunt there is not always a good catch in one place, and they must go from place to place. Thus the Aleuts may have to go a long distance from their settlements to catch sea otter, and these trips cannot be safely undertaken unless a large number of baidarkas go out together. Also, in order to make baidarkas one needs a forest, which does not exist on the Aleutian Islands. One also needs sea lion lavtaks, whale whiskers, sinews, line, etc.--items which the Aleuts cannot supply for themselves, at least not in the required amount. Thus in forcing the Aleuts to work, the Company not only provides them with the basic necessities, but also gives them the opportunity of improving their condition and way of life, and almost completely prevents them from starving to death.

On the other hand, that same concern has brought about the fact that at the present time the Aleuts actually will not do anything without pressure. They have become accustomed to certain luxuries and now these seem necessities to them; but at the same time they quite often do not have the money to satisfy their wishes. Obviously, if they worked more, they would have more means. But Aleuts will not work without being pushed, and consequently they do not blame their own laziness for not having those things they want; rather, they blame the Company, although they do not know precisely why the Company is to blame.

The new statute which the Governing Board has prepared does away with obligatory labor by the Aleuts, and suggests that the Company hire the Aleuts for hunting on mutually agreeable terms. I consider this measure absolutely necessary, even though the Aleuts will go hungry at first because they will not agree to work and thus will have no means to buy all the things they need. Later, however, when they realize that they cannot expect help from anyone, they will gradually learn to rely on themselves alone to earn their food. Thus by granting them full freedom it will be better than constantly supervising them, as the Company has had to do in the past.

Some Company reports state that Aleuts, who had formerly lived in small settlements great distances apart, are now grouped into several larger settlements and no longer live in crowded iurts but rather in neat, light and spacious homes. This is not precisely true. The Aleuts have indeed been grouped into large settlements now, but sometimes too many of them have been brought into one place so that it is difficult for them to prepare sufficient supplies for winter. Thus some have asked that their settlements be divided into two parts, allowing those who wish to select a place where there is enough fish and other food necessary for Aleuts, and the Chief Manager has issued a regulation pertaining to this. Regarding light and spacious homes, only a few Aleuts on Sitka and Kodiak who are in Company service have such homes. All the rest live as formerly in small little huts that are half underground, with the top covered over with dirt. These are built of all kinds of wood. It is true that some toions have spacious iurts, some even have a small Russian pech [stove]; but these are exceptions. However the Aleuts have become very accustomed to that kind of dwelling, so that one could encourage them to build according to a Russian design, especially if lumber could be brought in from Sitka. However I believe that this can be eventually achieved only if the Company seriously wants to achieve it. The requirements of a European style of life are beginning to manifest themselves among the Aleuts, so that one finds they all have teapots, cups and glasses, and many have samovars. They all care for these things quite properly. But the unbearable reek of the iukola and whale blubber that they eat, and of their dwellings, and of the Aleuts themselves, forces everyone to rush as fast as possible to fresh air in order to get out of the choking stench and overcome a wretched sense of nausea.

According to the latest reports, the present population of Aleuts is as follows (See Appendix 2):

	Men	Women	Total
On Unalaska	1,236	1,192	2,428
Kodiak Aleuts	1,115	1,102	2,217
Totals	2,351	2,294	4,645

Kurils, who live on the Kuril Islands, have a very small population, numbering 88 persons of both sexes. They resemble Aleuts in many ways, although in origin they are close to the Ainu who live on Sakhalin Island. They are almost constantly on the move from one island to another looking for a better supply of sea otters. They are humble and quiet by nature, and they are all Christians. It is obvious that because of their nomadic life they are totally unfamiliar with the various advantages associated with a settled life. Their families roam together with them. They get everything they need from the Company. The Company hunts on those islands with the assistance of Aleuts who request to be transferred there for a period of from three to five years; they come primarily from areas where there is a lack of good hunting and they are unable to provide necessities for themselves.

The *Chugach* live along the shores of Chugach Sound. They also belong to the Aleut tribe and are considered subjects of Russia. Actually, however, they do not acknowledge Russian sovereignty, and the sum total of their dependence on the Company is that when requested by the colonial administration they send small parties out to hunt sea otters, but only in places near their settlements. Sometimes they are also hired for Company work. Sea otter hunting parties are outfitted here just as with the Aleuts, and the catch is purchased from the Chugach at set prices. They are paid for their work as all natives are. On the whole, they consider themselves completely independent, even though they live near the Company redoubt. When they need something, or sometimes if there is a dispute, they turn to the Company prikashchik who is in charge of the redoubt. During my personal inquiry they asked to be paid more for pelts and also requested that pay for their day labor be increased somewhat because while they willingly hire themselves out to work for the Company, the pay does not adequately compensate them for the work, and they agreed to work only if they were to receive better terms. In reference to the hunt, they sell only part of their furs to the Company; the rest go to other natives and to foreigners. They also declared that they are quite satisfied with the treatment they receive from the colonial administration, particularly from the prikashchik who is in charge of the redoubt. They unanimously declared that if this prikashchik were transferred, they would all move north and end their relationship with the Company.

The Konstantin redoubt is administered by the Russian promyshlennik Grigorev, and it appears that a similar impression on the part of the savages who are in constant contact with him speaks quite favorably in his behalf. Nearly all the Chugach who live near the redoubt are Orthodox, a faith that they have adopted partly because of the zeal of the missionaries and partly, as is true with all savages, because they find some personal benefit in it. They observe religious ceremonies whenever possible, but in general they are rather nonchalant about this. They are gentle and quite honest by nature, but they also have a considerable inclination to the use of vodka.

The Chugach number about 226 males and 230 females, a total of 456.

The *Kenais* live along the shore of Kenai Bay and are also independent, in spite of the fact that many have accepted the Orthodox faith. They do not go on sea otter hunts, but they do hunt land animals. They sell part of their pelts to the Company at a set price, and part of them to other natives. The Company hires them to maintain baidara communication between Nikolaevsk redoubt and the coal mining post; they also make charcoal and do other work in the redoubt. They also ask to be paid more for pelts and day labor. They live quite humbly, as the Chugach do. They had no complaints of ill treatment by the Company or its prikashchik; on the contrary, they approve of the way the Company treats them.

At Nikolaevsk redoubt there are 430 male Kenais and 507 females, a total of 937.

The *Mednovtsy* live along the Copper River and are completely independent. They often lead a nomadic life because they are always hunting land animals and they try to find appropriate places where hunting is good for this nomadic life.

They sell part of their pelts to the Company, and for this purpose in summer they come to the Konstantin redoubt. Formerly they were hired there to use their baidarkas to transport goods and supplies from the redoubt to the Copper odinochka. But this odinochka is now abandoned, ever since the creole Serebriannikov--who was sent by Captain Tebenkov, former Chief Manager, to survey the Copper River from its source and to build up trade with the natives--was killed by the Mednovtsy Indians along with his three companions. According to the Indians, and from what we can tell from other accounts, the reason for the murder was Serebriannikov's arrogance toward the natives and his sexual relations with the daughter of one of their elders. It is apparent that the Mednovtsy Indians did not kill him to rob him, because they sent all of his belongings, and those of his men, to the redoubt. Nevertheless he was killed, and the odinochka was in danger, so they had to move both personnel and supplies back to the Konstantin redoubt. From that time on, trade relations with the Mednovtsy Indians have been more difficult.

A small number of the Mednovtsy Indians have accepted the Orthodox faith, but their nomadic life and the distance from the Konstantin redoubt, as well as their casual attitude toward their new religion, means that they very rarely participate in religious ceremonies, and many have even forgotten that they are Christians.

The nomadic natives near the Mednovtsy Indians insist that the latter are cannibals. If this is true, then it is certain that the Mednovtsy Indians resort to this form of food only in extreme cases, when they have no success in hunting. Then, faced with starvation, a Mednovtsy Indian will kill his youngest child, and the rest of the family will sustain itself on that meat.

It is difficult to determine how many Mednovtsy Indians live within the borders of our possessions, since none of the Russians has penetrated into their nomadic grounds. According to estimates, based on their own testimony, they believe there are between three and five thousand persons of both sexes. Only seventeen men and one women of these are considered to have accepted the Orthodox faith.

Next come the *Alegmiuts* in the northern part of Alaska; the *Ugolens* near Mount Saint Elias; the *Kolchans* in the interior of the mainland near our frontiers; the *Kuskovyms* along the Kuskovym River, which empties into the Bering Sea; the *Kvikhnakhs, Kiatents, Malegmiuts* and other peoples along the shores of the Bering Sea and along the rivers that empty into it, and also along the shores of the Arctic Ocean. All of these are completely independent, even though, according to the reports of the religious administration, there are more than 2,200 of them who are Orthodox (See Appendix 3). Many of these persons lead a nomadic life, and the Company receives only a very small portion of their furs. All the rest go either to Siberia or to foreigners, as will be described later. These people do not acknowledge Russian dominion over them, and they consider the land on which they live as their own property. Generally speaking these people are peaceful and do not endanger our settlements. It would not require too great an effort to bring them closer to us and to convey to them the idea that they are Russian subjects. But up to the present time the Company has not exhibited sufficient determination to do this, and to its own detriment it has allowed this very important source of trade to slip out of its grasp.

Among these independent people there is a populous tribe known as the *Koliuzh* or *Kolosh* [Tlingit] who live along the Northwest Coast of America from Yakutat Bay to the Stikine River, and on many islands lying along that shore. The tribes of these Kolosh are referred to under the general name of "Indians," who also inhabit the English possessions as far south as Oregon. Farther to the south the race changes and merges into the California Indians.

The *Kolosh* are divided into several clans, of which the most important are the *Crow* and the *Wolf*; usually however these are called by the names of the localities in which their settlements are located, as for example the Yakutats of Yakutat Bay, the Lituya, Sitka, Stikine, etc. The Kolosh have been the constant enemies of Russian entrenchment along the Northwest Coast and the adjacent islands. It is said that their hostility to the Russians was fostered by foreign merchants who feared that the entire fur trade would fall into the hands of the Russian Company. Whatever the reason, our first settlements encountered in the Kolosh fierce and relentless enemies. The Kolosh captured and destroyed the fort of Arkhangel Michael on Sitka Island and the settlement of Slava Rossii in Yakutat, and they killed nearly all the inhabitants and garrison personnel. For a long time after that the Russians had a constant struggle with these hostile neighbors. Until recently no Russian dared to go fifty paces out from the New Arkhangel fortress unarmed. At present this hostility does not exist, but trade relations are carried on only with the Sitka Kolosh who live only ten sazhens from New Arkhangel. The Kolosh who live in the straits are not hostile to us, but neither are they friendly. They themselves say that they "tolerate the Russians." In regard to the termination of trade with them, I shall have more to say in its proper place.

The Kolosh people are quite savage; they are courageous by nature, and accustomed to enduring every deprivation and physical pain. They are cunning and without scruple, because they have no religious convictions. They consider stealing as something of a virtue, especially if it is done to the detriment of an alien tribe. Drinking is widespread. In their view blood demands blood, and as a result a vendetta is carried from one generation to the next, and includes whole tribes. This causes frequent and prolonged wars between tribes, and this animosity contributes greatly to our safety in the colonies, for otherwise, if they were to unite under the leadership of a brave chief, the Kolosh would easily conquer our settlements and kill all the Russians.

They have an inborn passion for haggling. They are the chief middlemen for all pelts traded among all the natives. They are all superb shots, and thanks to the foreigners, they are armed with quite good rifles, pistols, revolvers and blades. A Kolosh will never part with his knife; at the first sign of an argument he will stab his opponent, but always if possible from behind, in a treacherous manner. Their diet is quite limited. Iukola and a little fat and shellfish make up their usual diet. However those who have come in contact with Europeans have acquired a taste for flour, treacle and rice. Tobacco is almost a necessity for them, and they will give up everything for a bottle of vodka. Their usual dress is a shirt and a woolen blanket, but many like to dress in European clothes. Toions or elders [starshiny] do not have the same kind of authority as is true in other natives. In general any person who is a member of a distinguished family is referred to as a toion; but the only ones with influence are those who are known for their achievements in war or because of their great wisdom and audacity. This influence, however, is manifested only in rare instances when some problem is decided by a general meeting. On all other occasions everyone lives as he wishes and does as he pleases.

Usually all toions have slaves who are called kalgas. A kalga is the property of his owner and can be disposed of at will; he is considered a chattel, not a human being. During certain ceremonies and special occasions it is the custom to kill kalgas. For example, when a toion dies one or two kalgas are killed so that the toion will have the service he needs in his next life. This kind of killing is no longer done on Sitka. The Chief Managers have been working at this constantly, and have finally succeeded in persuading toions that instead of killing a kalga they should sell him to the Company or free him. But if the killing is no longer in vogue next to the walls of the fortress in view of the Russians, this does not mean that this barbaric custom has been completely abandoned by the Sitka Kolosh. They say with total assurance that whenever a toion wants to kill a kalga he takes him to one of the settlements of a friendly tribe and kills him there in accordance with custom. The custom of killing kalgas is universal among all the other Kolosh.

When the former Chief Manager Baranov finally established himself on Sitka, he completely forbade the Kolosh to come to New Arkhangel. Not one of them was allowed to settle even at a considerable distance away from the fort. The main settlement of Sitka Kolosh was located on the Iablonnyi Islands near Sitka, but they lived there unsupervised and it was impossible to have advance warning about their plans and intentions, if and when they planned to attack the fort. It was likewise dangerous for the Russians to send men out to work in the forest or to go fishing. All of this led the former Chief Manager, Captain of the Second Rank [Matvei] Muraviev, to decide to settle the Kolosh near the fort, under its cannon so to speak, in order to keep all of their belongings and their families under control and thus to hold the Kolosh in some degree of supervision. There is no doubt that this measure would have been quite advantageous if at the same time he had gradually tried to bring the Kolosh and the Russians together, and to introduce them to luxury items, and thus to install in them the desire for new goods so that they would try to find a way to acquire them. This they could have done by working in the harbor, and by doing such work, without realizing it, they would have become accustomed to our way of life, to obedience, and they would have replaced Company laborers who are at the present time procured at great expense and with great difficulty. Unfortunately, such measures were accepted quite unwillingly; only during the administration of Captain of the First Rank [Adolph] Etolin, that is nearly 20 years after the Kolosh were permitted to settle in New Arkhangel, were they hired for harbor work. After Etolin's departure from the colonies, this measure was again almost completely halted. Captain of the Second Rank [Nikolai] Rosenberg finally dealt the matter a fatal blow when he allowed the Kolosh to see how much the Russians feared them. The result was that in 1855 they attacked New Arkhangel. The present Chief

Manager of the colony, Captain of the First Rank [Ivan] Furuhelm, has been persuaded to undertake again this plan that Etolin introduced 20 years ago. We should soon be able to see quite satisfactory results.

At present the Kolosh work willingly, and their needs increase more and more. Prior to this they used to receive 100 puds of flour from the Company per year, but now they receive more than 100 puds per month, and it has not yet been a whole year since they started working for us. Think of the result if this system had been adopted 20 years ago! There is no reason to doubt that it will be just barely possible to bring the Kolosh into complete submission over time by peaceful means. We must convince them, without resorting to force, that they will have no chance if they fight the Russians, and that no transgression against the Russians will go unpunished. Similar measures are particularly necessary in regard to the Kolosh who live in the sounds. But this cannot be achieved by increasing the garrisons in our settlements nor by constructing a number of forts whose upkeep would be expensive and ineffectual; rather, it can be achieved by the timely appearance of naval cruisers throughout the sounds. Once the Kolosh have become accustomed to seeing that the Russians are clearly superior in strength, they will gradually and willingly enter into relations with us, and not only will they be forced to acknowledge our dominion, but they will come to accept our customs without realizing it.

If, in addition to these measures, we will concern ourselves with edu- cating the Kolosh children, with the assistance of missionaries who would try to learn the Kolosh language and who would be willing to live with the savages and not hide from them behind the walls of the redoubts and forts, then naturally we will see good results over time. I also believe that it would be most bene- ficial to free the kalgas from the tyranny of the toions, and to accomplish this it is only necessary to assure kalgas that they will always find real protection in every one of our settlements. However this measure also cannot be realized without the assistance of naval cruisers. Later, in the chapter on trade and the defense of the territory, I shall have an opportunity to return to this subject.

In spite of deeply ingrained prejudices, superstition and total ignorance, many of the Kolosh have turned to Orthodoxy; or, to describe it more clearly, they have been christened, for one cannot consider this as true conversion. Those who accept a new way of life are usually guided by some sort of personal gain; real conversion over a long period will be hindered both by polygamy, which they will not give up without a struggle, and by the fact that our mis- sionaries do not understand the Kolosh language and thus cannot influence those people through the strength of their words or with persuasion.

Such are our immediate neighbors, whose number on Sitka alone is between 600 and 700 persons; in summer when they come in from other settlements to fish, there are more than *1,000* of them. As many as 400 of these, both sexes, are considered to have accepted the Orthodox faith. The total number of Kolosh in Russian possessions is between 15,000 and 20,000.

ADMINISTRATION

For administrative purposes, the colonies are divided into the following *departments*:

1) *Sitka* includes the Northwest Coast of America from Cape Saint Elias south to 54°40" and all the offshore islands in the region.

2) *Kodiak* includes the coast and islands in Kenai Bay and Chugach Sound, the coast of the Alaska Peninsula to the meridian of the Shumagin Islands, the islands of Kodiak and Ukamok and all the adjacent islands, and Semidi Islands. To the north it embraces the coast of Bristol Bay and the Nushagak and Kuskovym river basins.

3) the *Northern* or *Mikhailovsk* includes the Kuskovym and Kwikhpak river basins and the coast of Norton Sound to Bering Strait.

4) *Unalaska* includes the Alaska peninsula from the meridian of the Shumagin Islands, the Fox and Sinnakh islands, as well as the Northern or Pribylov Islands north of the Aleutian archipelago.

5) *Atkhinsk* includes the Andreanov, Rat, Near and Komandorskie islands.

6) *Kuril* consists of the group of islands of this name, from Urup to the Kamchatka peninsula.

The main colonial office is located in New Arkhangel on the island of Sitka. The headquarters of the Chief Manager and his assistant are located here, as well as the office, the admiralty, the main warehouses both for ships and for the storage of provisions, hunting equipment, furs and other goods. Here too the Company's ships spend the winter. Sitka is also the location for the main office which has direct jurisdiction over all officials who handle Company business and bookkeeping. This office also administers the Sitka Department. The manager of the office is selected and approved by the Governing Board of the Company. The Kodiak Department also administers the office located on Kodiak Island at Pavlovsk Harbor, while the rest of the departments are administered by prikashchiks appointed and approved by the Chief Manager of the colonies; these are located in the Mikhailovsk redoubt, and on the islands of Urup, Atka, Attu, Bering, Mednyi, Unalaska and Unga. In addition, in areas where there is need for such, there are colonial posts for barter with the natives, and there are special prikashchiks or baidarshchiks in the redoubt and odinochkas. All of these persons are appointed by the Chief Manager from among Russian or creoles in Company service.

LIBRARY
BRYAN COLLEGE
DAYTON, TENN. 37321

Russians and creoles are supervised by the main administration of the colony in accordance with the existing laws in Russia. Dependent natives are supervised by their toions or elders who are chosen by their own people and approved by the Chief Manager. As far as the independent tribes are concerned, they are self-administered, in accordance with their own customs, and the Company has only a very limited authority over the ones who settle near our redoubts or forts,

Accordingly, all matters involving business and all disputes are settled on the spot, either by the agreement of the group, as for example among the Aleuts and other subject peoples, or by the authority of the Chief Manager. Whenever the Chief Manager cannot decide on his own authority, a colonial council is convened, consisting of the Chief Manager's assistant, the administrator of the New Arkhangel office and several other persons in Company service. In the case of serious wrongdoings the colonial administration is only required to investigate immediately and then send a report of the matter to Iakutsk, along with a report on the accused.

When one studies the colonial administration in detail, one is struck by the fact that it is extraordinarily simple and direct, and since the Chief Managers are selected by the Company and the government, one really does not expect serious injustice, particularly premeditated. Of course the Chief Manager does have quite *extensive authority*, but this cannot be otherwise in a region so distant, which is half savage and barely developed. I am fully convinced that in respect to independent natives, especially the Kolosh, the Chief Manager should have even greater authority. It takes too long to ask Petersburg for a decision, when instant action is called for. At best a reply would take no less than eleven months. For this reason it would seem helpful not only to augment the authority of the Chief Manager, but to change his title and to call him the Governor, for the simple reason that he would be more of a person representing the government than a Company prikashchik, concerned with the well-being and administration of the region, not just commercial benefit to the Company. For its own operations the Company may have a special agent in New Arkhangel.

The duties of the Chief Managers are determined by the Company's charter, but in general the charter is quite unsatisfactory and unclear. It includes a large number of superficial formalities and loses sight of basic matters. Many paragraphs are self-contradictory. Consequently a Chief Manager of the colony who would use the quite extensive authority is completely hindered by the charter. Moreover this charter does not give any real guarantee to protect service personnel and inhabitants from arbitrary decisions of the Chief Manager, should the Manager wish to oppress them. Of course in its own interest the Company must be extremely circumspect in selecting its Chief Manager, and one should give it full credit that with the exception of Baranov, not one of them used his power for evil, and even Baranov perpetrated evil not deliberately, but as a result of special circumstances in which he was placed by the necessity of organizing a new region with the assistance of persons who for the most part were quite disloyal.

At the present time absolute arbitrary rule cannot be permitted, and in

extending more authority to the Chief Manager or Governor of the colonies, it is necessary at the same time to make him accountable before the law, not only before the Governing Board; that is, we must extend to everyone living in the colonies the right and the opportunity to submit petitions against sufferings and oppressions directly to the Governor, not to the Company.

In respect to the tribal administration that presently exists among the Aleuts and other subject natives, this of course should not only not be changed, but on the contrary, every effort should be made to strengthen it, and gradually to introduce it among natives who are presently considered independent, contrary to every reasonable notion. To accomplish this, it is essential to attract influential toions to the Russian side, and not to hesitate to give presents for this purpose wherever necessary, nor various visible awards for distinction, which all savages love. Finally, these toions should be protected not only by word but by deed. At the conclusion of this memorandum, I shall once again have the opportunity to return to this matter.

Kolosh toion.

PROVISIONING

In compliance with Imperial approval of its charter, a prime task of the Company has been to provision the region. One must confess that a very great deal still remains to be done in this regard. Unsatisfactory supply is partly due to climate and partly to a certain amount of indifference with which the Company has viewed this vital matter; once they had imposed a certain degree of order, they gave little attention to finding new ways to provision the region with all necessary items, even when this might often have benefited the country and profited the Company. The climate certainly is unfavorable. Constant rain and fog prevail in the Aleutian Islands throughout almost the entire year, with the exception of three or four months in winter when there are periods of freezing temperatures, although these are not constant. As a result agriculture is not possible. It is true that in some areas potatoes and radishes are grown, but cabbage, for example, has never been grown, even on Sitka, probably because of the ignorance of the gardeners. If potatoes were cultivated they could provide supplementary food for the Aleuts; but unfortunately the fact is that they have to go out to hunt right at the time gardens must be worked and cultivated, so that half of the people are away, and the other half are busy preparing fish for winter during this period. If the Aleuts were industrious, it would be possible for those persons who do not go out hunting, including the women, to do both: prepare enough fish for winter and also tend gardens and cut enough hay for cattle fodder. But the Aleuts usually do not want to work, and they are especially put off by the job of cutting and stacking hay. Every time it rains the hay has to be turned and brought in early so that it will not be soaked, and the Aleuts consider this constant work unacceptable.

At one time the Company passed a resolution to supply cattle to the Aleuts with the sole proviso that after the herd had increased the Company was to be given back the same number of head it had furnished. However, the experiment was a failure. Some of the Aleuts did not have enough feed for the livestock over the winter; others begged to have the cattle taken back, because, although they required only minimal attention, this interfered with their preparation of iukola for winter. The Aleuts actually do not ever use milk in their diet, and they have not become accustomed to eating beef; thus they felt they were being quite oppressed by having to care for cattle. And when they were given cattle they could not build barns because there are no trees on the islands, and so the

Aleuts had to keep the cattle near their iurts, right where fish were spread out over poles to dry. Naturally the cows hooked the poles with their horns, knocked the iukola onto the ground, and then trod on it with their hooves, and lay down on top of it, causing a shortage of provisions.

The Company also tried to propagate swine and goats on the islands, but pigs rooted under the iurts and ruined some of the vegetables in the gardens, while goats jumped up on top of the iurts and broke the roofs; consequently the Aleuts rejected both goats and swine. And thus neither agriculture nor livestock breeding were introduced on the islands, and the Company finally stopped trying to do anything about it.

Although the climate on the Aleutian Islands is unfavorable for agriculture or livestock production, other areas along the mainland starting with Kenai Bay have a completely different climate. Experience has shown that although the summer season in Kenai Bay is not long, it is nonetheless constant, and livestock can be raised there. Livestock can also be successfully raised all along the Northwest Coast of America and very likely even on the offshore islands as well as on the island of Sitka. The Russians are occupying only a small strip of land on this island along the shore of the bay where New Arkhangel has been built; of course livestock cannot be raised in this area because there is a total lack of the necessary forage, and thus it is impossible to provide hay for livestock here. But who can be certain that there may not be meadows with abundant grass in the inland areas, where to date no Russians have penetrated, and that livestock might not be raised there? No investigation into this matter has been made, and to the present time the interior of the island is quite unknown to the Russians.* Moreover, up until 1855 the colonial citizens Ovchinnikov and Makarov found it possible to keep a small number of livestock even near New Arkhangel, and although it was difficult, they managed to cut enough hay in small meadows within the forest.

If a substantial number of citizens were to settle along the American coast, it would be possible to develop both agriculture and livestock programs there; but the fear of the Kolosh is too strong among colonial citizens, and very few persons will volunteer to settle in such places where they can expect the savages to attack at anytime. The Company does not have the means to maintain special garrisons in these settlements to protect persons, or to build forts for that purpose. For this reason there has never been an attempt to establish these settlements.

Up to the present time the Company has also not been able to introduce agriculture along the Kenai shore because workers would be needed for that, and they are very expensive to hire. This is the reason that the Company is forever declaring that it is impossible to introduce agriculture and livestock breeding

---

* One of the hired navigators serving with the Company told me that out of curiosity he took a baidarka across the lake in the Ozersk redoubt on Sitka Island and went into a small creek that was fed from another lake located near Serebriannikov Bay; he saw fine pasture lands there. This information about the interior is not known by any of the Sitka inhabitants.

into the colonies because of the climate, and has never tried to make the necessary investigations to find suitable places for new settlements. As a result, the provisioning of the region relies on the importation of items from other lands, and on the possibility of getting some things from the Kolosh. Consequently self-sufficiency of the country has been forfeited, and provisionment, right to the present, is most unsatisfactory. Up to the present grain has been mostly brought in from Russia; only a small amount comes in from California. Rye flour brought from Russia has been sold in the colonies as follows:

1856 (per pud)	9.42 rubles, paper
1857	7.05
1859	6.47
1860	4.51

Delivered via the Amur:

1857	3.48
1858	4.13

Since bread is an item of critical importance, they decided to set a fixed price that was not changed even when the Company paid a higher price for flour. The set sale price is five paper rubles per pud of rye flour and common wheat flour; ten rubles for millet flour. These prices are still in existence at present. Since the Company quite often paid more for flour, naturally, by selling rye flour for five rubles the Company bore a considerable loss. As a result they adopted the rule that they would sell as little flour as possible in the colony; they refuse to sell to the Aleuts at all if possible, and sell only small amounts to persons who are not in Company service, and that only in extreme cases. They try to hold out enough from the annual supply to build up a large enough reserve to last for two years. This is the reason they adopted the rule not to accustom the Aleuts to luxuries such as flour, because this was unprofitable to the Company.

Up to now the colonies have received as much as 25,000 puds of rye flour and common wheat flour from Russia or from Hamburg. The cost to the Company, including freight to New Arkhangel, has been 1.66 silver rubles. Thus a chetvert of 9 puds cost six silver rubles, and freight is one silver ruble per pud.

Currently the Governing Board allows the colonial administration to bring in flour from California, and there is no doubt that this flour is secured less expensively than that brought in from Russia: first, because agriculture is developing each year in California to such a degree that at present a considerable amount of grain is being sent to Europe and thus the price for flour is gradually decreasing; second, it is cheaper to bring grain from California on Company ships than to bring it from Russia, especially since grain can be delivered to the colonies on ships that carry ice to California and previously had to return in ballast, for which it was necessary to pay a considerable amount of money, with no return. Of course it must be understood that in order to have an adequate source of grain supply from California, the Company will have to have a warehouse there, so that the agent who purchases grain when prices are low may store it until ships arrive, without having to pay additional money. Later on we shall see that it is entirely possible to build these, and that they should have been built long ago, if the Company had not lost sight of its own interest.

Let us emphasize once again that 25,000 puds is not enough for the colonies; this amount must be doubled, and it will probably have to be increased again.

It has been noted that up until now livestock production in the colonies has been insignificant, because all inhabitants of the colonies provide themselves with fish--either fresh, salted or dried (iukola). The latter is mainly used for food by the natives. Salt meat is also used. And persons in Company service get wild sheep from the Kolosh. The colonies abound in fish; they are especially plentiful when they swim up the rivers and creeks to spawn. At that time the Company puts up various supplies for winter. Part of the fish is salted to be sold or supplied to Company service personnel, and iukola is prepared for the Aleuts. Aleuts, who are left in the settlement after the others have gone out on the sea otter hunt, catch fish for themselves and dry it. A sufficient amount is distributed free of charge to all settlements, and there is also a large supply left in the colonial stores so that it will be possible to supply the Aleuts when they have used up their own provisions.

According to the rules, all Company service personnel receive salaries of less then 1,000 paper rubles per year, and in addition many of the common laborers who work for the Company and live in the colony receive food from a communal kitchen. Bread is also baked in a communal bakery and is distributed to service personnel at a price of five paper rubles per pud. In order to buy bread, everyone who is entitled to a ration receives 90 paper rubles per year, which means that each portion is 18 puds. By this calculation, the cost of food from the communal kitchen, including bread, is 166.9125 paper rubles per person per annum. Married persons who do not wish to receive food from the communal kitchen receive this sum in cash. The communal kitchen usually serves salted fish; salted meat is given out only on holidays, and fresh game only when it is available in a larger amount than is needed for distribution to top ranking persons such as the Chief Manager, his assistant, the office administrator, ships' captains and senior prikashchiks. But wild sheep is eaten only on Sitka; it is not available in other parts of the colony where fish and salt meat are the usual diet.

The Company has tried to find ways of getting good salted meat at low enough prices so that it would be available for everyone; this was the reason they tried to bring in salted meat via the around-the-world route, from Aian and from the Amur, as well as from California. Up to the present it has taken from 1,500 to 2,000 puds of salted meat per year to supply the colony. The most difficult and least satisfactory means has been the around-the-world supply route. This is the reason they began to salt meat in Aian. They would drive livestock there from various places in Siberia. It is obvious that the exhausted livestock driven to Aian, and killed shortly after it reached there, could not provide good meat. The salted meat was tough, stringy, and sold there for 9.80 paper rubles per pud. It sold in the colonies at a slightly higher price, 10 paper rubles per pud, or 25 paper kopecks per pound. But even that price was too high for people who were poor and had large families. Salted meat was prepared by the Amur Company and was floated down the Amur. It was considered somewhat better than that from Aian, even though the salting process was not always carried out very carefully, so that tails and other parts which normally would not be used for salting were sometimes placed in the barrels. The price was 10.56 paper rubles per pud. Salted meat from California was the best of all, but initially the price was 25.88 paper rubles per pud, and later it dropped to 15.48. In the colonies it sold for 20 rubles per pud. There is still hope that prices will drop, and then it will obviously be more advantageous to bring in salted meat from California. In any case, if livestock is not bred in the colonies, salt meat will only be available to a few, and the majority will have to eat salt fish, to which, it is true, they are accustomed; but this provides a food that is completely unappetizing and not very nutritious. I must confess that I have never eaten shchee or soup with such a foul taste.

Pork is of some use, but since pigs here usually eat fish and shellfish, their meat is disgusting. Pigs could be kept in the forest and allowed to run free, but people are afraid the Kolosh would kill them.

As far as poultry is concerned, there are only chickens in the colony, and they too are often fed on fish and have a bad flavor. Regardless of this, the price of a chicken on Sitka, for example, is from five to seven paper rubles. Ten eggs cost between five and six rubles.

Potatoes come in part from Company gardens, and in part from the Aleuts, from colonial citizens, and from the Kolosh. This is also true of turnips. Cabbage grows poorly and does not form a head, so that sauerkraut is either brought in from California or sometimes from around the world. For this reason it is given out in small amounts. Peas are cooked once a week in the communal kitchen, and either wheat or rice kasha once a week. Potatoes and turnips are cooked, and also dried fruit that comes in from Hamburg. This is good if there is nothing better.

Rum, which has replaced vodka here, is given out to service personnel in the amount of eight charkas per year. Beyond that, the Chief Manager has the right to give out one charka of rum after hard work, or in bad weather, so that actually service personnel receive one or two charkas per week. The rest of the inhabitants buy rum from Company stores in a designated amount at a set price. Lower rank service personnel may buy it only with the permission of their immediate superiors. Savages are not sold any rum whatsoever, but sometimes they are given a small amount as a kind of treat to reward them for work. The restriction on the sale of rum was established in order to control drunkenness among both savages and Company personnel, but this measure has never attained its desired goal. Foreigners give the savages rum in exchange for furs, which thus slip out of the hands of the Company. Workers and service persons get rum from higher ranking persons in spite of the fact that this is strictly prohibited and is supervised. In actual fact, if one has to hire a craftsman or a laborer, he must pay for this work either in currency, at an incredible price, or in rum, which is ten times cheaper. For example, for making a pair of boots a shoemaker gets either 30 to 35 paper rubles, or a bottle of rum, which can be bought in the Company store for 3.50 paper rubles. The temptation is very great. For a relatively small expenditure it is cheaper to pay with a bottle of rum than to pay 35 rubles for the work. Because of this, rum has become an object of illicit trade, and there is no way to halt it under the present conditions. At present a bottle of rum sells for between 30 and 35 rubles among the workers. This also creates additional harm because they secretly exchange rum with the Kolosh for wild game, greens, fish, etc., with the result that these supplies come into the market in short supply, and are insufficient for persons who need fresh supplies. Law-abiding persons who do not wish to carry on illegal trade are in want, and a few persons who are not so conscientious have plenty of everything.

Wild sheep is almost the only fresh meat the Kolosh bring in. They are the only ones who can hunt the chamois [iaman] in the high mountains which are covered by impenetrable forests. This hunting task was assigned to a group of Russians and creoles, but the attempt was not successful.

The Kolosh bring game, fish, greens, etc., to the market and exchange it all in the Company stores for blankets, rice, flour and other things they need. Everything that is bought from the Kolosh is sold to the inhabitants at a set price. Naturally such things go first to persons of high rank, then to those of lower rank, and then to ordinary persons. Anything left over is given to the communal kitchen. With this arrangement, if certain persons secretly buy fresh produce from the Kolosh in exchange for vodka, and then resell it under the table at three times the price to persons who want the produce, the result is that in the first place supplies in the market decrease, and second, the poor have to do without fresh food at all. To date all measures adopted to put an end to this illicit trade have been unsuccessful and have only led to an increase in the price of rum. I believe the main fault lies in the regulated sale of rum and in the Company's own prohibition against selling rum to the Kolosh. If the sale of rum in the colonies were to be carried on freely, then the Kolosh would not sell their supplies on the side since it would obviously be more advantageous to sell them in the market.

But this is not the only circumstance that sometimes affects the shortage of fresh food. Whenever the Kolosh are in any way unhappy with the Russians, or when they are quarreling among themselves, or when they celebrate their holidays, they stop bringing in supplies to the market, and New Arkhangel suffers accordingly. There is no need to explain how desirable it is for the Company to liberate itself from this dependence. The only way this can be achieved is through an effort to raise livestock, to train its own hunters so they can eventually supply wild sheep and other game, to increase the number of gardens, and even to force the Aleuts to plant communal gardens. If we have a constant sufficient supply of good salted meat and pickled cabbage, the Kolosh will realize that we can get along without them. Meanwhile, we must establish closer ties with the Kolosh, teach them how to work, and instill certain needs in them of which they presently have no comprehension. In general, it is necessary to give serious consideration to provisioning the region, look into this problem thoroughly, and after having done away with unprofitable aspects, to organize this area of activity that is presently in a very unsatisfactory condition.

During Shelikhov's time, all Russian settlements on the Aleutian Islands were enclosed by a stockade for fear the Aleuts would attack. On Kodiak, in addition to the stockade, they also built a wooden fort. But with the subsequent pacification of the Aleuts, these precautionary measures were unnecessary; the fortifications were allowed to fall into desuetude, and when the colonial administration was finally transferred from Kodiak to Sitka, the fort at Pavlovsk Harbor was likewise no longer maintained.

Meanwhile, the Company wished to establish permanent trade with the savage tribes who lived on the mainland within our possessions; the Company built trading posts at several places on the coast and then farther inland as it became necessary. The savages could bring their furs to these trading posts to exchange them with the Company for various items they needed. Since one can never rely on the peaceful and friendly disposition of most of the savages, these posts were fortified accordingly, and were called either redoubts or odinochkas. The name odinochka is also very often given to posts which are completely unfortified but located in secure places exclusively for trade purposes.

In New Arkhangel at the present time various persons serve on a permanent basis. There are 11 soldiers, 14 cowherds, stockmen, etc., and 73 men who work as carpenters, coopers, tanners, meat and fish salters, blacksmiths, and in other capacities as permanent Company master craftsmen: a total of 98 men. The rest, except for any who are ill, are put to work in general labor.

In the colonies the lower ranks are not issued uniforms because of a shortage of tailors. They receive credit on the Company for uniforms and ammunition in the amount of 27.44 paper rubles per year. When the lower ranks have completed their terms of service in the colonies, they are sent to their battalions where they are issued appropriate uniforms. Meanwhile, throughout the entire period of their stay in the colonies, soldiers have to clothe themselves at their own expense out of the allowance they receive. Inasmuch as they usually work in cold rainy weather, they wear out their clothing and footwear quite rapidly, especially since all of these items that are sent there are of poor quality; work boots are completely worthless. A working soldier wears out at least six pairs of such boots every year. According to current prices in the colonies, this means an expenditure of 60 paper rubles per year just for footwear. From evidence submitted by the military commander, Lieutenant Chausov, it is apparent that clothing for each soldier costs more than 200 paper rubles per year, even if they take very good care of their clothing. Thus it is evident that the amount designated for outfitting the men barely covers one-tenth of the actual cost.

On the other hand, it would also be disadvantageous to issue uniforms in accordance with government regulations, because working conditions in this climate would cause them to wear out in less than half a year. What the Company should do is to increase the allowance for the cost of the uniform to include the cost of issuing, every year, at current prices in the colonies, to each soldier: one work coat, one pair of dutchman's breeches, one warm shirt, two pairs of leather gloves and mittens, and one pair of work boots. At the same time they should try to see to it that these items that are brought in to the colonies are of good quality, and not substandard, as is presently the case.

In order for soldiers to appear on duty in proper attire, they should be issued one regulation overcoat, one uniform, a neckpiece and summer trousers. These should be issued periodically, and we should insist that these items be issued by military authorities in Siberia, to be paid for by the Company at established prices. Soldiers should be given money for the rest. Of course under such circumstances soldiers will have to pay for clothing out of their salaries. But since they receive an annual maintenance allowance of up to 440 paper rubles, and nearly every ablebodied soldier earns a substantial amount of money from hired work, and since the pay in the colonies is actually quite high, they should have money left over, if they practice thrift.

In the chapter on provisioning I have already stated that soldiers receive rations from the communal kitchen. This food consists of soup made from salt fish, or fresh fish in summer; occasionally there is salted meat, and once a week peas and kasha. But this food is issued only once a day, for noon dinner. For supper anyone who wishes may eat leftovers from the noon meal, warmed-up in the barracks if he chooses. Breakfast is not issued at all. As a result, all of the lower ranks without exception have to buy sugar and tea for breakfast and to extend the meager noon meal. Of course everyone who works in the rain all day needs a hot meal in the evening; because of this all the stoves in the barracks have kettles, tea pots and cups warming up from morning until night. This problem should be given immediate attention and should be more satisfactorily resolved than it is at present.

Few of the soldiers are indebted to the Company; on the contrary, almost all have credit with the Company. As of July 1, 1860 the total indebtedness of the soldiers amounted to 1,199.73 paper rubles. Soldiers had credit on the Company to the amount of 57,039.69 paper rubles, and a clothing credit of 22,592.88 paper rubles. Some soldiers have between 700 and 1,000 paper rubles credit, and two have more than 2,000 rubles credit apiece. Such considerable credit could obviously not be accumulated even by the most meticulous economy, and as far as the soldiers in the colonies are concerned, one cannot say that they are thrifty. The fact is that from the time they come to the colonies, all of them, almost without exception, are engaged in hiring themselves out in their free time, to individual persons, for any kind of work. They receive a considerable amount of money for this, or a set amount of rum with which they then buy wild sheep from the Kolosh and all kinds of food that they then sell to the inhabitants of New Arkhangel either for a high price, or again for rum, the price of which has risen in illicit trade to 30 or 35 paper rubles per bottle. Through these transactions they have accumulated substantial sums of money. So far the Chief Manager has taken no measures to put an end to this trade that is quite burdensome for the inhabitants, and up to the present time this trade is still carried on, although to a much lesser degree, and it will not be ended until the region is more abundantly provisioned, until the issue of rum from the warehouses is not so tightly controlled, until laborers and craftsmen are hired at fair prices, and, finally, when everyone is able to buy provisions from somewhere other than the Company store.

Presently many of the soldiers have asked to be assigned during the summer months as sailors aboard Company ships; probably the Chief Manager will have to agree to this because there appears to be a considerable shortage of sailors.

Nineteen men from the lower ranks of Siberian line battalions died between 1855 and January 1, 1861. It must be noted that in spite of the adverse climate the health of the lower ranks would have been quite good if many of them had not suffered from rheumatism and lumbago, which afflicted them during their trip along the Amur River when they were logging and building a road from Kys to DeKastrii. They had to work in marshes with no shelter, and suffered from the severe shortage of food. During the seven-year period they spent in the colonies, only one deserted.

Small islands near New Arkhangel.

SHIPS

Ships that belong to the Russian American Company may be divided into two
groups: those that can sail around the world between Kronshtadt and the colonies,
and the colonial ships, primarily designated for service in the colonies. At
present there are four ships in the first category: Tsaritsa, of 946 tons,
erroneously listed in the Company inventory as 1,900 tons; Kamchatka, 900 (?)
tons; Imperator Nikolai I, 595 tons; Tsesarevich, 529 tons. There are eight
colonial ships: the barks Kniaz Menshikov at 273 tons and Nakhimov at 278 tons;
the brigs Shelikhov at 270 tons and Velikii Kniaz Konstantin at 170 tons; the
screw steamers Imperator Aleksandr II at 500 tons and 70 horsepower and Velikii
Kniaz Konstantin, 300 tons and 75 horsepower; a paddlewheel for short voyages,
Imperator Nikolai I at 60 horsepower and 65 tons; the tugboat Baranov, 30 horsepower and 60 tons. There is also a 65-ton schooner, Tungus, but she is already
completely unseaworthy. Of all these ships, without doubt the best is Tsaritsa,
and also the steamer Aleksandr II. Both of these ships were built in the United
States of America, the first in 1854 and the second in 1855. The rest of the
ships have seen use but they are still good, except for the brig Velikii Kniaz
Konstantin, which is presently undergoing a complete overhaul; although it has
been used in Company service for twenty years, it will still be good for eight
to ten more years of sailing in the colonies. The bark Nakhimov, built in
Baltimore in 1848, was purchased during the recent [Crimean] war in San Francisco,
and sailed to the colonies under the American flag. Inasmuch as this vessel has
been used primarily to transport ice, it has become quite waterlogged and is old
before its time. Being in American hands it has not been kept in good shape,
and as a result it looks worse than it actually is; but it is in poor condition.
The steamer Velikii Kniaz Konstantin is ironclad; but her hull has not been
painted since she was purchased in 1856, and only rarely has it been tarred;
thus a large part of the plating has rusted. In 1859 when she was returning to
Sitka she began to leak and would have sunk if it were not for the fact that she
had double-hull construction. In this condition she managed to reach the island
of Attu where she underwent three months of partial repair, and in this manner
she finally managed to reach Sitka. This year she will be beached at New
Arkhangel, examined and repaired. The steamer Nikolai I and [the tugboat]
Baranov were built of cypress in New Arkhangel and they are in good condition.
The rest of the vessels are constructed of oak and pine; most were built in the
United States.

The Company deserves full credit for the fact that all of the ships are well maintained, and those which go around the world are meticulously cared for, in spite of the fact that all of them are commercial ships. For example, the ship Tsaritsa, aboard which I completed a 22-day voyage from San Francisco to New Arkhangel in the stormiest period of the year and under the most adverse circumstances, may certainly serve as an example even for most of our Navy vessels in regard to solid construction, beautiful fittings, neatness, cleanliness and order. We several times endured severe storms which went on for two or three days, with no danger to the rigging. The topgallants were frequently in such a wind that some ships would have had their sails blown to shreds, but the topgallant mast not only withstood this well, but did not even bend, because the tackle had been so well laced and tied down. Nowhere can one see ropes with frayed ends or running tackle which looks as if it is about to break and endanger other ropes or standing tackle. For all of this the Company obviously must express its great thanks to the hired Captain Riddell, who has commanded this ship for a number of years.

There is a good deal of complaint that the Company maintains its ships for commercial purposes and that one can scarcely hear a word of Russian spoken aboard them. In my opinion both of these charges are totally unfounded. The purpose of the Company ships is to transport goods, both to supply the colonies with all necessities and to export colonial goods. The faster the goods reach their destination the less expense there is, the lower the freight costs, and consequently the lower the cost of the transported goods. The markup imposed on these goods for freight charges is passed directly on to the consumer, because no commercial company can sell goods or make commercial transactions at a loss. Consequently if circumstances force them to sell goods for appreciably less, then it naturally follows that every effort must be made to avoid raising the cost.

The [Russian] American Company is at present in the situation that if they had to keep their ships in a semi-military capacity, they would be put to considerable expense. Thus they have adopted the policy of functioning like all commercial houses in the world. One cannot use the East India Company as a typical example; they were in a unique position, and there was a great difference between the policies of the East Indian colonies and our North American ones. Even if the Company were to continue to maintain their ships along military lines, as they have done previously, then the expense for this would be completely in vain, because the Company could never be in a position, with their ships, to protect the colonies from encroachment by any naval power.

Experience has dictated the direction which the Company should follow, and from the time when their ships began to operate along the lines of commercial vessels throughout the whole world, the provisioning of the colonies and the general transport of goods has been twice as fast and much less expensive than formerly. It is also true that Company ships are commanded for the most part by hired captains from Finland. But the Company should not be criticized for this. At present few naval officers are willing to join the Company. They demand a considerably larger salary, with the result that only two Company ships are commanded by naval officers; all the rest are under the command of hired skippers, either Finnish or creole. For a voyage around the world a naval officer demands a salary of not less than 10,000 or 15,000 paper rubles. Anyone who is quite unfamiliar with handling a commercial ship where a great deal of special training is required needs a navigator and a larger number of sailors. He also requires a supercargo, for a naval officer has none of the special knowledge and familiarity with the problems of accepting freight from Company agents aboard the ship, delivery of colonial goods to various foreign commercial houses, and the preparation of accounts for all of this. When a naval officer finally does acquire this necessary experience, then the period of his service with the Company ends; there are very few who will volunteer to renew their contracts for several more years, especially without a substantial increase in their salary.

On the other hand a hired captain who has in a manner of speaking grown up aboard commercial ships, has often begun his service on such ships with the rank of sailor and is thoroughly knowledgeable both with sailing such ships and with all the duties of the captain of a commercial vessel. He needs neither a supercargo, nor a large crew, nor a navigator. When necessary he can stand alone at the wheel while the crew and navigator handle the sails; furthermore he is satisfied with a fairly modest salary, in the range of 5,000 to 7,000 paper rubles. Only a few of the older skippers receive this amount, those who have served the Company many years.

In former times in spite of the fact that Company ships were commanded by fine naval officers, it took at least three years for these ships to complete a voyage from Kronshtadt to the colonies and return. Now it is true circumstances are different, but with hired skippers this same voyage takes eighteen months: eight months to bring goods to the colonies from Europe, and then after the ship has unloaded in New Arkhangel it is used to transport colonial goods to Aian, and from there back to New Arkhangel, and finally to Shanghai where a considerable amount of time is required to dispose of its goods and to take on a cargo of tea.

Of course the Company would gladly hire Russian captains, but where would it find them? Persons who have been schooled in commercial navigation are not experienced in it, and need quite some time before they are ready to properly command a ship. However the Company willingly takes them into service as navigators, and if they sail for several years and become very skilled seamen they remain in Company service and receive command of a ship and finally become quite exceptional skippers. At the present time there are three sea captains in Company service who had been trained in the school of commercial navigation; they commanded Company ships for a number of years and have now retired from sailing but continue to serve the Company usefully by accepting important posts in the colonies. But these gentlemen were trained in school, just as are the Finnish skippers who are now preparing young seamen for the Company. Of course it is too bad that these sailors are not fluent in the Russian language. But this is a common failing among all Finns and of course the Company cannot be blamed for this.

At present there is a shortage of navigators in the colonies, or as they are called here, senior and junior assistants to captains. This is due to the fact that if young men who have matriculated in the school of commercial navigation enter Company service, then when their period of service is up and they have become experienced seamen, they soon return to Russia, where, thanks to the development of steamship sailing, they hope to receive positions with good pay, and not be subjected to the difficulties and deprivations with which their service aboard Company ships is associated. The Company should either seek out navigators from among naval personnel, or train them at its own expense in the colonies, or train young seamen in Russia who would then be required to serve the Company for a determined period of time, or it should hire navigators from among these same Finns. On voyages around the world the majority of the crews consist of hired sailors who are Finns. In the first place there is no regulation which requires the Company to hire only sailors of the Orthodox faith, and actually, Finns are Russian subjects; finally, where can one find genuine Russian sailors to hire? Russian hired sailors are still very rare, and those who are hired are employed, for example, in Kronshtadt for short voyages, rather than being sent to serve aboard ships.

As of January 1, 1861 there were 36 Navy seamen in Company service. There are not enough sailors to man colonial ships; the total is about 130 in all, and some of these are creoles and at the present time they have even begun to hire some Kolosh, although only a few. Because of their disposition creoles find it very difficult to serve aboard ships, and for this reason they are unwilling sailors. Government sailors receive annual shore rations as follows: non-commissioned officers receive 500 paper rubles as salary, 90 paper rubles in shares [in the Company], and 22.20 paper rubles for uniforms, a total of 612.20 paper rubles; sailors receive a salary of 350 paper rubles, 90 rubles in shares, and 20.44 rubles for uniforms, a total of 460.44 rubles. All receive food from the communal kitchen, and by regulation they get eight charkas of rum per year plus an additional two charkas of rum per week during heavy work or foul weather. Married men with children under seven years of age receive six puds of flour per year, and those who have children between seven and fourteen years old receive twelve puds. They do not receive uniforms, but are required to outfit themselves on 20 rubles and some odd kopeks, as noted above. Of course this is not anywhere near enough money, and in this regard the situation of the sailors is similar to that of the soldiers who serve in the colonies. The only difference is that the soldiers' credit for uniforms on the Company is transferred to their battalions, while the sailors receive cash directly.

Government sailors who voyage around the world are quite well provided for in regard to food, since such ships carry special provisions. A usual ration for a sailor might consist of:

Salted beef	4 pounds*
Salted pork a total of 7 pounds	3 pounds

---

* Golovin uses "pounds" here and on page 46.--Eds.

Butter	3/4 pound
Coffee	1/2 pound
Tea	1/3 pound
Sugar	1 pound

Peas, groats, beans, potatoes, salt and pepper are added to the kettle without being rationed, and mustard and vinegar as needed. One-half cup of vodka is issued per [week]day, one cup on Saturdays, and one and one-half cups on Sundays. Fresh meat and greens are given out whenever the ship stops in port. In recent times, the captains of some ships belong to the Society of Sobriety and prohibit the use of vodka and wine altogether, and instead of vodka the crew members receive additional coffee. It is hard to tell how beneficial this measure is. Some persons believe that the use of vodka at sea is more harmful than useful. Others, on the contrary, hold that a moderate use of vodka is quite necessary. Even experienced naval hygienists differ in their views on this question. I believe, however, that a person accustomed to the daily intake of vodka will feel an acute deprivation at first, and this may have an adverse effect on his health. In any case, this problem should be thoroughly considered, and then a regulation should be issued which applies to everyone, so this is not open to abuse by captains, especially since crews are not always pleased with such regulations.

Sailors aboard Company ships receive quite poor rations; fresh meat and greens are given out infrequently, and only aboard ships that have sailed to Aian or who have carried ice to California; this involves only two ships. A usual one-month ration consists of:

Dry sea biscuits	35 pounds
Salt beef	14 pounds
Peas	8 pounds
Groats	8 pounds
Butter	5 pounds
Rum	19 charkas
Tea	35 zols
Sugar	3 pounds

Sometimes salt fish is boiled, and potatoes and dried vegetables go into the pot when they are available. Since this ration is less than that issued to sailors aboard Navy vessels, according to Rear Admiral Stepan Voevodskii, formerly Chief Manager [1854-59], the Governing Board decided to issue additional money for food to sailors in Company service. Noncommissioned officers receive 9.35 paper rubles, and seamen 6.37 paper rubles per month. The only stipulation is that this measure should not be publicized among sailors who are re-entering Company service, since they will be informed about it when they enlist.

Seamen, like soldiers, accumulate credit with the Governing Board during their period of service, and some of them also incur debts. Indebtedness of sailors as of July 1, 1860 amounted to 299.18 paper rubles, while their credit amounted to 27,128.25 paper rubles. The means for accumulating that credit were the same as those the soldiers had, except that in addition the sailors were able to smuggle rum in from California, and sell it at New Arkhangel at ten times the price.

At this point it must be noted that sailors who enter Company service immediately upon departure from Kronshtadt have no idea what their conditions of service will be. For example, some believe that they will only be serving during the time it takes to sail from Kronshtadt to Sitka, and that they will be returning on the same ship; but then they choose to remain in the colonies and consider that that fulfills their five-year obligation, sailing to the colonies and back. But it appears that they must serve a full five years in the colonies. The same thing has happened to men who go from Russia for a definite period--the time spent sailing around the world does not count as service. This creates frequent misunderstandings, arguments, and dissatisfaction. It would seem to be proper, when government sailors are being hired for Company service, that they be given enough information about all conditions so that they could think through the matter. Then there would not be any misunderstanding or argument. In fact, it is not only the lower ranks who are not fully informed about their contracts. We had the opportunity to investigate the complaints of several service persons in the colonies who insisted that they were given additional obligations or that their period of service had been extended, contrary to the terms they had agreed on with the Governing Board. During all this time, when the colonial administration encounters a vagueness in the contracts, it inter- prets them in accordance with previous examples, and sometimes not in accordance with the set rules, since there is no possibility of determining whether or not there is justice in the complaint, based on the contract. In accepting similar petitions to take back for review by the Governing Board, we intend to point out this problem to the Governing Board.

Although Company ships are well maintained, one cannot say that the same is true of the crews, especially aboard the ships that sail around the world. This is due to the fact that captains are in charge of provisioning the ships abroad, and some of them abuse this responsibility; such cases are rare, however. For the most, supplies are of satisfactory quality. It would be advisable, however, for the Governing Board and the administrator of the colony to question closely the crews of ships who have returned from voyages around the world.

The Company has a standing rule to deduct annually a certain percent of the initial cost of each ship, so that after a certain number of years the ship is fully depreciated. Repair and capital improvement costs are added to the value of the ship. This means that at present nearly all the ships which belong to the Company are carried on the books at a value quite a bit less than is actually the fact. In Appendix 4 I have indicated: 1) the price of each ship at the time of purchase, or the cost of her construction; 2) the value the Company lists for each as of July 1, 1860; 3) the actual value based on an appraisal in the colonies. In this last column, I have added my own observations.

According to Company calculations, the value of all ships amounts to:

       1,912,100.375 paper rubles

or

       546,314.393 silver rubles

The actual value, according to the appraisal, is:

       1,351,000 paper rubles

or

       464,571.429 silver rubles

Aleut mask.

PORT FACILITIES

The principal port in the colonies is New Arkhangel, where there are facilities both for the repair, outfitting and loading of ships as well as for the construction of new ships when this seems profitable and advisable. Port facilities at New Arkhangel are as follows: there is a small berth, or, more accurately, a small shed to haul ships up on shore and for construction purposes; up until now it has been necessary to build a new foundation for each ship; for normal inspection of ships' hulls the ships are usually simply drawn into shallow water and careened up as needed, and then any necessary repairs are made at low tide. Low tides go out as much as 12 feet, and a very low tide may be as much as 14 feet. New ships are rarely constructed here, and those that are are of small tonnage because it is more advantageous and profitable to have them built in the United States, because ships built of oak last five times as long as those that are built of unseasoned wood in New Arkhangel.

The colonies have no timber resources. Any lumber cut is nearly always used for construction of buildings either in New Arkhangel or elsewhere in the colony, or for ship repair, or for masts, or else it is sawed into boards and narrow slats. These latter are given out to Aleuts on various islands for making baidarkas. There is a sawmill for cutting lumber in New Arkhangel; it is powered by water as well as by steam. The water wheel is ten horsepower, and the steam engine generates five horsepower. The steam engine runs a planing mill and a machine to cut beams, cornices, window frames and wooden hafts. In this same place they build models for casting, and an air pipe leads to the cupola. There are circular saws ranging from four feet to one foot two inches, and one standing saw. The mill building is constructed of wood; it was recently repaired, and according to Company bookkeeping, it is valued at 3,000 paper rubles, while the machinery and equipment have a value of 19,824.35 rubles--a value that is quite realistic.

There is also a steam-powered barge [flashkout*] of 30-horsepower which has 25 saws. The main purpose of the barge is to cut lumber in places some distance away from New Arkhangel. It is in good condition, and the value

_____

* Probably plashkout.--Eds.

together with the machinery and equipment, is 100,000 paper rubles. A second
lumber mill is located on Serebriannikov Bay near New Arkhangel on the Kirinsk
River. It is water-powered, has 30 horsepower, and 20 blades. The instruments
and other inventory of the mill have been appraised at 6,976.50 paper rubles,
while the building is valued at 10,000 paper rubles. It is located in a convenient place, but it is rarely in operation because of the difficulty of floating
logs to it. Logs must be cut a considerable distance from the mill. The mill
was built there by a former Chief Manager, Captain of the First Rank Tebenkov,
to replace an existing one in the Ozersk redoubt, where there was also a flour
mill. But the place he selected was very poor, for although the Ozersk redoubt
was farther away from New Arkhangel than the Serebriannikov Bay mill, it nevertheless had all the necessary prerequisites for the construction of a lumber
mill.

New Arkhangel also has the following facilities: a machine shop for
repairing nautical instruments, a metalwork shop, a blacksmith shop, carpentry,
lathe, cooperage, tannery, ropewalk, paint shop, sailmaker's shop, and finally
a copper, iron and zinc casting shop. All of these are very small, but they
are enough to fill all the needs of the port. For example, all of the main
parts of the 30-horsepower engine of the tug Baranov were built there; only the
cylinders were brought up from California. Workers are hired everywhere, some
Russians and some creoles. Every shop has several young creole apprentices,
for the most part they are either orphans or sons of local service personnel.
Many of these work willingly, for generally speaking creoles are quite intelligent and have an aptitude for mechanical work. Thus the Company is constantly
training new master craftsmen; in exchange for their education they are required
to serve the Company at a set salary for 15 years, beginning at the age of 17.
Some areas of this education have been neglected so that there have been shortages
of craftsmen, but the present Chief Manager has given special attention to this,
and one hopes that his expectations will meet with success.

All the shops are located in quite rundown buildings, except for the
foundry; although that building is new, it was built in a careless manner from
blocks and boards. All buildings are appraised at 650 paper rubles, and the
instruments and equipment in them are valued at 28,109.27 paper rubles.

There is also a water-driven flour mill at the port which grinds grain,
as well as groats, into flour for service personnel. There are also a public
laundry where linen from the infirmary, as well as service personnel's clothing,
is washed; a place where furs are processed, a tent where lavtaks are dried to
be used for baidarkas and various other purposes. These buildings have been
appraised at 3,775 paper rubles, and the instruments, machinery and other
equipment are valued at 2,026.95 paper rubles.

The rest of the harbor facilities are appraised as follows: buildings,
67,426 paper rubles; machines and instruments, etc., 106,937.07 paper rubles.
This is a total of 174,363.07 paper rubles, or 49,817.73 silver rubles.

Port facilities in other departments of the colonies are quite insignificant. Almost all the buildings are used exclusively for local needs. Company

ships are repaired there only in unusual circumstances, such as if they undergo some damage at sea which prevents them from continuing their voyage. This rarely happens, however, and if it does, the ships are repaired almost entirely by the crew's own work.

There is a lumber mill in Kodiak which makes boards, but it chiefly produces the sawdust which is used to preserve, or cover, ice which is then transported by ship to San Francisco. There is also a small blacksmith shop, a carpentry shop and a metal shop. All of these buildings are in satisfactory condition.

At the Kenai coal mine there are a blacksmith shop, a metal shop and a carpenter shop which all make various items needed to mine coal or for local needs. There is also a 40-horsepower steam engine to pump water out of the mines, and it also runs a circular saw for cutting boards. The building which houses this machinery burned in 1860, and the machinery was partly destroyed, but it has now been put back into operating condition. The machinery has been valued at 18,307.80 paper rubles. There is also a bakehouse.

Near Nikolaevsk redoubt there is a small brickyard which employs Chugach workers, but it produces only a small quantity of bricks; generally they are bought in California.

In the Karluk odinochka there are a blacksmith shop and a tannery. Nikolaevsk redoubt and the Nushagak [Novo Aleksandrovsk] odinochka have a blacksmith shop and a metal work shop. There are blacksmiths and metal shops on the island of Unalaska in Mikhailovsk redoubt, and on Unga Island.

The islands of St. Paul, St. George, Atka, Attu, Bering, Mednyi, Shumshu and Urup have blacksmith, metal work and carpentry equipment in the warehouses for emergency use, but there are no buildings for these at all.

All of the above shops and buildings are kept in satisfactory condition, but they are generally small, so that they are only able to fill basic needs. The value of these buildings and equipment is included in the general capital of the Company, so that it is very difficult to ascertain the figure. But insofar as one can judge, the general valuation of all the Company property is made quite judiciously, and of course one cannot blame the Company for inflating the figures, considering for example that the building in New Arkhangel which houses instruments, the blacksmith shop, metal working shop, carpentry shop, lathe shop and copper foundry, is appraised at 100 paper rubles. The buildings which house the ropewalk and the tannery are appraised at 25 paper rubles each, and the laundry at 75 paper rubles. If these buildings were to be torn down, the lumber alone would be worth more than the appraised value of the buildings, even though the Kolosh are paid 11 paper rubles for a three-log stack of wood one sazhen long.

THE DEPARTMENT OF RELIGIOUS AFFAIRS

In regard to the religious administration, our colonies in North America belong to the Diocese of Kamchatka and are under the administration of His Eminence, Innokentii, Archbishop of Kamchatka, the Kuril and Aleutian Islands; he has his permanent residence in the city of Blagoveshchensk in the Amur oblast. The immediate supervision of spiritual affairs in the colonies is entrusted to His Excellency, Peter, Bishop of New Arkhangel, vicar of the Diocese of Kamchatka. Until 1858 the archepiscopal cathedral was located in New Arkhangel, and in 1845 the seminary was transferred there from Kamchatka; but in 1858 both the cathedral and seminary were transferred to Iakutsk.

At present in the colonies there are seven parish churches, two registries and thirty-five chapels under the jurisdiction of the church. Because some of the parish churches were built at Company expense prior to the organization of the diocese, the Company has promised to maintain them and to replace the buildings if necessary. But the iconostases, church plate, vestments, books, candles, communion wafers, wine and other supplies, for both churches and chapels, are paid for from special funds, which are added to the sum designated for church maintenance.

Churches and chapels are generally maintained through donations from parishioners and revenues from the sale of candles, which over time amounts to quite a substantial sum of money. In 1860 the general capital of the American churches amounted to 51,423.68 silver rubles worth of credit on the Governing Board of the Company, drawing interest at five percent. Donations from parishioners are partly in cash and partly in furs. Since the Company has the exclusive right to purchase all furs, it pays the church from 25 to 50 paper rubles (7.14 to 14.29 silver) for one sea otter pelt, depending on its quality. Candle revenue annually amounts to 5,500 paper rubles (1,517.43 silver) and goes almost entirely for the maintenance of the American churches.

When the diocese was organized, the Company pledged to set aside a yearly sum of 24,927 rubles (paper) for churches, but the actual cost for this purpose amounted to 32,938.70 rubles, if one adds in the cost of housing for clergy, servants, transportation and the like. In addition to this, the Holy Synod pays 3,085 paper rubles each year for the upkeep of the Kenai Mission. The churches and chapels are generally kept up decently. For the most part they have been built in areas where there are many natives, or in places where the natives dispose of their furs.

The total number of clergy in America in parish churches, the archepiscopal residence and in the missions amounts to eleven persons. There are sixteen additional church service persons.

According to the rules of the Holy Synod the Archbishop received 4,000 paper rubles (1,143 silver) per year for his salary and food allowance. In addition to this both he and all other priests and church service personnel are given a residence, heating, lighting, and also receive free fish, both fresh and salted, from the Company. Clergy receive a salary of from 720 to 2,200 paper rubles per year. The deacon receives from 420 to 480 rubles, the sexton from 340 to 360, and persons who bake the communion wafers receive from 60 to 160. Missionaries are allocated additional sums for travel, between 120 and 600 paper rubles per year.

Three missions have been established to convert the natives to Christianity: Nushagak, Kenai and Kwikpak. Missionaries were sent to the colonies as early as 1793, but in 1797 the Right Reverend Iosaf, who had been recalled to Russia to be consecrated a bishop, drowned with his entire crew aboard a Company ship on his voyage back to the colonies. Thus until 1810 there was only one elderly monk-priest in the colonies. In that year one more priest arrived, and in 1821, three more.

There was little difficulty in converting the Aleuts. This proceeded quite successfully in the Unalaska Department where the priest was [Ivan] Veniaminov [1797-1879], presently His Eminence, Innokentii, Archbishop of Kamchatka, the Kuril and Aleutian islands. Once he had mastered the Aleut language he translated many religious books into it, thus spreading literacy among the Aleuts. The conversion of other natives was more difficult. The Kodiak Aleuts were converted later than those on Unalaska and Atka. A primer was prepared for them, as well as a brief catechism, a short history of religion, and the Gospel of St. Matthew. According to the testimony of the Bishop of New Arkhangel, the tribes most adaptable to conversion to Christianity after the Aleuts were the Alegmiuts and the Ugalents in Nushagak parish; also the Kenais. This is primarily due to the fact that they are quite gentle and obedient people and are willing to be baptized when they have been persuaded that this is necessary; but in general they are indifferent to religion.

In regard to the rest of the natives who have been converted to Orthodoxy, there are some who come around the missions often and show interest mainly because they hope to receive some advantage or other, such as gifts, hospitality, or the possibility of occasionally asking assistance from godfathers or godmothers, whom they always try to select from among the most well-to-do and influential persons. However, it is no wonder that they are not convinced of the superiority of the Christian faith, for not one of the missionaries in the colonies has the slightest knowledge of their language, and consequently cannot converse with them. Even when they come to confession they do so with the help of interpreters who may know the native dialect, but little Russian. Often they are unable to express any of their thoughts at all.

If missionaries are only appointed in order to somehow christen a certain number of natives per year, and to show in their reports that the number of converts has increased, and once a year to go to visit a few settlements located close to our redoubts and odinochkas, then the colonial missionaries more or less fulfill their obligations faithfully. But if the appointment of mission-aries is meant to spread Christian teachings among the savages, and to set a fine example--by word and deed to modify their customs, and to help them in need, to heal them of bodily and spiritual ills, and systematically to teach them to adjust to settled and industrious lives, and primarily to influence the upbring-ing of their children, and finally to bring about a condition wherein the savages themselves will desire to be converted--then in that case, not one of our past or present missionaries has fulfilled his task.

Missionaries should not be appointed at random, but rather, selected from among those persons who feel a genuine call to fulfill this noble obligation. The first prerequisite should be a knowledge of native language, or at least a deep desire to learn it; for that purpose the missionary should not live in a redoubt, but rather should dwell among the savages, familiarize himself with their customs, roam alongside them. Only then will he be in a position to influence them. This is the manner in which Catholic missionaries go about their work. When they set out to convert, they are not frightened by hard work, deprivation or danger. When one dies, several others take his place.

The Bishop of New Arkhangel says there is now a wide field for missionary activity in spreading the gospel of Christ into distant places in the interior of the mainland, particularly along the Copper, Kuskovym and Kwikpak rivers and their tributaries, and in the far north along the shores of the Bering Sea. However there are great difficulties. Missionaries can penetrate into the interior only in summer by moving upriver in baidarkas, which cannot, however, carry a sufficient amount of provisions; consequently in barren areas they suffer hunger; in winter it is quite impossible to penetrate into the interior at all. Moreover missionaries have no way of telling where a large number of savages will come together at any given time, since they are constantly on the move in order to fish and to hunt. The deeper one goes into the mainland, the more vicious the savages one encounters. There are even cannibals there. It is dangerous to visit these, and even the natives who live near the missions will not consent to guide the missionaries there.

But none of these problems should stop a true missionary. The Mednovtsy Indians come to our missions to trade with the Company, and missionaries could go with them to penetrate the interior. For its part, the Company provides missionaries with the means of travelling to various parishes. For this purpose they are provided with baidarkas and guides, and if they are to visit places along the coast, they go aboard one of the Company's ships, which gives them the time and means of fulfilling their obligation. Precisely the same is true for priests who live on islands, who may visit their parishes either in baidarkas or aboard Company ships, but not oftener than once a year.

Of course it would be possible to increase the number of churches and church-related personnel, but in order to build churches or homes for priests and sextons lumber would have to be brought to these islands from New Arkhangel, which always involves a great deal of difficulty and expense because of the shortage of labor on Sitka. New expenditures of money would be required to maintain the priests. Consequently only such churches as are in existence at the present time are being used.

There are seven parishes in the colonies, including three missions: 1) Sitka, with 1,317 parishioners of both sexes; 2) Kodiak (Kodiak, Elovka and Ukamok islands and the small settlement of Katmai in Alaska) with 2,669 parishioners of both sexes; 3) Unalaska, which includes the islands of Unalaska, Umak, Borka, Akun, Tigalda, Unimak, Unga, St. George and St. Paul, with 1,658 parishioners of both sexes; 4) Atka, including the islands of Atka, Amlia, Attu, Mednyi and Bering, with 951 parishioners of both sexes; 5) Kenai Mission on Kenai Bay and Chugach Sound, the interior of the mainland up to the Copper River, with 1,633 parishioners of both sexes; 6) Nushagak Mission, all along the Nushagak River and along Bristol Bay up to Lake Iliamna in Alaska, with 1,635 parishioners of both sexes; 7) the Kwikpak Mission, in the areas inhabited by natives from Norton Bay and Kuskokvym River to the north, with 1,926 parishioners of both sexes. The Kuril Islands are under the diocesan jurisdiction of the Amur oblast, and number 217 souls of both sexes.

In order to provide religious services for the Sitka Kolosh, a special church was built in New Arkhangel under the jurisdiction of the cathedral. But the Kolosh almost never attend it, and when they do occasionally go inside, they do so out of curiosity; they squat down, smoke their pipes, and then walk out. At the time of the 1855 affair the Kolosh occupied the church as a vantage point from which they could inflict damage on our garrison; they held it until the end of the negotiations. They ransacked part of it and damaged the icons.

The following items have been translated into the Kolosh language: the Gospel of St. Matthew, the liturgy (excluding the priest's prayers) and various church hymns sung at vespers. But these translations are still in manuscript form because they are so unsatisfactory; there is not a single person who knows both Russian and Kolosh well enough to correct them. Moreover it is very difficult to translate anything into Kolosh because of the poverty of the language and the lack of words even for very simple things. For example, the Kolosh do not use tables and therefore there is no such word. In translating one must say "a board to eat on," which does not convey the proper meaning of the word. Any strange or incorrect expression makes the Kolosh laugh, which they do not bother to suppress, even during the service.

Appendix 3 indicates the number of natives who joined the Orthodox Church between 1841 and 1860; it is apparent that the number of converts decreases with each year, especially the Kolosh. For example there were 531 souls converted to Orthodoxy from among the various natives in 1846; but in 1854 there were only 38, and in 1859 only 42. Over a 20-year period 4,700 persons of both sexes were converted, but this number exists on paper only, because many of the nomadic natives who were baptized never even come near our missions and of course do not fulfill any of their Christian obligations, and their children have not been baptized for a long time.

In addition to the shortage of good missionaries, the major barrier to conversion of the natives is polygamy, which they are unwilling to give up; then too there is their nomadic life, and the efforts of the shamans who, because of their own personal ambition, try to prevent them from accepting Christianity. However, just within the present year the Kolosh have begun to be baptized more willingly. Forty men were baptized between January and April, and on April 2, one of the most influential toions of the Kukhantan clan accepted Orthodoxy. At the christening the d.s.s. [deistvitelnyi statskii sovetnik = Active State Councillor] Kostlivtsev was godfather, and the newly baptized man was given the name of Sergei. It is to be hoped that this example will influence many of the Kukhantans. However, if one wishes only to convert the Kolosh, without expecting anything more from the present generation, this would not be too difficult; if an appropriate ceremony were to be established, and each newly converted person were to be given a blanket and a shirt and were entertained, then the Sitka Kolosh would of course be converted one and all.

There is a Lutheran church and a pastor to provide divine services for the Lutherans, of whom there are quite a few in New Arkhangel.

Priests of the "white clergy" [secular] class are also sent to the colonies from Russia, mostly from Siberia. They too are wholly unconversant with the native tongue, although some of them live among the Aleuts all the time. It is however true that there are also creole priests, and if one were to select from them those persons of high moral character, then they would obviously be far more effective than the Russians. Generally speaking all savages are self-directed to a large degree, and they enormously enjoy every distinction and occasion on which they are singled out; thus one would hope that many of the outstanding native toions, including Kolosh, would as a result of this be willing to send their sons to the Company so that they might be prepared for the religious profession. It would greatly enhance the self-esteem of the savages to have a son become a priest before whom even the Russians would bow reverently. I therefore believe that it would be quite useful to recruit likely youngsters from the more distinguished clans of the Kolosh; after their elementary education they would be sent to Russia to be prepared for a priestly vocation. This would be very positive in its effect on the Kolosh; it would bring them closer to the Russians, and would modify their customs. There is no doubt at all that the youngsters could be very well trained, for generally the Kolosh are intelligent and quick to learn.

I believe that as long as the Kolosh remain illiterate and religious beliefs are not implanted in them and they do not feel a genuine need to accept Holy Baptism, it is not wise to entice them into Orthodoxy with the help of various lures, and that separate churches should not be built for them. Rather, they should have full freedom to attend the Russian church if they wish; of course not with their pipes in their mouths, as they do now when they attend the Kolosh church.

EDUCATIONAL FACILITIES AND SCHOOLS

Educational facilities and schools have been established in various
places to bring education and literacy to the colonies. The merchant Shelikhov
founded the first school on Kodiak Island to bring literacy to the Aleuts.
Simple promyshlenniks served as teachers. Subsequently a second facility was
established on Kodiak where they taught: God's commandments, the Russian language, arthmetic and navigational science. A few years later a similar facility
opened on Sitka Island, but up until 1820 it was in a quite deplorable condition.
Prior to 1833 one of the naval officers who happened to be in New Arkhangel was
usually placed in charge of the educational facility, but since that time the
responsibility has fallen on Captain-Lieutenant Etolin, former assistant to the
Chief Manager. It is obvious that education has begun to improve, especially
in regard to teaching the art of navigation. Some of the former students of
this facility are in the Company's service to the present time. This facility
has accepted all children without regard to rank. When they complete their
training, they are hired for various and sometimes quite diverse responsibilities.
In 1837, for example, seventeen persons graduated from this training center; one
became a scribe, four became sailors, four were copyists, five became master
craftsmen and three were apprentice seamen.

In 1841 a religious school opened in New Arkhangel, and in 1845 it became
a seminary. In addition to children who were preparing themselves for a religious vocation this school also accepted other children in order to give them
all an elementary education. But since the religious school and the seminary
were always in a most deplorable condition, the facility in New Arkhangel was
also neglected, and obviously needed to be reorganized. Therefore, until a new
permanent facility could replace the old one, a temporary school was opened
which took only children from families of high rank. Here they learned the
Commandments, Russian language, arithmetic, geometry, trigonometry, navigation
and some astronomy, English language, geography, history and bookkeeping. The
supervisor of the school was the hired navigator Petrashkevich, a graduate of
navigation trade school. I had a chance to observe that the various disciplines,
particularly those pertaining to navigation, were properly presented. The least
satisfactory of all subjects is the teaching of the Commandments, because of the
lack of a good teacher who is familiar with his subject.

Meanwhile a proposal was presented to higher authorities for approval which would organize a new school to be called the All-Colonial School. This project received Imperial approval in 1859, and on November 15, 1860 it came into reality. This facility has been instructed to accept children of persons employed in the colonies in various capacities, as a reward for their parents' diligent service which has been of benefit to the Company; it also accepts persons who have come to the colonies of their own free will who wish to audit the lectures. At first it was suggested that this school should have twelve lectors, eight to be maintained by the Company and four to be appointed by religious authorities from among the children of the clergy. The religious administration was to pay expenses for food and clothing, the same amount that the Company gives its own pensioners for those two purposes. The number of persons who wish to audit lectures is to be unlimited, and no payment is required for this; but their acceptance is subject to review by the Chief Administrator. In addition to the subjects which had been presented in the temporary facility, it was agreed that the All-Colonial School would teach the Commandments more fully, and the Slavic language, for those children preparing for a religious vocation. After five years of study the graduates go out according to their education: some enter naval service, others become office workers, and a third group will pursue a religious calling.

Graduates who have completed their training in this school at the expense of the Company are required to serve the Company in the colonies for ten years. In its scope, this school can be compared with uezd [county] educational facilities in Russia; the teachers are actually in the service of the Ministry of Public Education and enjoy all the rights of teachers in uezd schools in Siberia. For those who wish to enter the seminary, teachers are appointed by the episcopal diocesan authorities, and are supported from church funds. Navigational science, commerce, and the English language are taught by qualified hired navigators or other persons in Company service.

Students are accepted into the schools once a year prior to the opening of school, but this is also permitted on other occasions for those who have a satisfactory comprehension of the material which has already been covered. In order to enroll in this school a candidate must know how to read and write Russian, and must know the first four rules of arithmetic. At the end of each school year, all the students in all the classes take public examinations. Those who distinguish themselves receive books and certificates of commendation as a reward. Any who fail are allowed to remain in the same class for one additional year, but if they then have still not achieved any success in their studies, they may no longer attend the school.

Persons who have completed the courses and are hired by the Company receive 500 paper rubles as their beginning salary.

A supervisor for the educational facility is appointed and it is his job to oversee the business affairs and the school property. He is also required to look after the morals of the students, their cleanliness, and their orderliness. A matron is appointed to assist him, and she takes care of linen and clothing. Three workers are assigned to do the cooking and other work. The rest of the funds which the state sets aside for the upkeep of the school may, with the permission of the Chief Manager, be used for various improvements, or be given out as rewards to certain teachers for exceptionally fine work.

There is no doubt that if the colonial administration will give proper attention to this school and keep it from falling into disrepair as has been the case in the past, then in time useful persons will be educated, and the Company will not have their present burden of having to search for navigators and office personnel.

I do believe, however, that it would be much better if the administration would assume the responsibility of supporting not only this school but also all the other colonial schools. It would be possible to simplify education in accordance with the colonial style of life, and in the lower schools to give attention to teaching creoles mechanical skills, in which they are all quite adept. It is possible to choose one fine teacher who would assume the responsibility of training his helpers right there, and thus we could fulfill the needs of the country. This would mean giving him good support and complete freedom of action, and not burdening him with decrees from the Ministry of Public Education, which does not have the slightest real conception of the needs of the colony. The Governor of the colonies should be able by himself to supervise the performance and work of the teacher.

Obviously the greatest attention should be given to the moral upbringing of the children, especially the creoles, who often see examples of behavior at home which are far from edifying, and who easily adopt all the habits of their parents. Regarding this, it might be helpful if students with good potential could be sent to Russia to be educated, and could be assigned to schools there. Unfortunately, however, we have learned through experience that creoles have great difficulty in adapting to a change in climate and diet; those who are taken to Russia fall ill and die.

The Company sets aside the following sum of money for the maintenance of this educational facility:

Salaries to service personnel	13,450.14 rubles
Maintenance of teachers	9,364.63
Upkeep of the schoolhouse	1,563.00
Total	24,377.77

In addition to this All-Colonial School, in New Arkhangel there is a school for young boys and another for girls. The boys' school accepts children of lower ranking service personnel workers and orphans. These youngsters are trained to become scribes or craftsmen of various sorts. Those who are the more able, upon reaching the age of 17, are transferred to a special class in the All-Colonial School where they learn to become navigators. An administrative decision of 1842 states that there shall be 50 students in that school, and that the upkeep of each student will be budgeted as follows:

Food	102.285 paper rubles
Clothing, linen, footwear	64.65
Pens, paper, ink	10.00
Total, for 50 students	8,846.75 paper rubles
Maintenance of supervisor	140.00
Salary for teacher	800.00
Grand total	9,786.75 paper rubles

This does not include a budget for heat and light, which are provided by Nature.

At present there are 27 students in the school. Six of these are children of island administrators and other administrative units, and the rest are children of scribes, master craftsmen and laborers, plus one Kolosh. All are taught to read and write, and the Commandments. Nine attend a special class where they study arithmetic and grammar, in preparation for becoming, depending on their qualifications, either scribes or navigators. The rest are studying to become apothecaries, or machinists aboard steamships, or Kolosh interpreters, portrait painters, tailors, leather workers, painters, cooks, or craftsmen in the lathe shop, copper shop and pelt shop. The temporary facility is crowded and unsatisfactory, but in the fall a new one will be ready in the new barracks; it will be quite spacious. They are nicely supplied with clothing and linen; they receive food from the common Company kitchen, generally a soup made of salt fish. They are weak in reading and the Commandments, especially the latter. But they are quite eager students in the crafts, since all creoles are apt pupils in mechanics. The school is under the direct supervision of Captain-Lieutenant Prince Maksutov, assistant to the Chief Manager of the colonies.

The school for girls was organized in 1839 to train, completely at the expense of the Company, the young daughters of Company service personnel who were burdened by large families; it is also especially for orphans. The students come here from all parts of the colonies. The regulation of 1842 decreed that there be places for 40 students, and set aside the following annual budget:

Food	94.785 paper rubles
Shoes, linen, clothing	77.60
Total	172.385

At present there are twenty-two girls in the school, six of whom have come of age and have entered into service with families. Although the number has not been verified, four of those seem to have come as volunteers to learn reading and handicrafts. In 1860 the maintenance of these 22 girls amounted to 4,400 paper rubles: 1,200 paper rubles for the salary of the supervisor and 74 paper rubles for light and heat for her; Seliakhin, a noncommissioned officer of the Naval Artillery Corps, is the teacher there, and receives 250 rubles for his work, in addition to his salary from the Company. The school guard receives 440 rubles. This is a total of 6,364 paper rubles, and does not include light and heat, which Nature provides.

The pupils study the Commandments, in which subject they are quite poor, they learn to read and write in Russian, study arithmetic and handicrafts. They sew their own clothing and undergarments, do all the cleaning in the school and keep it in order, and learn how to prepare their own food. The school has set up a special fund from the sale of various handcrafted items the girls have made. When she marries, each girl receives from 150 to 300 paper rubles from this fund with which to set herself up in housekeeping. The capital in this fund presently amounts to some 1,600 paper rubles, and is deposited at interest with the Company. The school premises are adequate. In general the students behave decently, and this institution is without doubt very beneficial to the region, since it gives the daughters of poor parents and orphan girls the possibility of earning a living by the work of their own hands.

In addition to these institutions there are plans to open a boarding school for young ladies in New Arkhangel so that persons serving in the colonies, especially creoles, can give their daughters a proper education. Since it is almost impossible to find teachers in the colonies, and since creole parents cannot take on the education of their own daughters because they are indifferent and lack education themselves, up to the present time a large part of the young native girls are completely ignorant of reading and writing, and they have memorized only a few prayers. Their moral character has likewise improved very little, since their parents rarely set a good example. Consequently, in establishing this boarding school, the Company will be performing a very useful service. Everything is all ready for the opening of the facility, and only awaits the arrival from Russia of Captain-Lieutenant Gavrishev's wife, who has accepted the post of Supervisor.

There are also the following schools in the rest of the departments of the colony: Unalaska School, on Unalaska Island, was founded in 1825 by the priest Ioann Veniaminov (presently His Excellency, Innokentii, Archbishop of Kamchatka). Under the leadership of this distinguished mentor, the school made rapid progress and is still in beautiful condition. A tribute to this is the fact that every Aleut on the island of Unalaska is literate. This school is located in a Company building, and the teaching is done by service priests. In 1860 there were 50 boys and 43 girls in this school, mostly Aleuts.

The school in the Atka Department is located on the island of Amlia, the main Aleut settlement. Church service personnel teach there. According to the latest reports, up to 30 boys and girls study there.

Church service personnel have also been involved in teaching the children of Alegmiuts, since 1843, at the Nushagak Mission. Recently there were 12 boys and girls studying there.

A special schoolhouse was built at the Kwikpak Mission, and service personnel there try to help those who have been converted to Christianity become literate, but they have had only limited success so far.

There is also a schoolhouse on Bering Island, where one of the Company pensioners teaches reading and arithmetic.

The schoolhouse on Kodiak Island was vacated last year when the teacher left; but the Chief Manager has recently reopened it, and one of the service men from the Kodiak office has been selected to teach reading and writing.

As a whole, the Company deserves full credit for the fact that insofar as is possible it has worked to bring education to the colonies. If some of the schools and training facilities have declined at various times, this is due to the fact that not all the Chief Managers have felt obliged to see that they were kept up, and felt it was enough to mention in reports that the status of education was in satisfactory condition. One hopes that the present Chief Manager will devote proper attention to this matter, which it deserves.*

---

* Appendix 5 shows annual expenditures for the upkeep of schools, infirmaries, etc.

Kolosh carving.

INFIRMARIES

The climate in the Russian American colonies is quite deleterious to the health of the inhabitants. The constant rain, fog and generally foul weather act adversely not only on the body, but on the character of all the inhabitants of the islands, without exception. On the mainland farther to the north, and in the interior, although the climate is more severe, it is more constant; the inhabitants are stronger physically and livelier in character, as for example, the Mednovsty Indians, who are quite tall, healthy and muscular. In contrast, the inhabitants of the islands, the Aleuts and the creoles, are physically lethargic, weak, spiritless, and generally susceptible to respiratory disorders. A large number of creoles die early in life from consumption; in addition to their natural weakness, this is also caused by their undisciplined use of alcohol, and the early age at which they become sexually promiscuous. Russians who live here on a temporary basis suffer mostly from colds, rheumatism, gastric disorders and jaundice. Epidemic diseases are quite rare, and are altogether unknown to the inhabitants of the island of Sitka. Cases of scurvy are very rare, in spite of the climate, food and lifestyle, which obviously could aggravate this disease. In general, the treatment for it has a quick and successful result. At present smallpox is almost nonexistent, although it brought a terrible depopulation among the natives. They finally realized the advantages of being innoculated against smallpox, and the colonial administration makes every effort to vaccinate all the small children. For this purpose vaccine is brought in from California from time to time, and it is made available to all departments of the colonies. In areas where there are no medical personnel or feldshers, either prikashchiks or administrators have been taught how to give vaccinations. This subject has generally received special attention. It would be helpful if persons who are responsible for keeping smallpox under control would prepare detailed reports about their work; then it would be possible to tell from these reports how well this work is being carried out.

In former years syphilis was quite widespread among the Aleuts, but at present it is almost nonexistent on the islands. It frequently occurs on Kodiak, probably brought by crews of Company ships; but it is being encountered less and less as ship captains are being instructed to examine their men very carefully when they come into harbor. By contrast, this disease is still very widespread in New Arkhangel in spite of all the necessary measures the administration has

adopted. It is transmitted to the Russians from the Kolosh who get it from
other tribes who live in the straits; they in turn get it from foreign ships
engaged in contraband trade with the Kolosh. The Kolosh are not concerned
about this disease; they consider it an unavoidable evil, and take no measures
to treat it. Almost all the women who are engaged in clandestine debauchery in
the area around New Arkhangel are afflicted with this disease. At one time
syphilis was so widespread among the workers and soldiers in New Arkhangel that
when the present Chief Manager arrived in the colonies he had to resort to
forceful measures in an attempt to wipe it out. He destroyed all the huts near
the port, both along the shore and in the forest, in which illicit sexual relations were carried on; then he ordered a special building to be built near
Lebiazhe Lake, and put a sentry on top of it. From time to time the Kolosh
women who live in that area are taken to the infirmary for a medical examina-
tion. The sick are kept there to be treated and those who are healthy are
allowed to go. However a prolonged stay in the infirmary is very difficult for
the Kolosh women who are accustomed to complete freedom. As a rule, after two
or three days they run away from the infirmary back to their own settlement,
where it is very difficult to find them. Consequently the Chief Manager has
announced that any woman who runs away from the infirmary will have half of her
head shaved, which the Kolosh consider very humiliating. At first this measure
aroused dissatisfaction among the Kolosh, but when they became convinced that
the Chief Manager would carry through this threat, and when they finally
realized the benefits of medication, they capitulated; now, not only do they not
run away from the infirmary, they come voluntarily to request medical treatment.

Some of the laborers and soldiers, who are afraid of becoming infected
buy women slaves from the toions, keep them at their own expense, in spite of
the fact that the local priests condemn such alliances, and impose penance on
the guilty parties. It is quite expensive to support a Kolosh woman; it costs
from 25 to 30 paper rubles a month, which not everyone can afford. As a result,
most of the laborers and soldiers look for easier alliances, and there is no
possible way one can watch over them. They are complete fatalists. There are
even some who deliberately try to become infected so that they will be freed
from work to lie in the infirmary. The Chief Manager has ordered soldiers and
laborers to have frequent medical examinations, and he has also introduced a
rule that anyone who is infected with a venereal disease shall have his wages
and rations docked while he is in the hospital. By these and several other
similar measures, it has at last become possible to control the spread of this
disease, and although it still has not been completely eradicated, at least the
evil has been diminished. Of course there has been grumbling and dissatisfaction, but gradually they are becoming accustomed to the new order, and of
course the results will show how useful those measures are.

There are quite often serious injuries such as broken bones, sprains and
bad cuts and gashes on the limbs. These are the result of the constant construction and tree falling. Surgery is usually successful in these cases. The
Kolosh especially are likely to recover quickly and soon regain their health.

The following diseases are common among the Aleuts: gastritis, colds,
yellow fever, diarrhea, catarrh, lumbago, rashes, vereda, and particularly

carbuncles, which occur in the form of red eruptions of great size, especially along the spine and on the lower part of the body. Medical authorities attribute this problem to an excessive amount of whale meat and blubber in the diet. Fresh whale meat is not at all injurious, but often when Aleuts go out to hunt a whale they only wound it, not kill it. Salt water penetrates into the wound, and in two or three days the whale is dead. Often the wind and waves carry the corpse about for several days until it washes up on shore; then the Aleuts eat this dead animal. Consequently they nearly always eat meat and blubber that are already slightly tainted; the Aleuts actually consider this rather good, and use it immoderately. Sometimes after such a feast whole families become ill, especially with carbuncles; sometimes that illness has a tragic result.

Aleuts also suffer chronic inflammation of the eyes, a result of the smoke in their iurts. They also have respiratory diseases. Any change in place of habitation or diet or style of life always has an adverse effect on Aleuts. Those who enter Company service on Sitka frequently fall sick and die, in spite of the fact that they live in quite adequate barracks, receive enough to eat, which is obviously not the case at home, and only work when they prepare animal pelts or go out in baidarkas to deliver papers to the Lake Redoubt or supplies to men who work in the forest near New Arkhangel. It is not only the change in diet, but primarily the restraint on the freedom which they are accustomed to having on their islands which has a bad effect on them. In his own settlement an Aleut is the complete master of his own fate. Carefree and lazy by nature, he goes out to hunt only when it is absolutely necessary; he would not even go then if he did not have to. If he has even a small bit of iukola and blubber or shellfish and sea cabbage, he will not work. He can sit for hours looking at the sea. In a word, he does what he wishes, how he wishes. In New Arkhangel a bell summons him to work at a certain time. It is not difficult for him to comb the debris out of the fur pelts, but he cannot bear the sound of the bell which he must obey. I myself had the opportunity to question them as to why they do not wish to remain in the port. Generally at first they declare that either their father or mother needs them, but then they admit that they are simply homesick. Nonetheless, since there is good housing for them at the port, good food, a salary of 300 paper rubles per year, and the work is light, it would seem better for them to remain there than to go off to some place like Ukamok where they constantly suffer deprivation.

There are two infirmaries in the colonies to take care of persons who are ill. One is in New Arkhangel and has 40 beds; the other is in Pavlovsk Harbor on Kodiak Island and has 10 beds. The New Arkhangel infirmary is located in a two-story wooden building, which previously housed a seminary. The structure is fairly large, and there is fresh air in the rooms whose windows face the sea, but the air is damp and stifling in the rooms on the northwest side.

There are no facilities for women. They receive medical attention in their own quarters, but in exceptional cases they may be placed in a separate room, which at the present time is almost always occupied by Kolosh women infected with syphilis. The air is very close in that room, and the smell of dried iukola is unbearable. The Kolosh women eat iukola all the time; for them it is an absolute necessity.

The infirmary is adequately supplied with linen and other necessities, but it would be desirable for the linen to be changed more frequently. According to the established rule, the night shirts that the patients wear are changed on Wednesdays and Saturdays, while the rest of the linen is changed only on Saturdays. Because of the fact that the laborers are slovenly, this is not often enough. Linen should be changed more often, or else the sick persons should be required to be cleaner. Generally speaking, the infirmary cannot boast of cleanliness. Perhaps this is partly due to the fact that there are not enough hired hands; it costs too much to hire women to launder the linen and keep the floors clean.

Medicines are sent in part via the around-the-world route, and in part from California. However the pharmacy is not in satisfactory condition because there is no qualified apothecary. It is true that the Governing Board sent an apothecary by the name of Niebuhr to New Arkhangel; he was a man of quite some experience, but he was a hopeless drunk; in spite of every effort they could not reform him, and so the Chief Manager had to remove him from his post and cut off his salary. He has already written to the Governing Board to send another apothecary out from Russia. Unfortunately this will not happen in less than a year, and until that time the New Arkhangel pharmacy will remain the same condition in which it has been up to the present time.

The infirmary suffers from shortages of fresh food in New Arkhangel. Sick persons very rarely get wild mutton or other fresh meat. Their usual diet is a soup made of salted meat or salted fish. In summer they have fresh fish when there is a big catch. They also receive rice. According to the medical men, this diet does not prevent their recovery, but it sometimes slows the process. It is true that I personally noticed that persons who were infected with syphilis, but not severely, are cured rather quickly. But if this were a radical treatment, that would be another question. Although the colonial administration gives its attention to improving the lot of the sick, it is not enough, and it seems necessary that when wild mutton is available in the market, first of all a certain amount should be set aside for the infirmary. And for seriously ill persons, perhaps they should buy chickens, even though the price for them is very high. And, finally, there is no reason not to send to the infirmary some of the preserved foods that are to be found in no small quantity in the colonial warehouses.

There are two medical men in New Arkhangel. One is in charge of the infirmary, and the other takes care of the service personnel of the Company in their own quarters. There are three feldshers in the infirmary, and four apprentices. As noted, the number of sick persons always rises in the fall and winter.

In addition to the sick persons in the infirmary, every day at seven o'clock in the morning persons come in who are weak or who have some slight external or internal problem. They either receive treatment in their own homes, or if necessary they enter the infirmary as patients.

During 1860 the total number of patients and outpatients for the New

Arkhangel infirmary was 1,400. Of these 1,328 were cured; 22 had died as of January 1, 1861, and 50 are still in the infirmary. Maintenance of the New Arkhangel infirmary, including salaries for the medical men and feldshers, medicines, etc., costs the Company 45,000 paper rubles per year.

Neither doctors nor feldshers are appointed aboard ships built in New Arkhangel, because the crews are not large enough. Certain important medicines are given to the captains, along with a feldsher's instrument packet. They are also instructed on giving medicine to persons who may become ill. Obviously these measures are not adequate for serious cases. But is it reasonable to require the Company to have doctors or feldshers aboard all ships? This would be very costly, and the first prerequisite of commercial ships is that they must be maintained as inexpensively as possible, or otherwise they cannot carry out their mission.

The infirmary on Kodiak Island, as noted earlier, has 10 beds, and there is an additional small annex for women. This infirmary is headed by a medical official named Petrov, who was recruited from among the feldshers. From his reports it is apparent that in a year's time the infirmary treated 550 persons. Of these 535 recovered, 12 died, and in 1860, 13 were still there. The infirmary has two feldshers and five apprentices who when necessary go out to other parts of the Kodiak Department. All necessary medicines come from New Arkhangel. The maintenance of the infirmary amounts to 14,000 paper rubles per year.

There are also feldshers in other departments of the colonies: one on Unalaska Island; one on Atka; one at the Kenai mining site; and one in the Mikhailovsk redoubt. These feldshers receive an annual salary of 2,030 paper rubles.

In other less populous places responsibility for the health of the natives is placed on the prikashchiks, on the administrators, and on the priest and Church personnel. For this purpose the necessary medications, smallpox vaccine and feldsher pocket instruments are sent to such places. In summer one of the medical men travels through the colonies and personally inspects the condition of the health of the population and instructs the feldshers how to treat various ailments. But since it is impossible to visit all the colonies in the course of one year, the medical person vists the departments in consecutive order, going mainly to places with the larger populations. I find this form of supervision inadequate. It would be desirable to have medical personnel inspect parts of the colonies every year, although when the Aleuts are sick they rarely come to the medical men to ask for help but instead treat themselves in their own ways, which are similar to the cures used by simple Russians, who have a good deal of common sense.

In New Arkhangel and on Kodiak the Company, at its own expense, keeps midwives and their assistants to help in childbirth, especially for Russians and creoles. The assistants are being trained to take over this responsibility. In other places in the colonies where there are no midwives, the native women are assisted by some relatives who are experienced in this practice. But these women usually follow ancient customs, and sometimes they are simply charlatans, with the result that difficult births sometimes have a tragic outcome for both the mother and the baby. It would seem desirable to train a number of Aleut women in the art of midwifery, with the understanding that in their turn they would teach that skill to other women; thus gradually old beliefs and customs based on misinformation would be done away with.

It is interesting to note that the birth rate among the Aleuts is relatively small. It is rare for a family to have more than three children; usually they have only one or two. This should not be ascribed to infertility on the part of the Aleut women, because in places where they are close to the Russians and have illicit relations with them they generally bear many children. It is more likely due to the fact that Aleut men have an inadequate diet and are less potent. Iukola and blubber are not very nourishing, and there are times when the Aleuts are short of even these supplies and have only shellfish and roots to eat; at such times they become emaciated and weak. In contrast to this, the population of creoles increases rapidly in spite of the fact that not many of them live to an advanced age.

On the whole public health is quite satisfactory, especially taking into account the deleterious effect of the climate, particularly on Sitka, where seasons of the year are almost indistinguishable one from another and give the impression of a never-ending autumn, where there are no more than 90 clear days in the year, 200 days are rainy, and the rest are a mixture of clear weather, rain, snow and frost.

About 30 versts from New Arkhangel there are sulphur springs which are quite beneficial to the sick who suffer from rheumatism, scrofula, skin diseases, chronic ulcers, liver disease, etc. There are three main springs close together, and the temperature is a constant 50° Reaumur, and occasionally reaches as much as 52°. There is quite a substantial amount of sulphur there. The wooden troughs through which the water is conducted are covered with a thick coating of sulphur which is several layers thick. The chemical analysis shows that 100 parts of this deposit contain 97 parts of pure sulphur; the remaining 3 consist of lime, iron, chlorine, ammonium chloride and manganese. A clinic was built here earlier, and every year sick persons from New Arkhangel visited it and obtained quick and real relief. But in 1851 the Stikine Kolosh burned the clinic down, and up to the present time, for unknown reasons, it has not been rebuilt. Only the Sitka Kolosh go there to use it; they live in huts made of twigs. The present Chief Manager has decided to rebuild the clinic, however, if it is possible, in the spring of next year. He proposes to construct a building and to reinforce it against a sudden attack by Kolosh coming from the strait. He intends to build a barabora [hut] some little distance away for the Sitka Kolosh to use, in order to give them an opportunity to use the healing springs.

There are a number of hot and cold medicinal springs in other departments of the colony, especially in the Aleutian Islands that are all of volcanic origin; but the Aleuts almost never use them, and the colonial medical personnel have not examined any of them. Up to the present time, as far as I know, there has not yet been prepared a medical topographical description of all the colonies. Only New Arkhangel has been thus described by Dr. [Eduard] Blaschke in his dissertation, <u>Topographia</u> <u>Medica</u> <u>Portus-Novo-Archangelsinensis</u> (St. Petersburg, 1842).

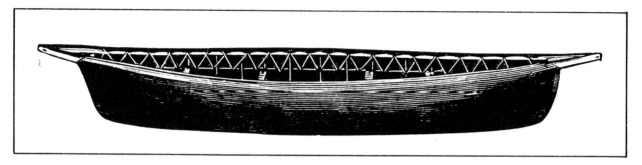

Baidara.

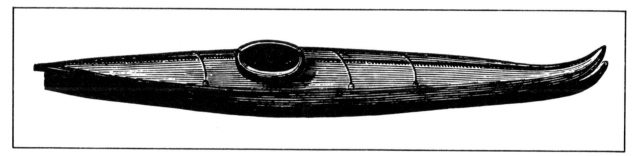

One-hatch baidarka.

CARE OF THE ELDERLY AND THE CRIPPLED

The customs and habits of the natives who live in the colonies, especially the Aleuts, are such that the aged, the crippled and orphans are never left without care. Everyone earns his daily bread by his own work, but considers it his obligation to give a part of it to persons who have none. This has been developed to such a high degree, especially among the Aleuts, that during a hunt experienced promyshlenniks will always give a portion to the young boys who are learning the trade under their tutelage, and also to the sick and the elderly who cannot hunt for themselves. When an Aleut returns from fishing, he leaves his entire catch in his baidarka so that anyone who is in need may take whatever is necessary to him; he is satisfied with the rest, knowing that in case of need he too may have a portion of the catch of his companions. This custom of mutual assistance is deeply lodged in the customs of the Aleuts, and they would find it very strange to see anyone begging for help. Everyone uses this system, by custom. As a result there are well-off natives, and poor ones, but none in need. The settlement is administered with the assistance of the elected toions, and the natives never allow their own tribesmen to fall into a condition of misery. They are always able to place orphans by general consent, and those who take them to care for them, do so as completely as they do their own children. Obviously the Company has had no reason to suppress this noble custom, or to take on the cost of setting up almshouses and orphanages since there is no one to put in them.

Consequently the Company has concerned itself only with supplying the Aleuts with all necessary goods during hunting, and gives them the ability to acquire everything they need from Company warehouses at a reasonable price, in case circumstance deprives them of the possibility of procuring their normal provisions at sea.

Then there remained the concern for incoming Russians and creoles. The Russians come to the colonies only in the service of the Company, for a definite number of years on terms determined in the contract concluded on a mutually agreeable basis. Thus the Company's concern for these people was to have been limited to the period of their obligatory service. At the termination of the contract anyone could freely return to Russia aboard Company ships and reassume his previous status. But many of those who come, when their period of service is up, renew their contract, marry native women, and then find it would be disadvantageous for them to leave the colonies. As long as their strength permits they continue to serve the Company, but with the years they finally become unable to work. To send such persons back to Russia would mean to throw them to their fate, as it were, without any way of making a living.

The Company has been concerned about this, and has set up a pension plan in the form of rewards for long and useful service. This has given assistance and the means for a new start to those who wish to be listed as colonial citizens, and gives pensions to those who have large families with young children. As early as 1802 [the Company] agreed to set aside 1/2% from net profit each year into a pension fund for that purpose. During the most recent period in the colonies, for the same purpose, a ten-ruble tax has been imposed on every vedro of wine, and one ruble for each pound of tea that is sold to consumers from the colonial warehouses. As a result, without hurting itself the Company has forced the consumers to provide protection for the elderly and the crippled among the Company's personnel, and for orphans.

Creoles who serve the Company enjoy the same rights as the Russians; but free creoles provide their own sustenance with their own work. Nonetheless, in special circumstances the colonial administration does concern itself with the well-being of the free creoles, and this is the reason that in the colonies there is really not a single person who is in dire need. There are presently 375 persons who receive a pension and necessary provisions; this number includes both men and women, colonial citizens, and also children of pensioners. This pension cost amounts annually to 30,000 paper rubles, and up to 1,200 paper rubles in shares. In addition, all pensioners and their families have living quarters provided at Company expense, and those who need it receive food from the common kitchen, or a supplement of colonial goods.

When one considers that over and above all of this, in New Arkhangel itself the Company is raising 24 boys and 22 girls at its own expense, in all fairness one must give the Company credit for its concern for the welfare of both service personnel and natives, even though as I have already noted not all of the expenses for that upkeep come from the Company's own coffers. The Company does not have a special permanent fund for pensions.

HYDROGRAPHIC SURVEYS AND VARIOUS EXPLORATIONS WITHIN
THE COLONIES FOR SCIENTIFIC AND COMMERCIAL PURPOSES

From its inception the Company, insofar as its means permitted, has attempted to ascertain not only the precise location of our various possessions in America and on the Aleutian Islands, but with the extension of trade in mind, it has sought to study the lands bordering the colonies. For that purpose expeditions were outfitted in 1803, 1806, 1813 and 1816. Although the government provided half of the financial support, nonetheless the Company was put to great expense and actually received little of value.

A consistent aim of the Company has been to survey the estuary of the Amur River and to organize a settlement in that area. All the efforts of Councilor Rezanov, a man not fully appreciated by his contemporaries during his lifetime, were directed toward that end; but they were not fulfilled because the leader of the expedition and its scientists were not in sympathy with his proposals. They were more interested in exploring the South Seas than in studying the northern regions where sailing was fraught with special hazards, deprivations and danger. The voyages of [Nikolai A.] Khvostov and [Gavriil I.] Davydov to Japan were made primarily to take the island of Sakhalin, if that should prove possible, and to entrench themselves there. The Company did not lose sight of this goal even in subsequent years. In all justice, the credit for opening the Amur belongs to colonial seafarers, particularly Lieutenant Gavrilov of the Corps of Naval Navigators, in 1846.

During Count Putiatin's expedition to Japan, the Company's ship Kniaz Menshikov was for more than a year at the count's full disposal, with no recompense from the government. The maintenance of the vessel and the expedition cost the Company more than 77,000 paper rubles. During the last war [Crimean], the Company lost two ships while carrying out the task assigned it by local Siberan authorities, who were forced by circumstance to use Company ships. The loss of those ships amounted to 133,000 silver rubles, and the Company did not ask to be reimbursed for this.

The shortage of equipment necessary to carry out a proper survey of the colonies forced the Company to engage the services of foreigners, and to prepare maps based on the surveys of Vancouver, Cook, Beechey, Belcher and other

persons, supplementing these whenever possible with findings made by colonial
seamen. In 1852 an atlas was published by Captain of the First Rank Dmitrii
Tebenkov, Atlas of the Northwestern Shores of America from Bering Strait to
Cape Corrientes and the Aleutian Islands, with the Addition of Several Places
on the Northeastern Shores of Asia. The plates were engraved and the work was
published in New Arkhangel.*

    In addition to this at various times the Governing Board published
departmental maps of various locations such as the Bay of Aian in 1845; in 1847
a map of part of the Pacific Ocean with the islands lying from 35° N. latitude
up to Bering Strait; in 1847 a map of the entrance to the mouth of the Anadyr
River; in 1849 a mercator map of the Kodiak archipelago; in 1850 a mercator map
of the west coast of the island of Sitka from Cape Ommaney to Klokachev Sound;
in 1851 a mercator map of Bering Strait and part of the Arctic Ocean; in 1853
part of Kodiak Island showing Pavlovsk Harbor; in 1854 the Pribylov Islands
(St. Paul and St. George); in 1856 the eastern portion of Siberia with an indi-
cation of the routes from Iakutsk to Okhotsk, Aian harbor and the Udsk ostrog;
in 1857 the Amur waterway--and a number of others. Although these maps are
small in scale, they are notable for their accuracy.

    Over the past twenty years expeditions have been organized in the colonies
for various research purposes. In 1842 Lieutenant [Lavrentii A.] Zagoskin
conducted one such expedition to explore the northern part of the mainland of
Russian America;** the expedition returned after two years having quite satisfactorily carried out its assignment. In 1843 two expeditions were sent north:
one was to explore the Susitna River which rises from Plavezhnoi Lake*** and the
other to go up the Copper River to investigate a river which rises from
Plavezhnoi Lake and flows into the Copper River. The first expedition returned
unsuccessful because they encountered difficulty in navigating the rapids; but
the second discovered the Tlieshitna River which empties into the Copper River,
and followed it all the way up to Plavezhnoi Lake.

    In 1843 and 1844 they explored Aian Bay and the mouth of the Anadyr River.
Between 1845 and 1850 expeditions were sent out to survey the following: the
west coast of Sitka Island, the American coast between Kenai Bay and Chugach
Sound, Kodiak Island, and the nearby islands. Nearly all the Aleutian Islands
were surveyed or accurately described. And finally, in 1848 Serebriannikov, a

---

* The copper plates for the Atlas were engraved in New Arkhangel by a creole,
Kozma Terentev; but the actual place of publication, although not noted on the
title page, was St. Petersburg.--Eds.
** Lavrentii A. Zagoskin, Pashekhodnaia opis chasti russkikh vladenii v.
Amerike, St. Petersburg, 1847. English translation, Lieutenant Zagoskin's
Travels in Russian America, 1842-44: The First Ethnographic and Geographic
Investigations of the Yukon and the Kuskokwim Valleys of Alaska, edited by
Henry M. Michael, Toronto, 1976.--Eds.
***Golovin was misinformed about the source of the Susitna River, which flows
from the Susitna Glacier.--Eds.

hired navigator, was sent to explore the upper reaches of the Copper River, but was killed by natives.

In 1848 the Governing Board sent a mining engineer named Doroshin to the colonies; he surveyed and examined the quality of the soil around Sitka, on Kodiak Island, and on the eastern side of Kenai Bay. As a result of his explorations coal was discovered in Kenai Bay. I will comment on this later.

Generally speaking, these explorations have been undertaken irregularly, without any real system, and have been quite superficial and not at all definitive.

From 1839 to 1849 the man who organized the zoological museum [Ilia G. Voznesenskii] was in the colonies collecting animal and plant specimens.*

In 1841 a small observatory was built in New Arkhangel to make magnetic and meteorological observations. The Academy of Sciences appoints the Director of this observatory, and the Company supports both him and his assistant, who is appointed from among the Company's service personnel. They undertake their observations very meticulously, and the results are submitted to the Academy of Sciences.

* See E. E. Blomkvist, "Risunki I. G. Voznesenskogo (ekspeditsiia 1839-1849 godov)," *Sbornik Museia Antropologii i Etnografii*, 13 (1951). English translation by Basil Dmytryshyn and E. A. P. Crownhart-Vaughan, "A Russian Scientific Expedition to California and Alaska, 1839-1849," *Oregon Historical Quarterly* 73 (June, 1972): 101-170.--Eds.

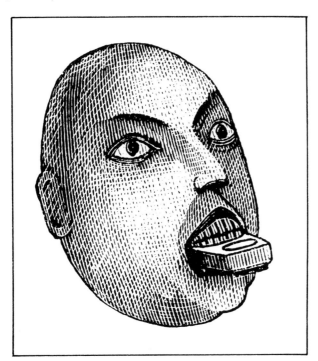

Kolosh mask.

BUSINESS ENTERPRISES AND TRADE

At the present time the business enterprises in the colony consist of: 1) hunting land and sea animals and fishing; 2) coal mining; 3) procuring ice; 4) logging. These enterprises can be divided into those which are *productive*, that is, which produce something that can be sold in the colonies, in Russia or abroad, and which can bring profit to the Company; and *non-productive*, that is, those that benefit the colonies but do not bring any monetary profit to the Company.

In 1799 an Imperial decree granted privileges to the Company and also gave it a monopoly on hunting land and sea animals in all our North American possessions, but at the same time it also obligated the Company to develop trade with neighboring countries and in general to develop trade in the Pacific Ocean. At that time the Company was chiefly concerned with hunting land and sea animals, the only source of its revenue, and focused all its attention in that direction. The small companies, which had existed up until that time, and which had hunted without any system or order, were dealt a death blow. In the beginning, the new Company also paid little attention to any kind of order, and it was only in 1805 when Councilor Rezanov visited the colonies that he introduced a system under which the Company would not face the extinction of fur-bearing animals, particularly fur seals. Sea otters and fur seals are the animals primarily hunted. The Company tried to find new places to hunt the former. For this purpose Baranov, Chief Administrator of the colonies, found ways to send out hunting parties even as far as to the shores of California. To accomplish this, he made use of the services of foreign smugglers. They came to New Arkhangel either empty or with a small cargo and goods for the colonies. He sent several baidarkas out aboard each of these ships, and assigned the necessary number of Aleuts; then the ships went to the coast of California and Oregon, let the Aleut hunting parties disembark in various places, and these latter then began to hunt river or sea otters. When enough animals had been killed, the ships picked up the scattered hunting parties and returned to New Arkhangel, where they handed over the furs and received half as pay for their work.* This arrangement ended when Baranov left the colonies.

---

* *Astoria, or Anecdotes of an enterprise beyond the Rocky Mountains*, by Washington Irving. New York, 1857.

When Ross colony was established in California, a certain number of Kodiak Aleuts were transferred there. The French voyager [Duflot] de Mofras, who visited California in 1841 and 1842, remarks that the Russians were hunting seals, sea and river otters all along the coast as well as in several estuaries in San Francisco Bay.

Meanwhile, on the Aleutian Islands, hunting went on with no thought to conservation. Only in 1822 did Chief Administrator Muraviev give the order to take measures to preserve the fur seals on the islands of St. Paul and St. George. But even here the goal was not achieved due to the total lack of organization and irresponsibility on the part of the prikashchik. Only in 1834, from the time that Captain of the First Rank Baron Wrangell (currently Admiral, and member of the State Council) was appointed as Administrator of the colonies, was proper conservation at last introduced. At present there are strict orders regarding this, and as a result, the number of animals is evidently not decreasing. On the contrary, there is reason to suppose that sea otters, for example, will increase in number; but a lack of hunters, and the constant movement of the otters away from the coast, means that the number of skins taken annually from 1842 at first decreased, but then remained constant; only since 1859 has this number begun to increase slightly.

Hunting sea otters is the sole occupation of the Aleuts, and of some of the Chugach. The Russians are altogether incompetent at this, and the creoles have still not learned how to hunt, although they have been encouraged. This hunt demands a special kind of patience, cooperation and skill, and one must begin to learn at an early age. Baidarkas are used, always a good-sized party of them, so that the sea otters will not be able to escape when they take fright. It is important to approach them with the utmost vigilance and in total silence; otherwise when they become aware that men are approaching, they will go far out to sea where it is all but impossible to follow them. Arrows are used for the kill; firearms are strictly forbidden because one can seldom aim properly when firing from a baidarka, and the noise of the shot frightens off the sea otters.

In former times it was easier to hunt them because they stayed closer to shore, and since there were many Aleuts, it was not difficult to organize large hunting parties. Under Baranov as many as 500 baidarkas were sent out to hunt every year just from the Kodiak Department. But at the present time even with great effort it is not possible to send out more than 300 from the entire colony, since the Aleut population has decreased by more than half since those earlier days.

According to its statute, the Company has the right to assign Aleuts to the hunt, provided that such individuals are not younger than 15 nor older than 50; also provided that not more than half of the able-bodied hunters from each settlement are sent out. However, this provision is not strictly adhered to. Without the old experienced leaders, the Aleuts will not go out to sea; the younger ones have to be trained to hunt at the age of 11 or 12, for otherwise they would rarely learn to become skillful hunters. The Aleuts are well aware of this, and therefore they begin to train their children in the art of managing a baidarka from the time they are very young; when they are 11 or 12, they are taken out to hunt under the supervision of the older hunters. Obviously none of these youngsters can take any sea otters at first, but the older hunters always give them a part of the catch regardless.

The colonial administration does not use force to organize these hunting parties. Discussions about the next year's hunt usually begin in December when the elders gather from all areas into the main settlements to deliver the pelts the Aleuts have taken, and to buy all their necessary provisions from the colonial warehouses. At that time every elder or toion announces how many baidarkas and how many Aleuts can be sent out from his settlement, and they come to an agreement about the leaders of the hunting party, etc. Then they reach decisions about when they should go and where they should go out to hunt the sea otter, when the archers should be sent out after birds, when the party should go out to kill sea lions, seals and whales, when the hunt for land animals should begin, and how many women and men should be sent to fish and prepare iukola for winter use, to provide food for the inhabitants of all the settlements.*

In order to outfit the sea otter hunting parties the Company provides the following at no cost: lumber and lavtaks for making baidarkas, whale sinews, sea lion gut and throat [for boots], cordage, two cups of rum per person for the entire period, and one and one-half pounds of tobacco. They also distribute for every 80 to 100 baidarkas a certain amount of weapons, powder and shot to kill birds that are to be used for food, and they also give out a small amount of tea, sugar and flour for persons who become sick while they are out on the hunt.

Since the sea otter hunting parties often have to go out as far as 150 or even 300 versts from their settlements, they send out a supply of provisions to the area near where the hunt will take place: seven and one-half pounds of flour per person, and whatever amount of iukola and blubber is necessary.

Each hunting party is assigned a certain number of women to help build baidarkas, care for the sick, prepare food, etc.; these women receive ten paper rubles from the Company for the entire period of the hunt.

If the Aleuts build baidarkas at their own expense, the Company pays them fifteen paper rubles for a three-hatch baidarka, ten paper rubles for a two-hatch, and five paper rubles for a single-hatch baidarka. Obviously the Company's effort to supply the Aleuts with all the equipment necessary for the hunt should not be looked upon as an unselfish act, for the reason the Company does this is that otherwise the Aleuts could not capture and kill animals, and consequently the Company would have no furs. Nonetheless these expenditures should be added to the payment which is given to the Aleuts for the hunt, which of course increases the colonial expenditures. Moreover the Aleuts could not

---

* Appendix 6 gives the number of Aleuts and baidarkas that were sent out to hunt from the Kodiak Department in 1860.

carry on without some such support, no matter what the administration. It would seem to be advantageous to send a small sailing vessel out with these hunting parties, which could carry everything the Aleuts would need for the duration of the hunt; in case of a heavy wind, it could help the baidarkas during their travel to the hunting areas. Generally all the hunting parties are ready and leave for their hunting areas by April 10, and they return during the first part of July. Meanwhile the Aleuts who have remained in the settlements go out in their baidarkas from time to time, also in parties, to hunt birds, sea lions, walruses and whales. All parties return to their settlements by August 15. Aleuts who stay in the settlements with the women and children prepare weirs to trap fish in the rivers from the month of May on, and they also use poles to fish at sea, and from the catch they prepare iukola for their settlement for winter.

The Aleuts may sell their catch of sea otters only to the Company, and at a set price. At present they receive 50 paper rubles for a good sea otter. The annual sea otter catch of the Aleuts, averaged from 1842 to 1860, is 984; added to those that the Chugach and Kenais take along the Kuril Islands, the total is 1,347. Formerly a certain number of sea otter pelts were also procured by barter from the Kolosh, but since 1851 this exchange has been completely terminated in the sound; only five skins were procured from them on Sitka between 1853 and 1860.

Appendix 7 gives the number of pelts procured annually between 1842 and 1860. It should be noted that the pay given to the Aleuts for sea otters as well as for other animals is rather small. It has already been increased twice, in 1836 and in 1852, but it still is not set at a proper level which would provide sufficient profit to the Aleuts without being burdensome to the Company.

Regardless of how large the expenditures are for the maintenance of the colonies in general, and all expenditures of the Company, nevertheless all hunts bring good profit; careful management of disbursements is possible and necessary to cover all costs.

Aleuts who are constantly involved in hunting or preparing for the hunt have not time for any other activity from which they could make some profit. As a result their well-being depends completely on the pay which they receive for these animal pelts. This is all the more true since the climate prevents them from developing agriculture or raising livestock. Moreover, the Company charges high prices for all the things the Aleuts need such as shoes, clothing, bread and other provisions. If one compares the number of sea otters caught with the number of adult Aleuts, it becomes apparent that each hunter does not even average one sea otter per year; consequently his annual pay is less than 50 paper rubles. This sum, together with the pay he receives for land animal pelts, is barely enough to pay for clothing and absolutely necessary supplies; after these expenditures, an Aleut has nothing left to use to build or improve his situation. This is a problem which cannot continue without proper attention.

In order to preserve the sea otters, a rule was made not to hunt in all places. The colonial administration must see to it that the sea otter breeding grounds are designated and untouched for some period of time. Thus the sea otters who are usually killed or frightened off in any given place will be allowed to multiply and calm down during a closed season. With this type of conservation it is possible to predict that they will never become depleted or permanently vanish from the shores of our islands.

At present the best sea otter hunting areas are Kamchatka Sound, Kenai Bay, along the shore of Alaska, near the Katmai odinochka, near Shumshu Island, and lastly near Iturup and Sakhalin. But they are also found in other places along the Aleutian Islands and the entire Northwest Coast of America south of Alaska. Without exception all sea otter pelts are shipped to Russia.

The fur seal hunt is one of the most important enterprises and sources of profit for the colony, to such a degree that the destruction of the seals would be a tremendous loss to the colonies. This is a constant concern and a dangerous situation for the colonial administration. Their breeding grounds are located on the islands of St. George and St. Paul, primarily on the latter. Seals come here from the south and appear at their old breeding grounds around April 18 or 20--these are the adult males; the females start to arrive from about the 26th of April until May. They breed here, and remain until the early part of October, when they migrate south for the entire winter; one does not see a single seal until spring.

In earlier times seals were killed on St. Paul and St. George islands with no discrimination or system, so that although they returned to their breeding ground every year, they began to decrease rapidly in number. As a result, in spite of all efforts, by 1828 it was not possible to take more than 28,000 pelts, although the administrator insisted that up to 40,000 pelts could have been taken without too much harm. Finally in 1834 certain prohibitions were instituted: from that year on, for a period of several years, no seal was to be killed on St. Paul Island, and on St. George the prohibition lasted from 1826 to 1827 [1836? to 1837?]. Now the number of seals has increased substantially; even if they do not continue to increase, at least they should not decrease, because there is a strictly enforced rule that when seals are killed, the males and females are to be separated from the young and driven into the sea. The young are then herded to the hunting ground and killed without regard. Of yearlings only the males are killed, and the females are driven back into the sea. From time to time prohibitions are issued, or only the most absolutely necessary number are killed. Seals also live on Bering and Mednyi islands, but in no great numbers. Recently between 8,000 and 20,000 seals have been taken each year without any great effort. The seal hunt is carried on by the Aleuts, who are sent out to the Pribylov Islands from various places in the colonies for several years at a time, by their own consent, and for an agreed amount of money. These Aleuts are maintained at the expense of the Company. Eight thousand seal pelts are sent to Kiakhta to be exchanged for tea there, and the rest are shipped by sea to St. Petersburg or to Shanghai or to the United States of America.

The hunt for land animals is generally carried on from September to the 15th of December. About September 20 the Aleuts receive all the equipment they need for the hunt from Company warehouses: traps, weapons, powder, shot, etc.;

each hunter also receives one pair of sea lion throats for boot tops, two pairs of lavtak soles, leather uppers, and, at the end of the hunt, a cup of vodka.

The Aleuts hunt only fox, river otters and arctic fox; in the Kodiak Department they also hunt bears, lynx, sables, muskrats, minks, marmots, wolverines and wolves. These pelts are also procured from the natives, both dependent and independent, at established prices. River otters are secured primarily from the natives. Between 1842 and 1860 the number of pelts acquired through hunting and barter by the Company from natives averaged annually: 1,350 sea otters, 8,475 beavers, 3,360 river otters, 3,890 foxes, 2,920 arctic foxes, 120 bears, 340 lynx, 1,390 sables, 1,000 muskrats, 130 minks, 17,820 fur seals, 150 puds walrus teeth, 2,435 pairs beaver castors, 40 marmot parkas, 380 sea otter tails, 20 martens, 75 wolverines, 5 wolves. For the period from January 1, 1849 to July 1, 1860, the entire hunt in the colonies, at colonial prices, amounted to 1,776,878.89 paper rubles.

From these hunts 2,000 beaver pelts are sent to Kiakhta and the rest go to Shanghai and America. River otters go to Kiakhta, foxes to Irkutsk and only a few to Shanghai. Blue fox go to Irkutsk and Kiakhta, and the white fox to America. Bearskins go by sea to St. Petersburg; lynx to Irkutsk; part of the sables are sold to service personnel on Sitka and part go to Shanghai, generally of rather mediocre quality. Muskrats, minks and marmot parkas are sold on Sitka. Walrus teeth and beaver castors are sent by sea to St. Petersburg. Sea otter tails go to Irkutsk and Kiakhta; wolverines and wolves go to the Mikhailovsk redoubt.

There has been some feeling that the Company's policy in regard to assigning Aleuts to go hunting has caused them too much hardship; but this is not altogether true. Of course the Company, according to the privileges that have been extended to it, has the right to order a certain number of Aleuts to go on the hunt, and then to purchase the pelts from them at a set price. But these assignments are made with the approval of the toions, and if the Aleuts go out to hunt not altogether willingly, at least they are not forced to do so. They are carefree to a large degree, and will endure all manner of need; the Aleuts would be more willing to sit at home doing nothing until hunger forced them to seek some gain. Furthermore, hunting sea otters, for example, is possible only in groups; the Aleuts themselves would never organize parties, in fact they would not have means to do this if they were not supplied with lumber, lavtaks and all the necessities for building baidarkas and all hunting supplies. A single hunter may only by chance kill a sea otter that has somehow strayed from the pack.

However, I do believe that it would be far more just to eliminate obligatory labor and increase the price paid for the pelts. The fact is that except for the obligation to hunt and sell skins to the Company at a set price, the Aleuts do not have any other committments. Whatever they procure is their own property. If one were to compare the situation of the Aleuts with that of natives who live in Siberia, or even with those who live in the northern parts of European Russia, such as the Tungus, Chukchi, Buriat, Samoyed and others, then it is no exaggeration to say that the situation of the Aleuts is in all respects far better, and that they have made tremendous progress.

If one and all had permission to hunt at will in our colonies, then in all probability within a few years the animals would be exterminated, and a large part of the furs would end up not with the Russians, but with our American and English neighbors. This would not only be a decisive blow to our colonial industry, but the Aleuts themselves would ultimately be ruined. If the government finds itself unwilling to extend the privileges of the *R. A. K.*, then no matter what measures are undertaken to administer the region, the sea animal hunt should be entrusted into the hands of some one company or other that could exercise the same kind of husbandry as the [Russian] American company now does.

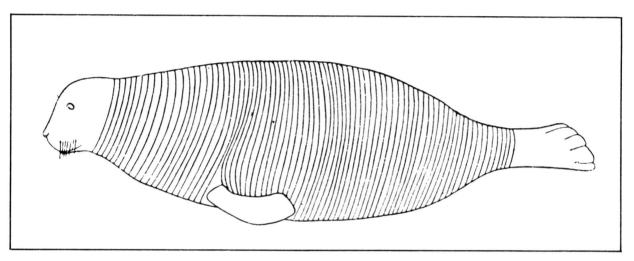

Diagram for cutting seal and walrus
pelts into thongs.

THE FISHING INDUSTRY

Fish are prepared in the colonies for the most part as food for the inhabitants; only a small amount goes abroad for sale. There are two kinds of fish here, one can be caught all the time, and the other appears seasonally. In the first category belong cod, halibut, bream, pike-perch and other kinds of small fish. Seasonal fish begin to appear along the coast in March, sometimes in February, especially herring. On Kodiak they come in June and November, on Atka in April, on Unalaska in fall. Red fish of the salmon variety begin to appear in May; these have various names in the colonies. This fish is generally salted and dried, in which state it is known as iukola.

For catching and salting fish, so far only one structure has been built near New Arkhangel in the Ozersk redoubt, and in New Arkhangel itself there is a shed to store it and to salt it. They also prepare barrels in that place. In other departments of the colonies they only prepare iukola as food for the local inhabitants.

When the fish are running, all service personnel receive fresh fish from the Company without cost. For the rest of the year salt fish is also given out free, and is used as food in the communal kitchen, while iukola is distributed free to the natives as it is available, for example, when the iukola initially prepared by each settlement seems to be insufficient for its needs. From the Company's supplies the Aleuts receive iukola during their sea otter hunts.

The present Chief Manager intends to organize fishing on a larger scale at Karluk on Kodiak Island, and he has already sent there a certain amount of lumber which is needed for building sheds and living quarters. When this industry has developed adequately, when salting can be done as needed, and when the demand for salt fish will increase in nearby markets, then this should provide the Company with a substantial and constant source of income. I shall have more to say about this below, and here will mention only the figures regarding the amount of fish prepared each year in the colonies, both for local needs and for sale. Judging by the figures over the past ten years, the amount of fish required each year for use in the colonies is as follows:

Salt fish, up to 114,000 fish, for a sum of 11,000 paper rubles

Fresh fish	64,000	9,500
Iukola	380,000	8,000
Total	558,000	28,500 paper rubles

or

8,143 silver rubles

In earlier times between 100 and 600 barrels of fish were prepared for sale. In 1858 1,070 barrels were prepared. Now, because of unfavorable market conditions, and since the present system of salting fish is quite expensive for the Company, between 300 and 500 barrels have been prepared for sale. When the fish processing building has been constructed at Karluk, it will be possible to prepare as much fish as is necessary, and the sale will be possible and profitable, especially if they set up a place to make barrels there, since at present the construction of barrels requires much time and expense for salaries for workers.

The whaling industry in the colonies is insignificant, and the entire amount of meat, blubber, whiskers, sinews, etc., is used for colonial needs. As noted earlier, this is carried on primarily by the Aleuts, although in part by some of the free creoles of the Kodiak Department. In addition, the Company carries on a whaling enterprise in association with the Finnish Company, but a review of this undertaking cannot be included in the present report.

Yakutat Indians paddling.

ICE

The ice industry began to develop in the colonies in 1852, when along
with the increase of population in California there developed a need to receive
this item more quickly and inexpensively than from Boston, from where it had
been supplied prior to that time. But since up to now ice has been shipped
only to California, the annual demand for it has been limited to 3,000 tons.
In time, if it becomes possible and profitable to sell ice to other ports in
the Pacific Ocean, and also to the Sandwich Islands and to China, then the
Company will undoubtedly increase its means of procuring ice in large quantity;
however, procurement depends a great deal on the climate. For example, on Sitka
and Kodiak, where ice is procured, the winters are often changeable and rainy,
especially on Sitka, so that there is no possibility of preparing a large amount
of ice. On Sitka sometimes it cannot be prepared at all. Consequently it
would be difficult to count on too large an operation, especially when it is
always possible to get large amounts of ice from the Amur without great trouble.
Under these circumstances, the American Company would have extraordinary difficulty in competing with any other company that might undertake this industry
on the Amur.

In the colonies ice is procured from lakes on Lesnoi Island near Kodiak
where two ice houses have been set up, each capable of holding 3,000 tons, and
in New Arkhangel, where there are also three ice houses each of 3,000 tons
capacity. Ice is procured by Company workers who receive a daily cup of vodka
while they work, and also by hired Aleuts from Kodiak; in New Arkhangel the
Kolosh do this work for one paper ruble per day. Workers only have to bring
the cut ice from the water, move it on wooden rails to the sheds, and pack it
there. Then when necessary they move it from the sheds on rails to the harbor
and load it aboard ships. The ice is marked and cut into appropriate sizes by
a special saw shaped like a plough which is powered by horses. This work goes
very quickly. If it should snow, then thaw and freeze again so that the ice
is covered with frozen slush, they then have to scrape off this slush with the
aid of a special scraper, for which purpose three horses are used. This is the
most difficult work because the frozen slush is often three or four inches
thick. Ice cannot be less than ten inches thick, otherwise it is useless. It
is seldom thicker than this on Sitka, but on Kodiak it reaches twelve or thir-
teen inches.

Between December 1, 1852 and July 1, 1860, 17,860 tons of ice were prepared on Sitka and 19,200 tons on Kodiak. The procurement of ice on Kodiak began in 1854. At present they usually prepare between 5,000 and 6,000 tons, so that if 3,000 tons are sold in a year, the rest is saved for the following year. The present value of ice storage and cutting equipment is about 50,000 paper rubles.

Russian blockhouse near New Arkhangel.

COAL

Coal is found along almost the entire Northwest Coast of America and in the English possessions its procurement is substantial in scope, but up to now there has still not been discovered a deposit of high-grade coal. Generally it is believed that the farther north one goes, the more imperfect the coal formation becomes. The mining engineer [Petr] Doroshin who was sent to the colony examined the eastern side of Kenai Bay, and in English Bay found deposits of coal which seemed easier and more profitable to mine. The need to supply Company steamers with coal at a lower price than California offered, and the hope to profit from the sale of coal, the consumption of which in California in 1855 had already reached 20,000 tons a month and was constantly increasing, forced the Company to give special consideration to this subject, and they began to increase mining operations wherever it seemed profitable to do so. Kenai evidently is the best place because of the large amount of coal which can be procured there. The strata of coal along the northern shore of English Bay are found in the form of kettle-shaped pits, and seams which can be seen at low water. It is possible to distinguish three basins, of which the middle is the largest. The strata lie along the shore for a distance of 2,000 feet. The depth into the interior has not yet been ascertained, but it is believed they extend for at least three or four miles. The seam is between nine and twelve feet thick, and bears up to 70% coal. It may be that the pit is even deeper.

All of these circumstances, plus the abundance of forest in the Kenai region, have led to the working of a small bay in the northern portion of English Bay called Coal Cove. Coal mining was first done with picks, but the coal which was obtained in this manner, although adequate for use aboard Company ships, was nonetheless found to be of low grade, and as much as 500 tons was shipped to California to be sold there on the basis of previous experience. It was sold at the relatively low price of 12.50 rubles per ton, or 21 paper rubles (6 silver) per pud.

In the meantime measures were taken to begin mining huge amounts of coal. In 1857 a water pumping station was built, and in 1858 all necessary structures were built to house machinery and service personnel and laborers. By the spring of 1859 they had reached a depth of 70 feet in the mine. Taking into consideration the slope of the strata as viewed from the sea, it has been calculated that at a distance of 600 feet inland from the shore, that is, where the shaft has been commenced, it should be possible to tap the coal seam at a depth of 160 feet. The use of picks to extract coal is still continuing. Between 1857 and 1860, 2,700 tons of coal were procured and used aboard Company steamers. In 1860 fire destroyed the building which housed the steam engine, and this has halted work, but they will soon proceed in the same manner as before. There is no reason not to expect that they will find coal of excellent quality, although it may be at a considerable depth.

The coal strata in English Bay are of tertiary formation and are believed to have come from a coniferous forest. However even this quality of coal will find a market in California. The question is whether the Company will be in a position to extract this coal as economically as coal which is mined in other places where it is less expensive to work than in our colonies. Mining cannot flourish in places where circumstances prevent the introduction of pay for manual labor, and our colonies are very much in this situation. Workers for the most part are sent from Russia, and in addition to a salary, they receive food and all necessities from New Arkhangel and Kodiak, where all of these items are brought either from Russia or from abroad.

It is considered absolutely necessary to have a minimum of 93 workers who are experienced and knowledgeable in this venture. If these persons were to work diligently day and night, it would be possible to mine 70 tons of coal per day. But in addition to these workers, it would be necessary to have 28 service personnel for administration, supervisors, and other purposes. It would not be inexpensive to maintain these persons.* Moreover, Coal Cove is open to the north and northwest winds, which are quite severe and prolonged here, so that ships anchored far out from the shore cannot be loaded, but must proceed into the interior of the bay. This requires that rails be constructed from the mine shaft to another point along the shore where ships can be loaded at all times, or that a special floating coal warehouse be built which could be loaded when convenient and then be floated out into deep water in the bay so that incoming ships could be loaded with coal without delay. It is also essential to sort the coal, for otherwise it can never be sold.

Coal deposits have also been discovered on the Alaska Peninsula and on the islands of Unga, Kodiak and nearby islands; also at Cape Ansburn, in Norton Sound, and on the islands of the Koloshenko Archipelago. But all of these places have been only superficially surveyed by persons who were insufficiently knowledgeable in this matter, and as a result nothing definitive can be said in this regard.

_____

* 45 miners, 18 hod carriers, 6 carpenters, 6 loaders, 3 steam engine maintenance men, 2 stokers, 1 blacksmith, 6 boys to sort coal, 6 to carry coal, for a total of 93; 1 chief engineer, 1 head miner, 1 assistant head miner, 1 maintenance man and his assistant, 1 secretary, 1 feldsher, 1 pilot, 1 guard, 2 cooks, 2 signalmen, 1 baker and his assistant, 1 man to care for the horses, 1 stockman, and 10 men to load coal aboard ships; a total of 28 [Golovin lists only 27 here, having failed to record one of the positions]; and a grand total of 121.

It is entirely possible that there is coal on the island of Sitka, but as noted earlier, this island has been explored only along the coastline, and up until now the interior remains quite unknown. Generally speaking, judging by statements in the official report, it is very, very dubious that coal will bring the Company the kind of profit it hopes for.

Kolosh grave.

89

FORESTS

Forests grow in abundance along the entire American coast beginning in Alaska, and on adjacent islands offshore: in small amounts on Kodiak and on Lesnoi Island. In the interior of the northern part of the mainland it covers large areas, especially along the Susitna, Knyk, Kwikpak and Kuskovym and other rivers, and during the spring floods a great many uprooted trees drift down these rivers and out into the sea. There is no forest on any of the Aleutian islands; their only wood comes from driftlogs tossed up by the sea. Up to the present time trees are cut primarily on Sitka, and only for colonial needs. A rather insignificant amount of lumber was sent out for sale, but this was only done on an experimental basis.

Yet the colonies are requiring more and more lumber to build various structures on Sitka as well as on the Aleutian Islands, for ship construction, for ships' masts, baidarka frames and the like. Forests on Sitka and the nearby islands produce fir for the most part, but it is of exceptionally fine quality. Larch and wild cypress also grow there, and are used mainly in ship construction. Birch grows in various places on the mainland, and occasionally oak. Logging is done mainly by soldiers. They are sent to perform that work in groups of 15 to 20 men for a month at a time, and occasionally for longer. In the forest they live in earthen dugouts [zemliankas], and they receive their food from New Arkhangel. Throughout the period that they are working they receive one cup of vodka per day. In spite of the fact that the work in a forest such as that on Sitka is terribly difficult, because it is virgin timber where trees grow on top of fallen trunks which have decomposed in time, many of the soldiers volunteer for work in the forests and remain there for several months at a time, only infrequently visiting New Arkhangel.

Cut lumber is put to use almost immediately because there is such a great need for it. The Kirinsk lumber mill in Serebrennikov Bay and the mill in New Arkhangel are in almost constant production preparing boards for baidarka frames and the like, for there is constant need not only for cut lumber, but also for sawdust for storing ice, and to pack it aboard ships. Without sawdust, ice melts very rapidly, and when it is stored in the hold or in sheds, the corners of the blocks are broken off, and a great deal is lost thereby.

Lumber is not always cut in the same amount, but only as need requires on Sitka or in other colonial departments, therefore there is no extra reserve supply in New Arkhangel except for a small number of boards necessary for the construction of ships' decks and planking. From the appended table, Appendix 11, it is apparent how much lumber was cut on Sitka from 1852 to 1860. However it is difficult to ascertain the value of that lumber, because, as noted above, it is cut by soldiers who receive payment not on a daily but on an annual basis, which is generally true for all work.

Shipment of lumber to New Arkhangel and other places is done via the harbor. Only firewood is purchased, because such a large amount is required, as much as 2,300 cubic sazhens per year, and there are very few persons who prepare firewood. Consequently, they contract with the Kolosh for it, who receive 11 paper rubles per sazhen, which includes delivery aboard their own barges, and stacking. If the harbor lends them a barge for firewood transport, then for every 10 sazhens of wood, they add one additional sazhen to pay for the rented barge.

Thus far, this has comprised the entire forestry operation. A certain amount of boards and shipmasts has been sent abroad for sale, but this has been just an experiment.

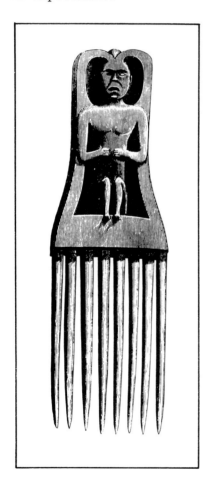

Kolosh comb.

INLAND TRADE

From the time the Aleutian Islands were discovered, the promyshlenniks and private companies who were engaged in the fur trade there sent nearly all of their furs back to Russia, without exception. Sergeant Basov and the merchant Trapeznikov alone sent 112,220 rubles' worth of furs to Russia in 1747; in 1750 they sent 39,376 rubles' worth. A large part of the furs were then sold in Kiakhta, and part went to Turkey and to Persia. When the Russian American Company was at last organized and brought permanent settlements and administration to the colonies, this led to the provisioning of the colonies with food and other supplies; since the Company did not have sufficient means to accomplish this, it had to turn to foreign assistance. Foreigners supplied the colonies with food and other goods and received furs in payment. In this fashion a substantial portion of the pelts were transferred into the hands of Americans and other foreigners who sold part of the furs they received in China and part in the United States of America.

The Company found that this form of business was unprofitable. Foreigners brought food to the colonies but also tried to sell goods in the colonies which the Company did not need and had no use for; but often the Company was forced to accept these, since foreigners would agree to sell food only if the Company would also purchase other goods. Thus the Governing Board in 1820 prohibited the colonial administration from entering into transactions with foreigners, and undertook to supply the colonies by using its own ships which could sail around the world.

The Company's fur trade was profitable up until 1820, except for losses incurred in transactions with foreigners who supplied the colonies. Furs procured in the colonies were sent to Siberia where part of them were exchanged for tea in Kiakhta; the rest were sold in St. Petersburg and Moscow, or in some cases in Siberia and in the interior gubernias; the tea received in exchange was sold in Moscow and at the fair in Nizhnyi Novgorod.*

---

* Also known as the Makariev Fair, since it was begun in conjunction with the Makariev Monastery.--Eds.

In 1818 the Company had 900,000 rubles worth of goods in Russia and 520,000 rubles in cash, for a total of 1,420,000 rubles. Its obligations totaled 1,700,000 rubles. In 1820 the capital of the Company in cash, checks and goods totaled 4,147,960 rubles. In 1818 and 1819 the Company paid an annual 7-1/2% dividend on each share. At that time, because of the lack of a supply system, they began to deduct for supplying the colonies with Company ships, a decision which led to very high expenses for the Company since it was very expensive to build and maintain ships and they sailed lightly laden with less than full cargo. The slow turnover did not cover costs, in spite of the fact that the amount of furs began to increase, and goods that the Company sent were twice as expensive as those the foreigners bartered there on the spot.

In 1820 and 1821 the profit amounted to only 4% per annum, and in 1822 and 1823 the Company suffered a loss of 286,000 rubles. These circumstances forced the Company to withdraw its prohibition against foreigners trading in the colonies. This new rule also had harmful effects: it was found to be unprofitable to pay foreigners in pelts, because fur seals, for example, could be sold in Russia for between 15 and 25 rubles, while they were worth only 8 rubles in America. For this reason in 1831 they began to pay by check, which was both difficult and disadvantageous. At the same time the size of the catch began to decrease, while expenses for the maintenance of the colonies began to increase each year. Finally in 1838 an agreement was concluded with Hudson's Bay Company, who agreed to supply our colonies with food and other necessities at an agreed price.

Then a regulation was issued regarding hunting, and this aspect of affairs came to be properly handled. The Company received its revenues exclusively from the sale of furs and of tea which they had traded for in Kiakhta. Consequently it was necessary to procure the largest possible number of furs, and while protecting the colonial trade, to acquire furs from natives who lived in our colonies. Through an agreement with Hudson's Bay Company, at their instigation, vodka, weapons and gunpowder were completely excluded from goods traded to the savages. The Kolosh who lived in the sound willingly disposed of their furs to the Company, as did other natives in the north. The Company organized trading posts called odinochkas or redoubts for the purpose of bartering with these natives in various places. However this part of the trade gradually began to fall off. Foreign whalers who came to our shores to take whales brought supplies of rum, weapons and gunpowder aboard their ships, and traded these things with the savages for their goods. Hudson's Bay Company also did not live up to their obligations, and secretly supplied the savages with the prohibited goods. As late as March of this year [1861] a steamer belonging to that company came into our sound and persuaded the Kolosh to bring everything they had to exchange since the steamer was well supplied with goods including vodka and weapons. As a result, the Sitka Kolosh were drunk for several days.

Finally the announcement that the English port at Victoria was a port open to free trade diverted the Kolosh there, with the result that from 1851 on they almost completely stopped trading with the Russians. Prior to that time Kolosh from the sound area had come to Sitka. Now they are afraid to come, since the Sitka [Kolosh] killed the visiting Stikines and became belligerent toward other tribes. It was also the custom to send a steamer into the sound every year to exchange goods with the savages, but [Nikolai] Rosenberg feared the Sitka Kolosh would attack New Arkhangel, and instead of adopting more reasonable measures, decided to keep the steamer at Sitka. Thus when the current Chief Administrator [Ivan Furuhelm] arrived in the colonies in 1860, he sent the steamer out to exchange with the Kolosh, but although the steamer remained there for a considerable period of time, it only brought back 40 cheap pelts. It is true that the Kolosh did come aboard to trade, but they demanded vodka, gunpowder and firearms in exchange for their furs; according to regulations the Company cannot sell these items to them.

The fur trade in the north is faring no better. At a certain time established long ago by custom, the natives come to the shores of the Bering Sea and exchange their goods with the Siberian Chukchi and the inhabitants of the islands of Uziak, Ukibok, Ugiiak and Gvosdev, all in the Bering Sea, which have not been occupied by the Russians. Both the Chukchi and the islanders then go to the American coast and barter goods with the savages in exchange for reindeer hides and certain other items which the Chukchi receive in part from merchants on the Lower Kolyma [Nizhne-Kolyma] and partly from whalers, as the islanders do. The Company has tried to promote some sort of trade with the Chukchi and the islanders, but like the others they demand vodka, firearms and gunpowder. Even the Lower Kolyma merchants cannot trade profitably with the Chukchi, so they sell them Russian goods and vodka just as they did formerly, and they also buy foreign goods from them.

According to reliable information received this spring in the Sandwich Islands, where whalers always gather prior to their departure for hunting, we know that the brigs Kohola and Nero and the brigantine Victoria--all three flying the Hawaiian flag--and the bark Zoe, under the American flag, as well as two or three schooners that, except for Zoe, had been outfitted by the whalers, were preparing for trade in the north mainly with such items as rum, low-grade cognac, tobacco, gunpowder and firearms. Ships trade these goods for furs, whale whiskers and walrus tusks. Any time American newspapers mention whalers they state that such and such a ship, engaged in whaling in the north, had an unsatisfactory catch but nevertheless found business very good. Quite often there are articles concerning the harm done by whalers who give vodka to the savages. The Friend, a newspaper published in Honolulu, has an article entitled "Life on board a Man of War," which tells the story of a skipper who visited a small Chukchi settlement on the Asiatic shore and found every person, even small children, in such a state of drunkeness they were on the verge of insanity.

Not content with buying furs from the natives and killing whales and walruses in our possessions, to the obvious detriment of the native inhabitants who are thus left without the basic means of existence, the whalers have more than once tried to take fur seals on our islands. In 1841 and 1843 they sent out hunting parties to Bering Island, and in 1849 they put several whaleboats and a crew of 45 men ashore on the island of St. Paul with all the equipment they needed to hunt seals; however, they were forced to withdraw when the administrator appeared with armed Aleuts. They also often take lumber that the Aleuts have prepared for winter with great labor; they even take the supplies of iukola that the Aleuts prepare during the sea otter hunt, so that often a whole group is left without food.

Such lawlessness is truly harmful to the Company's trade and to the inhabitants of the Aleutian Islands, and can only be ended by sending naval cruisers into these waters. It seems only just for the government to protect its subjects and its trade in these waters, as part of its obligation to protect them everywhere. A further statement will be made on this subject in its proper place. Meanwhile, it would seem useful to completely revoke from the charter the prohibition against the Company selling alcoholic beverages, weapons and gunpowder to the natives, and leave this to the judgment of the colonial administration. The harm has already been done. All the savages have firearms, carbines, pistols, revolvers, powder, shot and vodka. There is no possibility of completely halting this illicit trade. Cruisers will be able to prevent its growth and protect the inhabitants from the lawlessness of foreigners, but the contraband trade will continue to some degree in spite of this, and hunting will simply become more costly. If the colonial administration had the right to sell these items freely to the natives, then of course they would willingly bring their furs to us rather than to foreigners, for when they trade with those persons, they risk having the fruits of their labor confiscated. Furthermore, this would result in no lawlessness, because furs would be purchased from the savages at a set price, just as Company goods would be sold to them at a set price. Thus a savage would never have to give a pelt worth more than three rubles for a bottle of vodka priced at three paper rubles.

In regard to the moral issues involved, in my opinion one cannot expect any good to come from the present generation of savages such as the Kolosh, no matter what measures may be adopted. It will be sufficient for them possibly to become accustomed to our ways. The next generation will no doubt be better; perhaps one can expect good results only in the grandchildren of the present Kolosh.

In order to improve its situation, the Company attempted to establish trade operations in various places in Russia. In 1843 they made an attempt to trade in Kamchatka; in 1844 they brought 50,000 silver rubles worth of consumer goods and other things there. But there also they encountered competition from foreigners who found it possible to sell their goods more cheaply than the Company could, and as a result they placed whatever price they wished on goods which were for some reason unavailable in the Company store, while the Company was selling all of its goods at set prices. This stability of prices gradually caused the Company's trade in Kamchatka to develop. At the same time the Company brought into Kamchatka substantial quantities of government goods aboard its ships, and by 1847 it was making a substantial profit. Nor did the government lose anything by allowing the Company to bring in its shipments. As evidence of this one can see that for example rye flour that the Company brought aboard its ships sailing around the world was much less expensive than that carried via Okhotsk. Almost all the goods were brought to Kamchatka aboard ships sailing directly from Russia or from Hamburg. When the port of Petropavlovsk closed [during the Crimean War], the Company terminated all trade in Kamchatka because the goods they had delivered could not be sold and so they did not realize any profit.

In the meantime the Company began to ship goods to the mouth of the Amur River, beginning in 1855; there was a profitable market for them there. Later it had to give up that operation as well, for the Company encountered competition from foreigners and from the establishment of the Amur Company. Once the Aian harbor had been established, the Company entered into trade relations with the Tungus, and began to supply nomadic natives in that area with food, gunpowder and the like, at set prices. For this purpose they built warehouses in Aian, Nelkan and at the Aldan station. The Company's intention was to gradually gain control of the entire fur trade by providing the savages with all their needs, at set prices. But here again they encountered competition from Siberian merchants and other persons who found it profitable to exploit the naivete of the natives to exchange trivia for furs.

In general, the Company should be given credit for never having abused its authority. It never resorted to harmful and illegal means to develop trade; this was the reason it could not compete with the Siberians. Like all savages, the Tungus, Iakuts and others were addicted to vodka, and would willingly dispose of their furs to anyone from whom they could get it. At first one only had to give a savage two or three ounces of rum in order to make him a bit intoxicated, and then he would be willing to trade everything he owned for trinkets if only he could have more vodka. This is not a new scheme, but rather, a very old one; anyone who has ever had dealings with savages knows of it. There is another scheme which the Siberians use. If a Tungus brings in a pelt and asks 25 silver rubles for it, and the pelt is not worth more than 10, a Siberian will not bargain, but rather, will take the pelt and give the Tungus the goods he wants, but will praise those goods in such a way that he makes them seem worth the price of the pelt, plus his profit. Attempts have been made to show the savages that they are being hoodwinked; [Company men] will explain to him that his pelt is not worth 25 rubles, that it is only worth 10 rubles, but that he will actually get his 10 rubles worth of goods [from the Company], whereas if he sells to a Siberian merchant, he will only get 6 rubles worth of goods, and they will be poor quality. But the savage cannot understand this. He says, "You will only give 10, but he will give me 25. I will sell to the one who gives me 25."

Under these circumstances trade could not be developed there, and the Company had to terminate all its operations in that region. If and when the life of Siberian savages is examined and described, a great many sad pages will have to be read in that description. Perhaps then the natives themselves will give credit to the honesty of the Russian American Company.

At present Company stores and commissaries are located in Moscow, Kazan, Tiumen, Tomsk, Irkutsk, Kiakhta, Iakutsk and Aian. There is a special store in St. Petersburg where sea otter pelts are sold at a discount of 30% over earlier prices. Lately the demand for sea otters has decreased considerably, partly because imported river otters, known under their German name, can be had for quite a modest price; partly because the military has completely done away with using sea otter for uniform collars.

TRADE IN THE COLONIES

One of the most important sources of profit for the Company is from supplying the colonies with all their necessary provisions and other goods. I stated earlier that at present special attention is being given to procuring food items for the colonies as inexpensively as possible. Other goods which are necessary in the daily life of the inhabitants are shipped to the colonies; some come from Russia and some from abroad, especially from Hamburg. When one analyzes the special reports which the Company has submitted to the government at various times for a review of its activities and as evidence of its condition at certain periods, one is struck by the diverse meanings given to the term "supplying the colonies." For example, in the initial stages of the Company's existence, both food and other goods were supplied to the colonies via Siberia. This operation was both difficult and costly, and the Company was forced to turn to foreign sources of supply. But foreign ships that came to the colonies brought little food, and as noted above, they forced the Company to accept goods for which they had no use. Furthermore, under such terms of trade, the furs which represented the prime source of Company revenue fell into the hands of the foreigners, the more so since foreigners were not prevented from obtaining furs from the natives, a fact that was obviously detrimental to the Company's interests.

Finally in 1813 the Governing Board concluded an agreement with [John Jacob] Astor, a citizen of the United States, to establish a factory for the fur trade at the mouth of the Columbia River. Under the terms of that agreement Astor was to supply the Company with all necessities, and in exchange to receive furs at an established price; also he would transport Company furs aboard his ships to Canton and sell them there, charging a commission and receiving a set fee for freight, then giving the remainder to the Company. Both companies promised to respect the trade of the other as well as their respective hunting places, and they pledged not to give gunpowder and firearms to the natives. They agreed to act jointly against contraband ships, and in case of trouble they would aid one another. However this agreement was abrogated because of the hostilities which broke out between England and the United States of America, and the eventual transfer of the factory into other hands. Subsequently the Governing Board completely terminated trade with foreigners and decided to supply the colonies aboard its own ships that sailed around the world.

In this spirit the Governing Board prepared a review of the Company's activities from 1797 to 1819. A report concerning later years, in which the Company requests new rights, clearly states that it was very detrimental to the Company to prohibit foreigners from trading in the colonies because it was extremely expensive for the Company to supply all the necessary goods aboard its ships. This practice eventually involved the Company in such expenditures and burdensome costs that it was finally forced to repeal that prohibition. But a report for the past twenty years again points out the damage done by giving foreigners permission to trade freely in the colonies, so that all the profit that could have gone to the Company went into the hands of foreigners. It also points out that the Company suffered considerably in transactions with them and in discount transfer; that even the agreement with Hudson's Bay Company, which had agreed to supply the Company, was quite unsatisfactory for the Russian American Company. Therefore the Company at first tried to supply the colony with all necessary goods by bringing them in from Europe aboard freighters; but since 1853 all goods and supplies have been brought to the colonies on Company ships, and only rarely aboard freighters.

There is a discrepancy in all of this: the Governing Board reviews the advantages and disadvantages of supplying the colony with Company ships, but has not made it clear why it was disadvantageous to do this. The point is to deliver goods to the colonies as quickly and as cheaply as possible. In a commercial operation where everything is accounted for, the cost of maintaining the ship used in carrying goods, and the time consumed in that transport, represent a very important factor. Naturally, any cargo carried on a commercial ship that has been outfitted with the greatest economy and has as its objective reaching its destination as quickly as possible in order to reap the greatest profit possible is going to have considerably lower freight charges than cargo carried on a ship outfitted almost on a military basis that is not concerned with costs and delays in sailing.

The Company only now seems to have understood this. It is organizing its ships in a commercial fashion and is instructing them to make quick sailings. It has finally realized that it is no more expensive to carry freight on its ships than on commercial ships; having eliminated all foreign merchant participation in trade in the colonies, naturally it now realizes all of the profit for itself.

The Company imposes a 42% markup on goods imported into the colonies to cover freight, loading and unloading, etc. This completely covers the expense of outfitting the ship and even allows a surplus. These goods are then sold in the colonies with an additional markup of approximately 35%; that is, on certain essential items a lower markup is imposed, while on other things, for example luxury items and trinkets, a larger percentage is taken. On an average it amounts to about 35%.

Of course not all of the goods are sold. Some stand in the warehouses for several years. There is also damage and spoilage and drying out to consider. But nevertheless the profit is substantial, in fact so much so that the Company is in no way inclined to give up that trade, because the profit from this particular venture comprises almost the only means for maintaining the colonies.

Once the goods delivered to the colonies are priced, they are sold at that established price; this does not change until a new shipment is received. It is unfortunate that the St. Petersburg and Hamburg agents are not concerned with the quality of their goods; very often they supply merchandise which is sold only because there is nothing else available. For example, boots for laborers are sent from Russia and are sold in the colonies for ten paper rubles per pair. But they are absolutely worthless. One pair will not even wear one month. Consequently a laborer pays more than 100 paper rubles per year for footwear.

It would also be worthwhile to import shirts made of Russian linen from Russia, for laborers, soldiers, and for other persons with little money. These shirts could be sold for no more than 2.10 paper rubles, or 60 silver kopecks. They would be much more serviceable than the sailcloth shirts which sell for 4.50 paper rubles or cotton shirts for 6 paper rubles; these are of no use whatsoever to a working man.

I must say a few words about the following problem: the colonies have no coins or commercial paper. All salaries of service personnel and laborers' wages are paid in colonial marki, which are of value only in the colonies. The natives will not accept these marki. All trade with them is carried on by barter. Service personnel and the inhabitants of the colonies in general receive all their goods from the Company stores in exchange for these marki. Naturally, since they do not have any other money, they have to get everything from the Company, no matter how poor the quality of goods may be. If someone wishes to buy something in California, for example, he needs hard cash. Thus there are speculators who are able to get gold one way or another and sell it to persons who need it, for a very high price. However neither this circumstance nor the prohibition against bringing anything in from California deters the inhabitants; in fact this serves as good evidence of the fact that a great many more goods can be had on the side, even if for a high price, than from Company stores, where they are always of poor quality. The Company stores have very few things the inhabitants need.

I am not venturing an opinion as to what degree it is more profitable to the Company to have marki in circulation rather than currency. The marki are made of parchment in denominations of 10, 25 and 50 kopecks, and in 1-, 5-, 10- and 25-ruble denominations. It is true that persons who save can bring these marki to the office and then their savings are considered a credit on the Company on which they can earn interest. But marki are little valued in the colonies; they are spent more readily than would be the case with hard cash. This is profitable to the Company, but how does it affect the pocketbook of the workers?

THE TEA TRADE IN KIAKHTA AND SHANGHAI

From the very beginning of its existence the Russian American Company exchanged tea in Kiakhta for its furs, then disposed of the tea in Russia at a considerable profit. These profits decreased substantially when the decision was made that in exchanging tea a certain amount would be paid in items of national [Russian] manufacture. In adopting this measure, at the request of certain Muskovite manufacturers, the government intended to support and develop manufacturing in Russia, but this aim was definitely not achieved. Several manufacturers became rich from sales to consumers of tea, but did not improve their products at all because they had an assured permanent market for their goods, in spite of their shortcomings. So naturally they had no incentive to go to any extra expense or to be concerned with improving things. Tea merchants likewise paid little attention to the quality of the manufactured goods, and only sought to secure them as cheaply as possible. The Chinese would pay very little for them because they were of no use, and in Shanghai, for example, Muskovite fabrics could be bought more cheaply than in Moscow itself. Naturally, everything they lost on manufactured goods the tea merchants had to add on to the price of tea.

Such a form of trade for a Company that had as its prime objective a market for its furs could not be sufficiently profitable, especially when there was competition from other tea merchants. Moreover, beginning in 1842 expenses in Kiakhta began to increase because of packing and shipping costs.

Of course all of this affected Company business and decreased its revenues. For example, from 1835 to 1841 the Company made a profit of 50 to 80 silver rubles on each chest of tea. In 1845 the profit per chest amounted to only 6.04 silver rubles. And in 1845 the duty on common tea was lowered from 60 silver kopecks to 40, but on choice tea, it was raised from 60 to 80 silver kopecks per pound. Since the Company received two-thirds of its whole amount from Kiakhta in choice tea, and only one-third in common tea, the increase in duty on the former exceeded the lowering of duty on the latter. The difference, for 6,200 chests, represented a loss to the Company of up to 10,000 silver rubles per year. This problem, the difficulty of exchanging tea in Kiakhta, and the increase in expenditures for maintaining the colony, forced the Company to request certain privileges from the Government: these included permission to pay only 40 silver kopecks per pound on choice tea, this to be limited to 6,000 chests, and customary tax to be paid on the rest. Also, the Company asked permission to pay duty after the sale of the tea acquired through barter, but not later than nine months after it was transferred from Kiakhta, with no interest for that period; it asked to be excused from paying any duty on furs brought to Kiakhta.

Eventually, in 1850, the Company was permitted to bring 2,000 cases from Shanghai by sea over a two-year period; after that period had elapsed, it had permission to export 4,000 chests annually instead of 2,000, until the termination of its privileges.

During this time the Company continued to exchange tea at Kiakhta, and also tried to establish barter trade with the Chinese at Kuldzha and Chugachak;* but the Chinese in those places were completely unfamiliar with the value of furs, and thus trade could not be established there.

Permission to carry tea by sea gives the Company a tremendous advantage, because it gets choice quality tea less expensively than in Kiakhta and saves a good deal in shipping it by sea; furthermore that tea can be sold in Russia at the same price as Kiakhta tea.

The Government granted the Company this permission, to bring tea by sea, in order not to undermine the Kiakhta merchants. Nevertheless, it appears that trade in Kiakhta will shortly be completely terminated. With the opening of Chinese ports, foreigners will supply China with all necessities in such quantity and so inexpensively that our merchants in Kiakhta will not be able to compete, and then it will be advantageous to allow all Russian merchants to bring tea by sea. This would lower the cost of tea in Russia, and increase the demand for it, by giving poor persons the opportunity to use it.

In addition to the tea trade, the Company plans to send logs and lumber to Chinese ports; it has already sent a small amount of lumber on commission to Shanghai on an experimental basis, but the results as yet are unknown. It is uncertain whether the Company will be able to develop this trade to any significant degree. It would be necessary to have special ships and warehouses for this. At present the Company faces competition from the Americans who have forests in Oregon which are in no way inferior to ours; they can undersell the Russian American Company because there are workers available in Oregon, and they cost much less than is the case in our colonies. Later, when the Oregon forests have been cut, our Company will undoubtedly make a profit and quite a substantial one, by supplying lumber to China, the Sandwich Islands, and mainly to California.

---

* Both located in Sinkiang Province, Kuldzha (Kuldja), on the Ili River, and Chugachak are known today as Ining and Ta Cheng respectively.--Eds.

TRADE WITH CALIFORNIA

Commercial relations with California, although quite limited in scope, have existed almost from the very beginning of the Company's existence. The Company received grain, meat and produce from there. Meat in particular was procured inexpensively; frequently it was possible to secure livestock free, and the only labor involved was in skinning it. All this trade was carried on with the Spanish missions, which was of advantage to both parties. When the Ross factory was established, there was reason to hope that the advantages the Company would receive from the California trade would gradually increase, and that the colony would in some manner secure a permanent source of provisionment for itself.

When there was a change of government in California--that is, when Mexico declared its independence--our relations with the new government grew more and more strained. Finally the Company was forced to give up its factory, almost for nothing to a Mexican subject named [John] Sutter. After conceding Ross, and before gold was discovered in California, trade with that country was almost completely terminated.

The great influx of population to California at the time of the discovery of the gold fields gave birth to new demands in that country. Anything brought there from Europe, the United States and elsewhere found an immediately profitable market.

The Chief Administrator of our colonies, Captain of the Second Rank [Mikhail] Tebenkov, took advantage of this circumstance, although rather belatedly, to send a shipment of various goods to California in 1848 that had accumulated over the course of several years in colonial stores. For the most part these were dilapidated goods of poor quality that could not be sold in the colonies. All of these goods sold. At the same time there was a mining engineer named [Petr] Doroshin in the colonies, who was sent to California with the necessary number of men in an effort to work gold fields if possible. In three months they produced 12 pounds of gold, but he did not keep on lest the men he had with him might run away.

In 1850 and 1851 some goods were also sent to California for sale, but trade in these goods was not nearly as successful as it had been formerly. In February, 1852 an American ship came to New Arkhangel to take on a cargo of ice if possible. Hitherto ice had been supplied from Boston, which of course was very expensive. Ice is in considerable demand in the United States, where it is used in great quantities. That ship took 250 tons of ice, for which the Company received $18,750, or $75 per ton. Of course the Company had to pursue the idea of developing this profitable trade, and in October of that same year the Company's agent concluded an agreement with a commercial firm called the American Russian Trading Company, by terms of which the Russian American Company undertook to send 1,000 tons of ice per year from its colonies aboard American ships, at $35 per ton, until September, 1855. This was very profitable for the Company, for they could get ice for no more than two to three dollars per ton. Of course they first had to use part of that money to build ice storage houses and to acquire the equipment necessary for working with ice, but all of these expenditures were recovered within a very short time.

However, in 1854 the director of the American Russian Trading Company, [Beverley C.] Sanders, who was a sly and clever fellow, managed to get letters of recommendation from the president of the federal government, from our envoy to Washington, and from several other prominent persons, and he appeared in St. Petersburg with these letters. Here the Russian American Company was *actually forced* to sign a twenty-year contract with Sanders, in spite of the fact that the Company's privileges were due to expire in eight years, and it was not yet known whether these privileges would continue to be extended to the Company.*

The contract with Sanders was concluded and went into effect October 9, 1855. The Russian American Company had to sell all the ice it procured, not only in our colonies but in any of the Russian possessions around the Pacific Ocean, to the American Russian Trading Company at the same price our Company paid, and to divide any profit equally. In addition, our Company had to pledge to sell lumber, coal and fish to the American Russian Company on the same terms as ice.

Of course it was detrimental to our Company to have to agree to such a contract for a twenty-year period. It was soon discovered that except for two or three persons who had some capital, the rest of the partners of the American Russian Trading Company, including Sanders himself, had entered into this business venture with no cash, and at the expense of our Company had built an ice storage house in San Francisco as well as everything else needed for the ice trade. Our Company, in fulfilling its obligations, built icehouses on Sitka and Kodiak at its own expense, and all the while was giving over half of its profit and paying half of the expenses.

Disagreements arose constantly, caused by one side or the other. The

---

* I think, however, that when they signed this contract, our Company planned to request that the privileges be continued, once they expired, on the basis of this contract, for the Emperor had to approve it.

Russian American Company insisted that according to the agreement the sale of ice should not be limited to California, but rather that they should try to develop the trade along the entire coast, to Panama, and even farther. But since the Americans did not have any capital, they did not think about this, and Sanders himself, the director of the company, entered into other speculative ventures. He opened a bank without having any money, and when that venture proved totally unprofitable, he finally had to run away from the law.

The affairs of our Company proceeded in this manner until 1859 when the Governing Board finally decided to entrust Captain of the First Rank Ivan Furuhelm, who had been appointed Chief Administrator of our colonies, with the task of trying to abrogate the contract, even if it should be necessary for the Company to take a loss. Of course the proposal that Furuhelm made to the American Russian Trading Company was at first decisively rejected because the contract was too profitable for the Americans. But Furuhelm's persistence, and a certain knowledge of American customs, triumphed over all obstacles. Noting that the Company's privileges would expire much sooner than the duration of the contract, and that the Americans were not rigidly adhering to all conditions, Furuhelm proposed either to abrogate the old contract and draw up a new one, or to resolve the matter in the courts. It would have been tremendously expensive to bring legal action in America, and judgment is always given in favor of the party who is in the position to pay more. The American knew this very well, and decided not to proceed.

As a result the contract was terminated by mutual agreement, and a new one was concluded, beginning January 1, 1863. Under the terms of this contract the American Russian Trading Company receives ice only from our Company. It pays seven dollars per ton and must take at least 3,000 tons per year; in any case, it must pay for 3,000 tons. If it buys more, the price is the same. Ice may be hauled aboard freighters belonging to the American Russian Trading Company or aboard our Company ships, in which case our Company receives eight dollars per ton for freight charges. Twenty percent is added to compensate for loss [by melting] that means our Company supplies about 20% additional, or 3,600 tons, rather than 3,000. Furthermore the Russian American Company has the right to sell ice wherever it wishes, at whatever price, except for California, Oregon and the coast of Mexico where ice may not be sold for less than $25 per ton.

Obviously this contract is very advantageous to our Company. When it expires even greater benefits can accrue. Needless to say, the present Chief Administrator plans to exploit this, if he does not encounter competition from the Amur. However I believe that by using its resources, the Russian American Company will then be in a position to carry on its ice trade without loss.

From January 1, 1852 until July 1, 1860 the amount of ice exported was 20,554.50 tons, for a sum of $121,956.04, or approximately 162,181.54 silver rubles; that is an annual average of 18,090.16* silver rubles (See Appendix 10).

---

* For the eight-and-one-half years the average should read 19,080.18 rubles. --Eds.

Furthermore, ice is for the most part carried aboard Company ships, and thus the freight charge of eight dollars per ton brings in a very substantial sum.

In addition to ice, they contracted to send lumber, salt fish and coal to California, but only a small amount of the latter, really on a trial basis. However at present neither lumber nor fish can be shipped profitably, first, because Oregon lumber can always be supplied less expensively, and second, because the Company does not have any place in San Francisco where it can build a lumberyard or fish storage building. Without these, it is impossible to sell at a profit. As a result one must take the price which is paid when the ship anchors. That price is never high, for they know that the goods have to be sold immediately. Consequently the lumber and fish trade has been ended for the time.

Now that the Governing Board has permitted the colonial administration to purchase grain, salt and certain other items in California, it is to be hoped that trade between our colonies and that region will become more fully developed. It is regrettable that when the Company established commercial relations with California they did not immediately think of appointing a special agent there who spoke foreign languages. The agent they sent* was totally unfamiliar with the customs of the country and with the English language that was predominant there. Furthermore he was an older man who could not move quickly and could not turn circumstances to his advantage. He bought a house for the Company in San Francisco which required yearly expenditures for repairs and brought no profit at all; yet he did not think of acquiring a site on the shore for the construction of docks and warehouses. This is now almost impossible to remedy, and the Company has to pay very dearly to unload its ships in foreign harbors. And since it does not have warehouses where goods destined for the Company can be stored, or where goods sent to California to be sold in exchange for colonial items can be warehoused, it has to acquire the former and sell the latter at prices that are very unprofitable.

The position of agent cannot be considered a sinecure or a reward for a long term of service; it demands an active, resourceful man who has the knowledge to take advantage of circumstances--in short, the very qualities that the Company's agent in San Francisco does not have. Thus our Company's trade in San Francisco proceeds poorly.

---

* Petr Kostromitinov, manager of the Ross colony, 1830-38; vice-consul and commercial agent in San Francisco, 1852-61. Although Golovin criticizes his efforts in the latter position, Kostromitinov had very successfully promoted and increased agricultural production during his years at Ross.--Eds.

TRADE WITH THE SANDWICH ISLANDS

        In precisely the same manner the Company has also sent lumber and fish
to the Sandwich Islands, but prices were very low there also, and the sale of
fish was hindered by the fact that the salting was not satisfactory. Now it is
done better, and the Company's commissioner in Honolulu hopes to find a good
market for it.

        As far as the ice trade is concerned, its use there is still too little
developed so that it is impossible to sell more than 100 tons per year, and the
profit from this is so small that it does not pay to become involved in it.
Nonetheless, trade relations with the Sandwich Islands are constantly kept up,
and the Chief Administrator of our colonies even receives regular letters and
reports from the Hawaiian government officials on the progress of trade in those
islands.

Aleut carving
of an American
sailor, 1845.

CONCLUSION

The Company's existence is based on dual foundations: the first consists of the *rights* or *privileges* that give the Company the character of <u>private</u> enterprise; the second is the series of *obligations* that the Company has assumed in order to organize the region, which gives it the character of a *governmental* institution.

From this it follows that if the Company received the *rights* and *privileges* as a reward for *obligations* it assumed, then the following basic questions must be posed and answered:

a) Has the Company used its past and present privileges within legal limits?

b) To what degree has the Company fulfilled the obligations which it has assumed, both in regard to indigenous tribes inhabiting the colonies, as well as in regard to the government, in matters such as welfare and administration of the region?

c) What steps has the Company taken to develop a moral-religious education for the natives as well as a general and technical education?

d) What measures has the Company adopted to develop trade and industry in this far-off land? And, finally,

e) Does the present condition of the colonies justify the privileges granted to the Company and the continued use of these privileges? If not, what has hindered the development of commerce? And what measures should have been taken to overcome these obstacles to a successful business venture?

To conclude the above review, it is necessary to examine each of these questions, and thus formulate a general overview on the conditions of the colonies at the present time.

From the above, it is evident that in the beginning of its existence the Company had quite limited means of fulfilling the obligations it had taken upon itself. The organization of the country was undertaken with the help of individuals who were far from moral, and of course as a result there were many abuses. Even Chief Administrator Baranov himself often transcended his authority both in regard to the natives, the Aleuts for example, as well as in regard to Russians who were in Company service. When Baranov was replaced, abuse and lawlessness on the part of authorities became less frequent, and at the present time only the Chief Administrators of the colonies can be abusive in their actions, and this happens only rarely. They are careful to watch the activities of the prikashchiks and of persons who oversee the natives, but they do not have any authority. The abuse of power on the part of Chief Administrators stems from the obligations and rights they have in regard to the natives, and also in regard to the rights of service personnel of the Company, which have been set forth very vaguely in the Company's charter. Everything pertaining to the rights and obligations of the Chief Administrator abounds, as does the entire charter, with verbiage, contradictions and reservations.

The scope of the obligations imposed on the Chief Administrator in commercial operations is very far-reaching. He is expected to have a fundamental knowledge of the subject matter pertaining to the trade and industry of the country, as well as a broad knowledge of administrative order. Consequently it would be desirable to have at least one learned jurist along with the Chief Administrator, a person wholly concerned with the welfare of the people. Unfortunately not only are such persons not to be found in the colonies, but only the Religious Administration is subject to the Code of Laws. The office of the Chief Administrator has no decrees, no laws, no military or naval statutes. In short, it has nothing but the charter of the Company.* Because of this, it is apparent that all matters are resolved either on the basis of the charter, or if the charter has no provisions regarding a particular subject, then it is decided according to the will of the Chief Administrator or by the Colonial Council, according to its interpretation. In all justice it must be stated that there have been no serious complaints about lawless behavior on the part of Chief Administrators. All disputes stem from the lack of clarity in regard to statements in the contracts which the Chief Administrator concludes with persons who enter Company service--obligations of the Company as well as of the persons signing the contracts. In settling such disputes, both the Chief Administrator and the Colonial Council will of course always defend the rights of the Company, so that even the most well-meaning Chief Administrator may make a mistake and resolve a problem unjustly.

---

* During my stay in New Arkhangel one of the noncommissioned naval officers who was in Company service was apprehended with several bottles of rum which he had brought from California and hoped to smuggle into the port, which is strictly prohibited in the colonies. The colonial administration wanted to make an example of the guilty man, but had difficulty in deciding what form of punishment to mete out to him. They did not know the rules regarding punishment of naval personnel, that is, what was an appropriate form of punishment for infraction of the rules. In effect they wondered, is it permissible to demote a noncommissioned officer to ordinary seaman and take away his bonuses for service? Should he also receive corporal punishment? Such problems arise frequently.

In regard to the natives, one can say that the colonial administration would always be in a position to be oppressive in the obligations which the charter imposes on them in relation to the Company; this could come about without overstepping the law, and in this, everything depends on the personal character of the Chief Administrator. It follows that even if there are no abuses now, there could be. The best way to prevent them is to establish a judicial institution in the colonies which is independent of the administrative authority. A conscientious and knowledgeable jurist should be assigned to be there and look into the question of how to organize such a colonial court. No matter how it is done, essentially only in exceptional cases would the decisions of the colonial court be forwarded for review to the highest state judicial chamber, the Senate. And even this right of control over the colonial court should be quite limited because of the remoteness of the region.

In the colonies where there has been no court system at all up to the present time, it would be quite appropriate to try such an organization on an entirely new basis. Would it not be a good thing to experiment with oral justice proceedings there, so that the court's activity would be completely independent from control by local authorities?

Furthermore the Aleuts and all natives in general should be relieved of any obligatory labor for the Company. The Company should be directed to hire Aleuts for hunting at a mutually agreed upon wage. The Company should, however, retain the exclusive right to buy sea animal pelts from the natives at established prices; these prices should be raised.

The Company was organized under the direct patronage of the government, which delegated a portion of its own authority to enable it to administer the colonies, with the understanding that it had a responsibility to earn trust and respect. If public opinion in Russia has not always justified the activity of the Company, it must be acknowledged that in foreign countries the credit of the Russian American Company has been solidly established. The Company has acquired unlimited trust and respect by fulfilling all of its obligations in an irreproachable manner in its dealings with foreign commercial houses. Its credit is accepted willingly and profitably in Europe and America and China. There is no commercial house which would think of terminating its business with it. There is no doubt that the Imperial patronage which the Company enjoyed has contributed a great deal to sustain this respect with which the Company has wished to surround itself. But nonetheless one must acknowledge that the Company has performed a service, because many companies who have enjoyed the same degree of patronage have not succeeded in gaining respect nor enjoying this trust.

The Company assumed the administration of the colonies that are spread out over such tremendous distances, and has managed to keep them as one unit without any participation or sacrifice on the part of the government. Thus for example during the last war [Crimean] our colonies were the only ones not subject to attack by the enemy. The initiative in this matter was taken by the Russian American Company who also found the means, although at a great sacrifice, to provision the colonies with food throughout the war, transporting it aboard neutral ships, at the time when several of their own ships were given over without charge for use by the government.

When one examines further the problem of the obligations that the Company assumed, both in regard to the peoples inhabiting the colonies as well as in regard to the government, in all aspects regarding the welfare and administration of the region, one can draw the following conclusion:

The administrative system that now exists for natives subject to Russia, the Aleuts, for example, does not need any major changes. It seems just to give them the right to choose their toions without any interference from the colonial administration, so that once the tribe has selected a toion they do not have to wait for the Chief Administrator to approve him for that position. In precisely the same manner the removal of toions should be left to the decision of the tribe. Furthermore, I consider it quite unnecessary to set up any sort of governmental police authority. In fact, this would be more detrimental than beneficial. It would be sufficient if in determining the toions' obligations to the government, the toions were to be supervised initially by regional officials in order to preserve law and order and organize public services and amenities. In this manner, every complaint and request from the natives would go directly to the top in the colonial administration, where necessary measures must be taken to satisfy the just demands of the natives and to maintain order. Regional officials should not be given the right to interfere in the affairs of the natives. They should rather be obligated to accept all their petitions and send them to the colonial administration for review.

As far as any improvement in the living standard of the Aleuts is concerned, it seems to me that this will come about naturally when they are freed of all obligations to the Company; that is, when their condition of virtual serfdom is ended, and the Company has ceased to be a wet nurse to them. Of course at first the Aleuts will suffer more want than they do now, because they are lazy and indifferent to the future. It is possible that some of the Aleuts will die under the new arrangement; but then the rest will gradually organize themselves as they think best and most advantageous. It is impossible to change the way of life of an entire people artificially through enforced measures. Change will come about by itself, from the pressure of external circumstances. What force would induce an Aleut to drink milk and eat meat, when he wants to eat whale and sea lion blubber? Or how will he be pressured to eat bread before he has been weaned from iukola? Give them the opportunity to work and to earn whatever they want and need, and let them decide for themselves how to get it. If the Company had concerned itself earlier about ending this aid, it would have been better for both the Company and the Aleuts.

Insofar as independent indigenous peoples are concerned, especially the Kolosh and others who remain in an altogether savage state right up to the present time, the Company has achieved very little, as I have remarked earlier. Any measures that have been taken to establish closer relations with these natives have always been inadequate, unsatisfactory and useless. It seems as if the Company has never had any determined, well-conceived plan to reach the independent natives who live in our possessions, nor a plan to subjugate them eventually. Consequently every Chief Administrator has acted in accordance with his own understanding of affairs, depending on circumstances, without realizing that in so doing he has often negated any good his predecessors have done. Under these circumstances the Company lost a substantial part of the furs, which now go from these natives to foreigners; the Company has taken absolutely no measures to protect their settlements from these same natives, so that fear of the Kolosh prevents organization of new settlements in those very places where it would be useful. Because of this, neither livestock breeding nor agriculture can progress, and it remains expensive to provision the region in spite of the fact that this is most inadequately done. Formerly there was trade with the savages, although it was carried on in a somewhat haphazard manner. Now there is no trade, and the Kolosh who live in the sound have become estranged from the Russians.*

Measures to be taken should include: an endeavor to establish permanent commercial relations with the Kolosh and with all other natives who live in our colonies, in an attempt to develop new wants among them and thus make them dependent on us; solicitude for the education of their children so that future generations will lay the groundwork for the eventual transformation of tribes who are still savage at present; finally, slaves must be freed to show genuine protection to all who escape and seek security from the Russian government--this will weaken tribes who are hostile toward us, and we should organize these slaves as settlers who are dedicated to us. Up until now our mission has not had any real influence on these savages, regardless of the figures submitted by the religious authorities in the colonies about the sizable number of natives who are converted to orthodoxy each year. I have already stated that in my opinion it is not enough to convert the savages to orthodoxy, that is, to be satisfied that they have succeeded in converting a number of persons through gifts and entertainments. They must direct their attention to the goal that savages will be imbued with respect for our missionaries, and will gradually realize our superiority; thus eventually we will destroy the influence of the shamans. Then the savages will willingly send their children to be educated by the Russians, and they themselves will change a number of their customs and ways. But this will come about only when missionaries are persons of better moral character and better education, who are more able to understand their vocation, who will not hide behind the walls of the redoubts, but who will try to be closer to the natives, learn their language and their way of life, and serve among them as a fine example, helping those who suffer and seeing to the education of the children.

---

* John Dunn, in his work History of the Oregon Territory and British North-American Fur Trade, says the following about our trade with the natives in 1846: "The Russians and Americans are the only two nations that come, even remotely, in contact with the British in those countries; and both are equally powerless and uninfluential with the natives. The Russians, for the most part, confine themselves to their own territory--a strip of sea coast, beyond 54° of north latitude. Even here they can hardly be said to exercise direct power, or even to have much influence. They have posts, it is true, stationed there; one especially at Sitka, in the Kamchatka country--a large one, which is worthy of some notice, and to which the Hudson's Bay Company, by a commercial contract, entered into lately, supplied provisions. They, however, are barely traders; carrying off the products of country, without taking much interest in the condition of the natives: neither caring for them, or cared for by them."

Almost from its inception the Company has given appropriate attention to providing general and technical education for the natives. It has been noted above that thanks to the establishment of schools in various places the Aleuts willingly studied reading and writing, and now there are many of them who are literate. The independent natives to date have not become literate, but nevertheless at the present time the Kolosh come to the port at New Arkhangel and are learning the carpentry trade; some become sailors on Company ships. Many of the creoles are trained to be seafaring men or master craftsmen of various kinds. The reorganization of the colonial schools gives hope that there will be good results in the future. But here again one must state that the obligatory term of service for creoles educated by the Company is too long. If it is not eliminated entirely, it should at least be shortened to five years. It would be a great advantage if the government were to assume full responsibility for educating the children in the colonies.

I feel obliged to add that the spread of literacy among the Aleuts was most of all due to the efforts of the priest [Ivan] Veniaminov, who is currently [Innokentii,] Archbishop of Kamchatka, the Kurils and the Aleutian Islands. He learned the Aleut tongue and translated into it the Book of Matthew, a brief catechism and several prayers, and he managed to stimulate the Aleuts to learn to read and write. Even to the present day the name of Veniaminov is spoken by the Aleuts with deep respect and love.

At present there is a priest in New Arkhangel who has recently come to the colonies. He has begun to learn the Kolosh language, and intends to take on the responsibility for teaching the Kolosh children. The Bishop of New Arkhangel has given him a small accommodation for this purpose, where he can bring the children together. Of course this undertaking will be beneficial, but it would nonetheless be desirable if in addition to this the priest would visit the Kolosh settlement often, would become more deeply aware of the needs of the savages, and would gradually help them become accustomed to the idea of sending their children to be educated, not only to New Arkhangel where they are too close to their families, but even to send them to Russia. I maintain that real progress can be expected only from those children who are completely separated from the harmful influence of their parents at a very early age, so that they will forget the savage, uneducated way in which they lived as young children.

In the chapter on trade I discussed its current status. I will add only this: the Company has been preoccupied by profits to be realized from the fur trade and has consequently focused its attention exclusively on that subject; therefore all other areas of endeavor have forged ahead very slowly.

The Company assumed responsibility for provisioning the colonies through its own means with all necessities. There was no competition from anyone. This has led to the situation that all items supplied to the colonies are to a large degree either cheaply made or of a very mediocre quality, and they are sold at very high prices. This is one of the main sources of revenue for the Company in maintaining the colonies, and naturally the Company will not readily give up its rights to such profits. There is also the problem that many of the goods sent to the colonies are procured by the Company abroad, primarily in Hamburg.

If one were to take into account the expenses for the upkeep of an agent, travel abroad by the administrator, the cost of discounting checks, etc., then it would not be any more expensive to procure these goods in Russia from Russian factories. Furthermore the Company would be able to supervise the quality of the goods and the money would remain in Russia. The Hamburg agent not only supplies goods of poor quality, but they are carelessly packed, and frequently the amount sent does not correspond with that shown in the bill of lading and other documents.

Of course it would be good to allow anyone who wished to trade freely in the colonies, but this raises the problem of what the inhabitants of the colonies and the natives would use to pay the merchants for goods. If they paid in furs, then that enterprise could no longer continue to be a monopoly of one company; if that occurs, the trade will quickly decline and within a few years will have completely vanished.

There is no official currency in circulation in the colonies. If coins were to be introduced, then in a short time they would fall into the hands of the savages who would make them into rings, bracelets and all sorts of other ornaments. Paper currency would actually be used only for trade with Russian merchants. Any trade in such currency with foreign merchants would be very detrimental to the inhabitants, and the government would then have to pay out gold abroad in exchange for the paper notes. This problem needs careful study. Finally, could Russian merchants supply all needs everywhere? Would they find sufficient profit in bringing goods and supplies to such places where the demand for them is very small when they are needed, and where natural conditions make it extremely difficult to supply the localities?

If the fur trade were to remain in the hands of the Company, as formerly, then the advantages to the Company itself would induce it to supply the Aleuts with all necessities in order not to be deprived of the only workers qualified to carry on the sea otter hunt. Otherwise, one could hardly expect that all localities would be supplied as needed.

Lately the question has again arisen about permitting foreigners to come to colonial ports. The argument in support of this is that Americans would have every right to close their ports to all Russian ships if our ports were to remain closed to American ships. This problem has been raised in San Francisco by Senator [William M.] Gwin of California, one of the so-called *politicians* whose every effort and impulse is focused on attracting the largest possible number of voters in order to be elected a congressional representative and thus win an advantageous position, and line their own pockets. Senator Gwin was trying to be elected to a four-year term and thus raised various questions which could influence his election. This is the reason that he is concerned about advantage to his country. In this vein he expressed the real desire of the California merchants to have free access to the Russian colonies. He tried to justify the legal requests of the Americans on the basis of existing agreements which permit the Russian ships to use the same facilities in America as are extended to the Americans in Russia, so that if the Russians close some of their ports to foreigners, then the Americans will have the right to close any of their ports to Russians that were not yet open at the time these agreements were signed.

However Gwin's arguments provoked no response in the United States. Public opinion is usually expressed in print in magazines and newspapers, but so far not a single line has been published about this situation. The government will never become involved in any problem unless it senses that public opinion demands it. Whalers and contrabandists are the only ones who would perhaps like to have official permission to visit our ports and thus have even greater opportunity to carry on illegal hunting and trading. But they are not currently prevented by any prohibition, and they cooly declare at the Customs House in San Francisco that they are going to trade in the Russian possessions, and for that purpose they are carrying a supply of rum, powder, lead and various fire-arms and blades.

In giving careful consideration to the question of allowing foreign ships into our colonial ports, I come to the conclusion that some ports should be open, but only those where there is some colonial authority, that is, where appropriate supervision can take place. Generally the rule has been adopted that only certain designated ports will be open to trade where there are police and customs officers available. Trading vessels are not allowed to visit other ports. I see no reason to change these rules for our colonies.

Consequently I believe that at first the following ports should be open to foreign ships: New Arkhangel on Sitka Island and Pavlovsk Harbor on Kodiak Island. These are the only ports where it would be possible to organize police and customs supervision over visiting vessels. Then, every ship involved in trade in other parts of our colonies, or involved in transporting trade goods in our waters, should be declared contraband and should be seized and subjected either to a monetary fine, or to confiscation, in accordance with the decision of a special commission that should be set up either in New Arkhangel or in Nikolaevsk on the Amur. Thus our cruisers that seize the ship should have the right to tow it into one of these ports, depending on which is more convenient.

The willfulness of whalers and contrabandists who hunt and trade in our waters, not only in our colonies but also in the Sea of Okhotsk, and along the entire Asiatic coast, knows no bounds. More than once our envoy has asked the government of the United States to cooperate in ending the illegal hunting and trading by American ships. The response of the federal government has always been the same. It has declared that there is no possibility of taking any measures whatever to end this willfulness on the part of whalers and smugglers, and it can only announce to American subjects the prohibition against hunting and trading in Russian waters; but it says that of course this prohibition will not be heeded, and the Russian government will have to take its own measures to protect its shores from hunting and trading.* Actually, the government has a

---

* Last year the American ships Lizzie Thompson and Georgine, which were taking on guano illegally in a prohibited place, were seized by the Peruvian government and confiscated, in spite of a protest by the government of the United States. If Peru considers such measures completely legal, then should the Russian government be less energetic?

direct obligation to protect its subjects and to enforce the hunting and trading restrictions; it is not only necessary to send naval cruisers for this purpose, it is an obligation. However cruisers should have been instructed in this matter so that they could have acted decisively, as circumstances demanded, in honor of the flag that these ships fly, rather than being given cautious and indecisive memoranda that only aroused laughter among those persons against whom they were directed.

I even believe that one appearance of our naval ships in Honolulu and in San Francisco, where whalers and contrabandists usually provision, would be enough if it were announced that they were being sent to pursue contrabandists and whalers who ply their trade in Russian waters. If there were a permanent station for our warships in the Sandwich Islands or in California, so that cruisers could be sent from there to the Sea of Okhotsk and to the colonies, this would give a very satisfactory impression. It would also put an end to the lawlessness of the whalers and smugglers. The savage tribes who live in the colonies would realize that we are strong in deeds, not words. And the influence of the Russians in the Pacific Ocean would be a fact, whereas at present it does not exist at all. The Sandwich Islands offer every advantage for maintaining a permanent station there. From there the way is open to America, Japan and China; the commanders of our warships would be able to familiarize themselves fully with the sailing conditions in such places where in case of war all their activity might be concentrated.

And is it not obligatory for us to study our own colonies? If we accuse the Company of indifference, must we then follow its example?

I further believe that communication with Europe must be promoted on a faster and more regular basis to insure the success of our trade in the colonies and the general welfare of the country. The easiest and fastest way to accomplish this is to communicate through California. The English have established regular communication by ship between San Francisco and the port of Victoria. Why should not the colonial administration enter into an agreement with the English so that they would transmit our papers and dispatches from San Francisco to Victoria and back, so that we would only be responsible for establishing steam navigation between Victoria and Sitka? This effort would not require any great expenditures. Small steam schooners with very small crews could maintain this communication directly by sea during the summer months. During the stormy period in the rest of the year they could go through the straits [Inside Passage].

In regard to hunting, one may say that except for sea otter, hunting has developed very little under the influence of the Russian American Company. In fact, the entire region still needs careful study. There is no doubt that if people with energy, persistence and adequate financial resources were to come to our colonies, they could uncover riches here that have never hitherto been tapped.

Consequently it seems reasonable to give the Company jurisdiction over such places where it already has some business, and to give all Russian subjects permission to prospect and to exploit any discoveries they may make. To this end, persons wishing to have land for their permanent use should not be faced with all manner of barriers to prevent this. Only under conditions of complete freedom of action can we hope for good results.

California flourishes more and more each year. Trade, hunting, industry, livestock breeding and agriculture are being developed on a gigantic scale, primarily because there are no oppressive measures to hinder the citizens, and because each knows that he is working for himself, for his own profit. Apparently this division of labor fuses imperceptibly into a whole, providing prosperity for the entire country.

There is yet another question to which I addressed myself at some length earlier. It is argued that the monopolies granted to the Russian American Company destroyed our commercial navigation in the Pacific Ocean. In fact we have seen that during the first years after the discovery of the Aleutian Islands, many enterprising persons began to outfit their ships for trade with the newly discovered islands. It would therefore seem to follow that gradually poor ships should be replaced by better ones, their number should constantly increase, and in time a real commercial fleet should be formed.

Promyshlenniks who were sent to the Aleutian Islands and the Northwest Coast of America were lured there solely in the hope of acquiring furs. Not one of them ever thought of analyzing whether this source of wealth might someday disappear, or whether it would be forever inexhaustible. The whole question was how to obtain the most furs with the least effort. Under such conditions, the fur trade was bound to disappear in a relatively short time. Until the Russian American Company introduced proper conservation measures the number of animals decreased every year, and one could even then foresee the time when there would be no more animals at all. But all this time the Company continued to kill animals regardless, although they did not take as many as the Aleuts used to kill to sell to small promyshlenniks and companies before the Company was founded. Sea otters used to be found along the California coast in great numbers and now there are none whatsoever. Likewise beavers, river otters and fur seals and other animals have also disappeared. When the fur trade ended for our promyshlenniks, as a means of quick and easy riches, not one of them gave a thought to any other kind of enterprise and trade in the colonies. If some private persons had decided to invest money in producing lumber, fish or coal, then where could they have disposed of these products? California was sparsely populated by a small number of Spaniards and did not need lumber, fish or coal. Japan and China were closed to us. The Sandwich Islands were still in a primitive condition. What could have spurred the Siberians to build ships and to organize a merchant fleet? Whaling was always free to all, and at one time one could make huge profits at it, but how many Russian whaling ships were outfitted for this enterprise?

I believe that we did not build up a commercial fleet in the Pacific Ocean, first, because there was no way for it to develop; if there had been reasons for it to have been developed, it is impossible to conceive that navigation and shipbuilding would have progressed because of the lack of persistence and the indifference with which our trade people have regarded any improvement up until now.

It would seem that trade with Persia and relations with the Caucasus could encourage a merchant fleet in the Caspian Sea, but even to the present day the ships sailing there are just like those that were sailing there a hundred years ago. A monopoly granted to the Russian American Company might be detrimental to development of the colonies in general, or to the welfare of the region; but of course it could not hinder the development of our merchant fleet in the Pacific Ocean. This fleet disappeared by and of itself. During that period the Company always had the necessary number of ships there, on which fine skippers and outstanding sailors were trained. Many naval officers owe their training to the hard school on Company ships. On many occasions the government used Company ships for its own needs; to carry out such assignments required knowledge, devotion to duty, and sometimes sacrifice.

In regard to the question of whether the present condition of the colonies is in accord with the spirit of the privileges the Company has received; whether the period of these privileges should be extended; what are the factors that impede business; what measures might negate such factors as hinder successful enterprises, one can make the following observations:

In every case when the well-being of the colonies or improvement in the life of the natives and of visiting Russians offered the Company some direct profit, it did not shrink from expense. In all other cases, when profit was dubious, or required special effort and ingenuity, the Company either did not act at all, or adopted half measures. Thus, since the hunt for fur-bearing animals comprised the chief source of its revenues, the Company paid special attention to that undertaking and to everything directly related to it. This resulted in its concern for the Aleuts, the desire to increase the population of the colonies, and various other such measures. It is true that goals were not always attained, because they did not always conceive of plans early enough, which should have been followed through constantly.

In order to have available, at a reasonable wage, good skippers, master craftsmen, mechanics, prikashchiks and various other specialists, the Company had to build training centers and schools. And their wish to attract useful persons into service led the Company to be concerned about retired service personnel and their widows and orphans.

On the other hand the lumber and fish trades did not represent any direct profit. It would have required a considerable investment to develop these, with no assurance of quick success; thus these enterprises were not developed.

One might have expected to be able to get furs from the savages in the colonies by entering into friendly relations with them. But this would have meant penetrating into the interior of the country to organize new factories and keeping several garrisons there--in short, it would have meant expenses with no assurance of profit. It was not profitable for the Company to keep up the St. Dionysius redoubt [near the mouth of] the Stikine River at its own expense, so it was very pleased to have an opportunity of leasing this border point to the English. The development of agriculture and livestock breeding, prospecting and exploration in order to find new wealth in the interior of the country would have demanded both expenditure and persistence, with no real assurance of success. The Company found it more profitable and advantageous to supply the inhabitants with imported grain and meat rather than make serious research efforts.

Should the Company be blamed for this?

No. It acted as a commercial company, for profit, because it could not have existed otherwise.

Consequently I maintain that in order to organize the colonies properly and to develop their industry and trade, it is necessary to adopt the measures which I shall outline briefly.

The government should appoint a Chief Administrator or Governor of the colonies. If there is no competition from other companies, the government may select and appoint a Governor from among the candidates submitted by the Company, on the condition that the Company may not request his replacement unless it demonstrates beyond any doubt that his presence is detrimental to successful business enterprises in the colonies. His power should be quite broad, especially in respect to the independent natives, but they should be protected by definite laws. It is necessary that he be an independent person not subject to any governor-general, and that he submit reports of his activities only to the highest governmental bodies. The number of officials assigned to him should be limited. No guberniia administrative units should be introduced unless the needs of the region absolutely demand it. The Governor should supervise general order in the colonies, and the security of the inhabitants, and if he finds it necessary, he may oversee these through the use of naval cruisers that are at his disposal at all times during his administration of the colonies. In addition, he should personally inspect each department of the colonies every year.

Settlers, who should include creoles, should be administered by elected elders on the basis of tribal customs. The term "free creole" should be completely abolished, and all settlers should be subject to recognized obligations in regard to the government. These obligations should be of such a nature that Russians and creoles are not dissuaded from settling in the colonies. Places set aside for settlers should be given to them for their permanent possession, with all advantages.

Subjected natives, such as the Aleuts, and eventually others, should be governed by elected toions, as they are at present, in accordance with tribal customs. Land which they now occupy should become their own property. All disputes involving property should be resolved by tribal agreement, with no interference from the colonial administration. Only in exceptional cases, when the natives themselves request it, should these disputes be submitted for review and decision by the Governor.

The colonies should have no special police or officials except for naval cruisers. Port captains should be appointed only in harbors that are open to foreign ships. These captains should be given police supervisory powers.

Supervision of whaling ships and contrabandists should fall under the jurisdiction of naval cruisers which should be equipped for that purpose with exact and forceful instructions.

Wherever possible new settlements should be established along the entire Northwest Coast of America and along the principal rivers; in accordance with the desires of the settlers, they should be protected against attack by the savages. Settlers who secure lands should receive them in perpetuity.

Missions should be established there on a different basis. One should use the missionaries to influence independent tribes, should take in the native children to be educated, come into close contact with them, free the slaves, and if necessary act with overt force. I believe that at first a distinguished member of the clergy should be chosen who would have the responsibility for gradually building a mission, preparing the first missionaries from among the creoles, and then from various natives who live in the colonies.

Colonial training centers and schools should be kept up at the expense of the government treasury. Obligatory service should not be a condition of education. Perhaps some small fee should be set which would assist in rapidly moving the training institutions and schools from under the treasury to the tribe, which would be a good thing.

The Russian American Company should be given in perpetuity the use of those localities where it presently has settlements or various kinds of enterprises; the limits of those possessions should be set. The Company should have the right to hunt sea animals for a precise but extended period, in those places where it has been hunting up until the present time; that is, in places where it already has an economic interest. It should be clearly stipulated that the Company should maintain and improve the territory. The Company may hunt land animals within its possessions, and buy furs from the savages, following the same general rules as do other promyshlenniks or companies who may wish to engage in this enterprise in the colonies. Since the prohibition against selling vodka, weapons and gunpowder to the natives has not attained its goal, it should be abolished for everyone.

All Russian subjects who wish to engage in some aspect of hunting (except for the sea animal hunt in places that belong to the Russian American Company), trading and prospecting should be given freedom of action in all parts of the colonies that are not an integral part of the property of settlers. Whatever discovery they may make should belong to them exclusively. Anyone desiring to cultivate unclaimed lands should be given the land in perpetuity providing he makes an improvement on the land.

The extension of agriculture and livestock breeding in the colonies should be supported in every possible manner.

The harbors at New Arkhangel and Pavlovsk should be opened to foreigners who should be given the right of free trade with the inhabitants. However the export of sea animal pelts should be prohibited since this enterprise is one of the privileges of the Russian American Company.

Good communication should be established with California and eventually with Russia, because communication via the Amur and Siberia is more difficult, since the Amur River and the Sea of Okhotsk are closed by ice for seven months of the year.

These, in my judgment, are the most important measures that could serve to improve conditions within our colonies. But I believe that it is necessary for this question, which is of such importance, to be carefully studied by a special committee made up of persons who have the good of the country at heart and who understand the problem and whose goal is not just to bring about various changes for the sake of change, but to organize the region on solid foundations and to provide for the protection and well-being of its inhabitants.

Russian cemetary at New Arkhangel.

Mikhailovsk redoubt from the bay. The Company flag established authority in this remote outpost where Russians, Finns, Yakuts and Aleuts and other company employees lived together.   (From William H. Dall, *Alaska and Its Resources*)

Mikhailovsk redoubt. A typical fortified post enclosed by pickets and flanked by bastions. Storehouses and employee quarters(including bath and cookhouses), are located within the palisade. (From Frederick Whymper, *Travel and Adventure in the Territory of Alaska*)

Village on the lower Kwikhpak(Yukon) during fishing season. The catch is dried into _iukola_ for winter use, and stored in elevated wooden huts where it will be protected against scavengers. (From William H. Dall, *Alaska and Its Resources*)

Redoubt on the Andreanov Islands, under the jurisdiction of the Atkhinsk Department. This lonely outpost served for the collection of furs and for trade.(From William H. Dall, *Alaska and Its Resources*)

(Left) Russian Orthodox Cathedral of Saint Michael in New Arkhangel.

(Opposite) A Kolosh toion in full ceremonial regalia. The Chilkat blanket is woven of worsted spun from mountain goat wool; the pattern represents the toion's own totem. His headdress is topped by a ring of seal whiskers, within which an amount of down is placed. When the toion dances, the down drifts on the air like snowflakes. (From Albert P. Niblack, *The Coast Indians of Southern Alaska and Northern British Columbia*)

(Below) Barracks for the garrison at New Arkhangel.

Drawing by Ilia G. Voznesenskii, which he entitled,"Sunday on Unalaska Island."
It is not clear whether the twelve Aleuts (all wearing finely made oilskin gar-
ments) have gathered at this small wooden structure for worship, instruction or
conviviality. Voznesenskii, was a Russian scientific explorer, sent to Alaska in
the mid-19th century by the Academy of Sciences.   (From Voznesenskii, Archive
MAE AN SSSR, Leningrad)

Illiuliuk settlement on Unalaska. Aleut iurts and wooden Company houses stand
on the shore beside the Russian Orthodox Church of the Ascension.(From Voznesenskii, Archive MAE AN SSSR, Leningrad) (*See* Blomkvist, "A Russian Scientific
Expedition to California and Alaska, 1839-1849,"*Oregon Historical Quarterly* 73
[June 1972] pp. 101-170)

Illiuliuk settlement on Unalaska. To supplement meager fare and add variety to
a monotonous diet, most Company employees had their own kitchen gardens to grow
root vegetables such as potatoes, radishes, and turnips (Voznesenskii, Archive
MAE AN SSSR, Leningrad)

Unalaska. The water-driven mill could grind grain into either flour or groats.
The two cattle grazing on the right were a rarity on Unalaska. (From Voznesenskii. Archive MAE AN SSSR, Leningrad)

Kolosh village next to New Arkhangel. Out of sight in this view are the Russian cannon aimed at the village; an attempt to maintain order and discourage attack.(From William G. Morris, *Report upon the Customs District, Public Service and Resources of Alaska Territory*)

The Russian American Company post at Aian, on the Sea of Okhotsk off the coast of Siberia. Capture of this post during the Crimean War posed supply difficulties for the Russian American colonies, and hindered the trade between the Company and the nomadic Siberian natives that was conducted here--the Company supplying food and gunpowder in exchange for Siberian furs. (From Voznesenskii, Archive MAE AN SSSR, Leningrad)

The Iablonnyi (Apple) Islands, off the coast of Sitka Island, in a squall. The
Kolosh, in a typical dugout craft, endure the downpour, protected by their woven
cloaks; the "eye" ornamentation on the prow was often used by this tribe. (From
Voznesenskii. Archive MAE AN SSSR, Leningrad)

Island opposite New Arkhangel. The staff for the magnetic observatory on the
right were sent from the Academy of Sciences in St. Petersburg. The paddlewheel vessel in the foreground is the 60-hp *Nikolai I* (From Voznesenskii, Archive MAE AN SSSR, Leningrad)

The main street of New Arkhangel, with the Russian Orthodox Cathedral of Saint Michael at the end. (From William G. Morris, *Report upon the Customs District, Public Service and Resources of Alaska Territory*)

Kodiak Aleuts whaling in tiny, superbly maneuverable baidarkas. Wooden hunting hats were made to resemble bird heads, and kept sun from the eyes of the daring hunters. (From Duflot de Mofras, *Exploration du Territories de L'Oregon*)

Ivan Veniaminov, great Russian Orthodox missionary priest to Alaska and the Aleutian Islands.(Later Bishop of Kamchatka, the Aleutian and Kuril Islands; after the sale of Alaska, Metropolitan of Moscow) (From Academy of Sciences of the USSR, *The Pacific*)

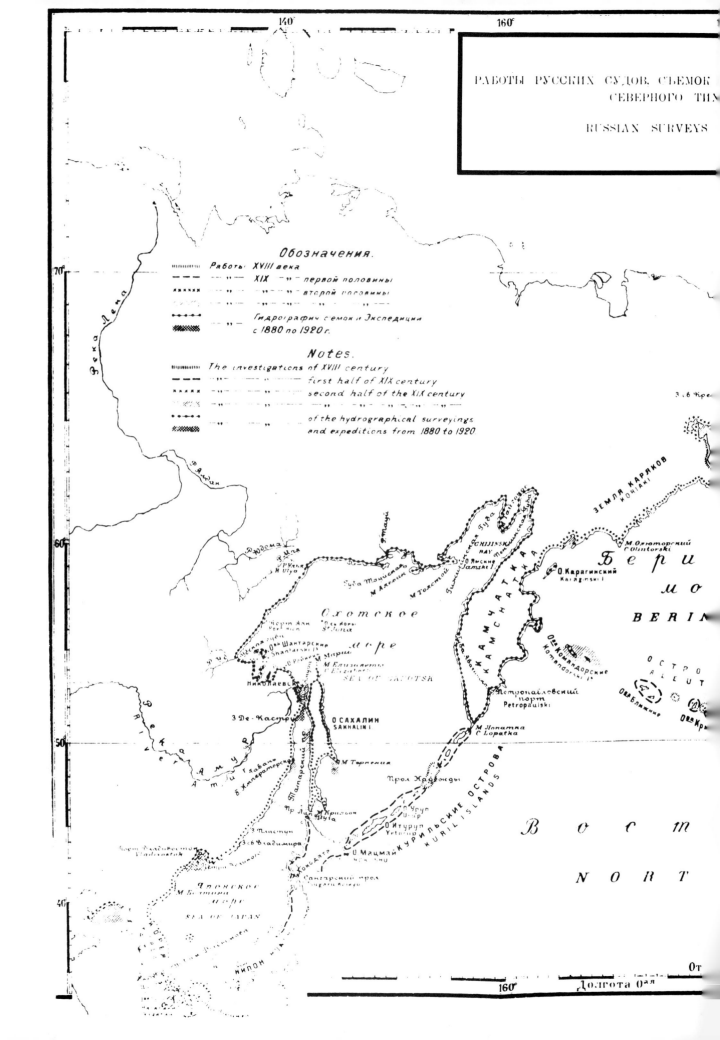

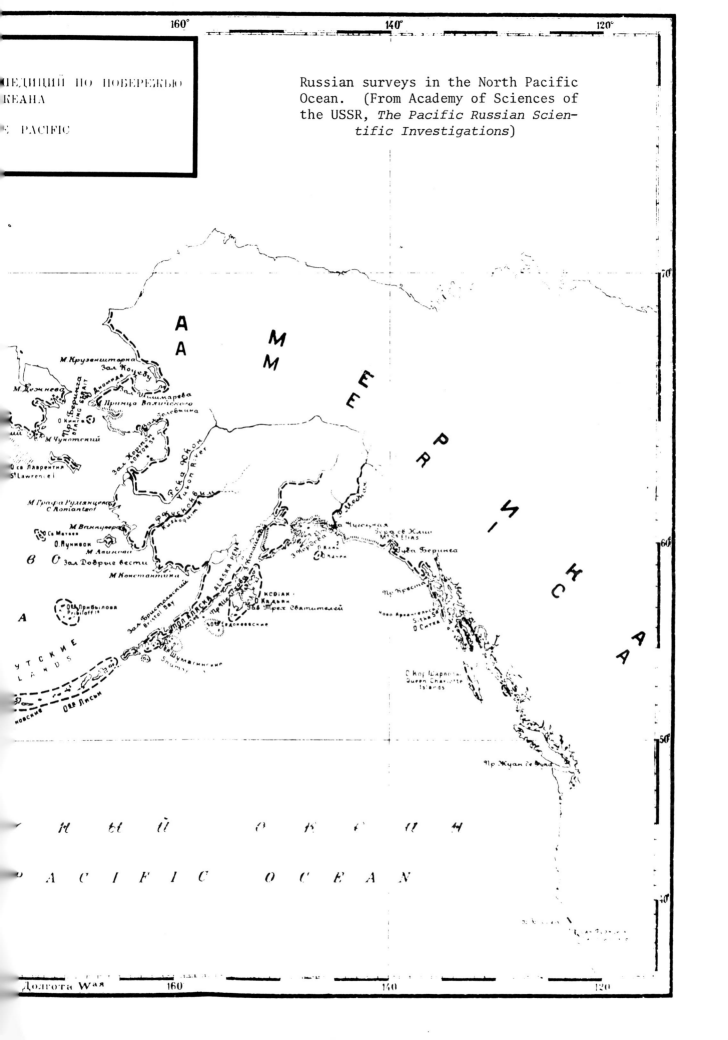

Russian surveys in the North Pacific Ocean. (From Academy of Sciences of the USSR, *The Pacific Russian Scientific Investigations*)

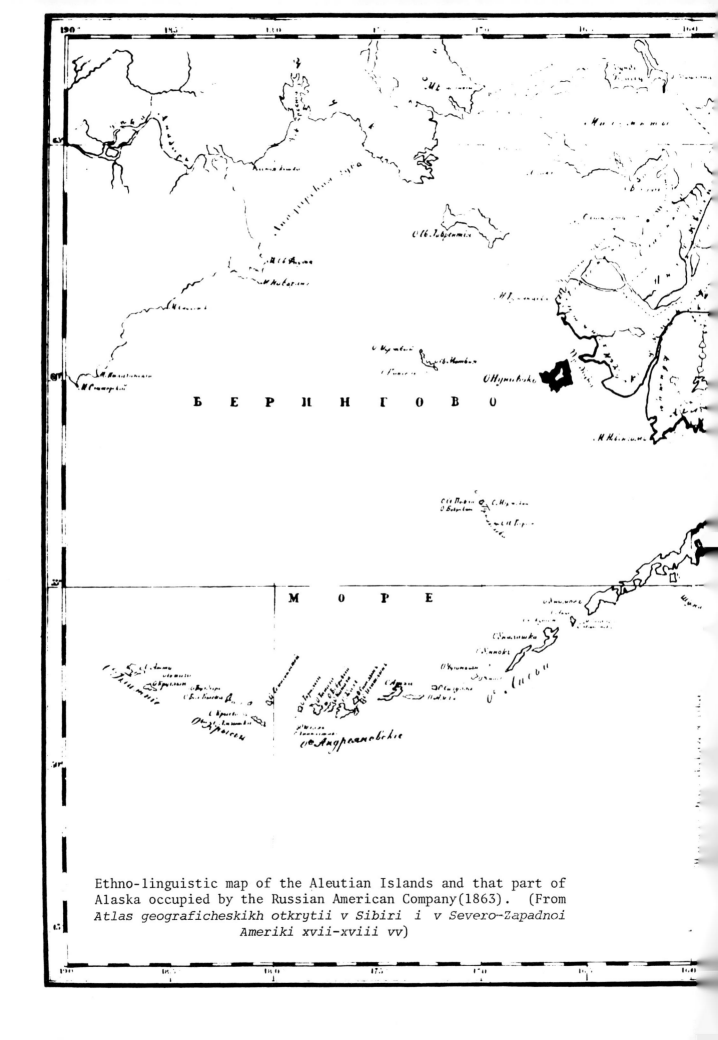

Ethno-linguistic map of the Aleutian Islands and that part of
Alaska occupied by the Russian American Company(1863). (From
*Atlas geograficheskikh otkrytii v Sibiri i v Severo-Zapadnoi
Ameriki xvii-xviii vv*)

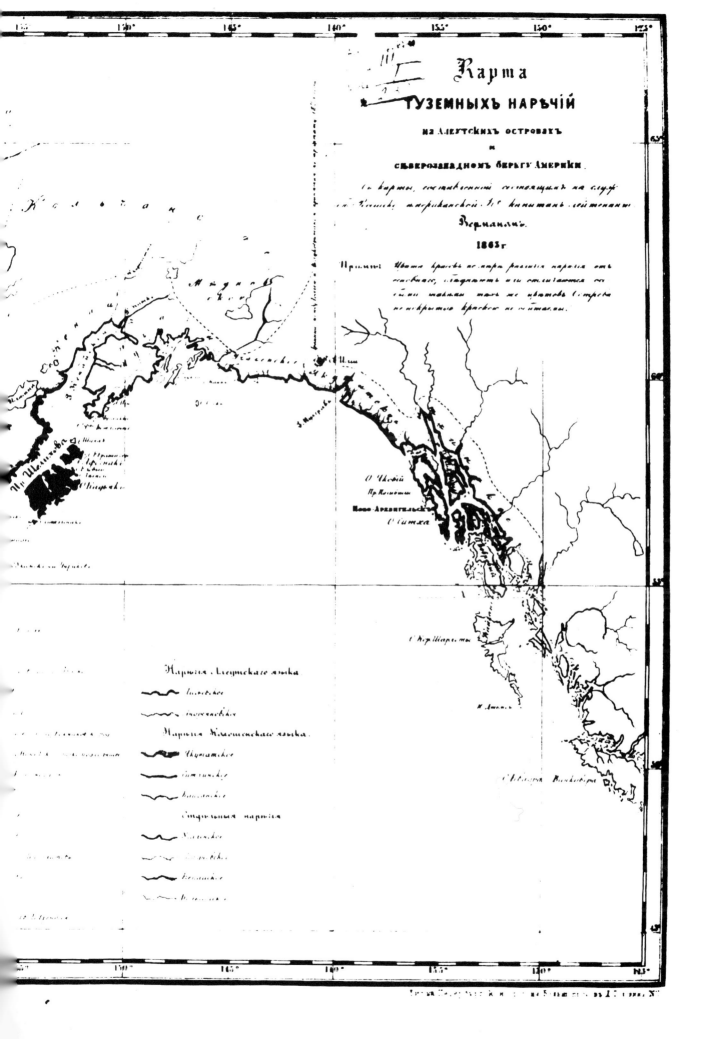

Карта
ТУЗЕМНЫХЪ НАРѢЧІЙ
на Алеутскихъ островахъ
и
сѣверозападномъ берегу Америки.

Map of Russia's colonial possessions in North America in 1821.
Drawn by Captain-Lieutenant M. B. Berkh. (From *Atlas geograficheskikh otkrytii v Sibiri i v Severo-Zapadnoi Ameriki xvii-
xxviii vv*)

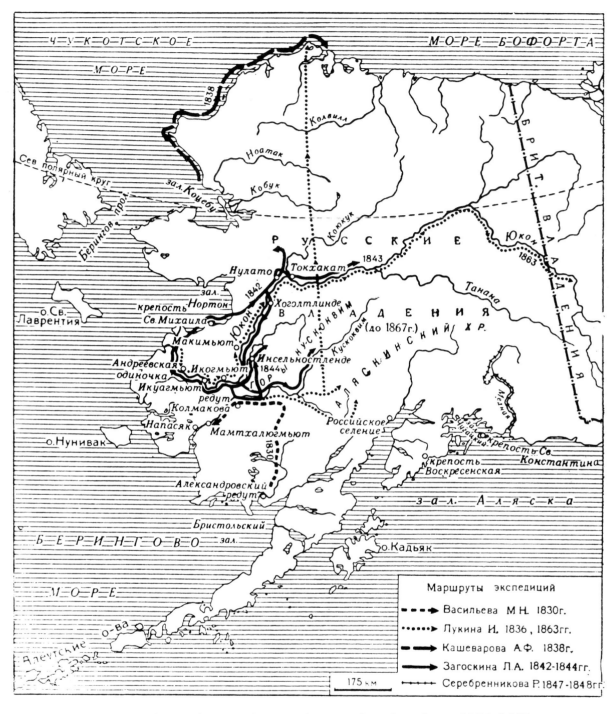

Routes of Russian explorers in Russian America, 1830-1863.
M.N. Vasilev, 1830; I. Pukin, 1836 and 1863; A.F. Kashevarov, 1838; L.A. Zagoskin, 1842-1844; R. Serebrennikov, 1847-
48. (From D.M. Lebedev, *Russkie Geograficheskie Otkrytiia*)

APPENDICES

APPENDIX 1

A LIST OF INDIVIDUALS IN SERVICE IN THE COLONIES
AS OF JANUARY 1, 1861

Chief Administrator, Navy Captain of the First Rank	1
Navy Staff Officer	1
Navy Commissioned Officers	2
Corps of Naval Navigator Commissioned Officers	2
Siberian Line Battalion Commissioned Officer	1
Retired Commissioned Officer	1
Civil Officials	2
Mining Engineer	1
Miner	1
Church Personnel	27
Doctors	2
Medical Officials	2
Apothecary Assistant	1
Medical Assistants	7
Medical Apprentices	7
Midwife	1
Assistants to Midwife	3
Ship Captains (Skippers) and their Senior Assistants (Hired Navigators)	12
Junior Ship Assistants (Hired Navigators and Students of Navigation)	10
Master Craftsmen: Shipbuilders and Gunsmiths	2
Machinists and their Assistants	10
Supervisors at the Sitka Magnetic Observatory	2
Office Administrators and their Assistants	4
Accountants and their Assistants	10
Office Personnel	5
Prikashchik (Special Agents/Supercargoes)	22
Administrators of Departmental Posts and Commands	31
Scribes	27
Seamen	39
Conductor of Corps of Naval Artillery and Noncommissioned Officer of Laboratory Units	2
Lower Rank Siberia Line Battalion Personnel	179
Hired Servitors, Master Craftsmen and Workers: Russian	184
Native	240
Supervisor and Teacher at the Public School of the Russian American Colonies	1
Supervisor and Teacher at the Boarding School for Girls	1
Hired Workmen at the Schools and Infirmaries	4

TOTAL 847

APPENDIX 2

GENERAL INFORMATION ON THE POPULATION OF THE COLONIES
OF THE RUSSIAN AMERICAN COMPANY, 1860

		New Arkhangel & Lake Redoubt	Kodiak Department	Unalaska and Unga Islands & Odinochas under their Jurisdiction on St. Paul & St. George Islands
RUSSIAN	male adults	366	66	4
	male minors	23	-	-
	female adults	34	1	-
	female minors	29	-	-
	total	452	67	4
CREOLE	male adults	129	237	54
	male minors	120	194	71
	female adults	123	243	69
	female minors	133	195	61
	total	505	871	255
ALEUT	male adults	23	660	421
	male minors	8	421	331
	female adults	21	640	424
	female minors	12	427	335
	total	64	2,148	1,511
FOREIGN	male adults	3	-	-
	male minors	-	-	-
	female adults	-	-	-
	female minors	-	-	-
	total	3	-	-
KENAI	male adults	-	303	-
	male minors	-	137	-
	female adults	-	347	-
	female minors	-	144	-
	total	-	931	-
KUSKOKWIM & AGLEGMIUT	male adults	-	465	-
	male minors	-	203	-
	female adults	-	470	-
	female minors	-	200	-
	total	-	1,340	-
CHUGACH & MEDNOVTSY	male adults	-	213	-
	male minors	-	93	-
	female adults	-	199	-
	female minors	-	82	-
	total	-	587	-
KURIL	male adults	-	-	-
	male minors	-	-	-
	female adults	-	-	-
	female minors	-	-	-
	total	-	-	-
TOTAL	male	672	2,994	881
	female	352	2,050	889
GRAND TOTAL		1,024	5,944	1,770

Atka Department: Atka, Amla, Mednyi, Bering & Attu Islands	Kuril Department: Shumshu & Urup Islands	Mikhailovsk & Kolmakovsk Redoubts	Kenai Mining Camp	California Agency	Totals
4	1	30	29	1	501
-	-	-	-	5	28
-	-	-	-	1	36
-	-	-	-	1	30
4	1	30	29	8	595
39	3	15	6	-	483
48	1	6	2	-	442
46	3	7	12	-	305
64	3	8	2	-	466
197	10	36	22	-	1,896
210	58	3	-	-	1,375
194	22	-	-	-	976
203	41	2	-	-	1,331
156	33	-	-	-	963
763	154	5	-	-	4,645
-	-	-	1	-	4
-	-	-	-	-	-
-	-	-	-	-	-
-	-	-	-	-	-
-	-	-	1	-	4
-	-	-	-	-	303
-	-	-	-	-	137
-	-	-	-	-	347
-	-	-	-	-	144
-	-	-	-	-	931
-	-	21	-	-	486
-	-	8	-	-	213
-	-	17	-	-	487
-	-	12	-	-	212
-	-	58	-	-	1,398
-	-	-	-	-	213
-	-	-	-	-	93
-	-	-	-	-	199
-	-	-	-	-	82
-	-	-	-	-	587
-	25	-	-	-	25
-	15	-	-	-	15
-	32	-	-	-	32
-	16	-	-	-	16
-	88	-	-	-	88
495	125	83	38	6	5,294
469	128	46	14	2	4,850
964	253	129	52	8	10,144

Of the tribes treated in this appendix, the Kenai, Kuskokwim, Aglegmiut, Chugach and Mednovtsy are not regarded as tribes that benefit from Company privileges to the same degree as the Aleuts; rather, the Company considers these tribes as dependent primarily because they are not hostile. Actually none of these tribes is very dependent on the Company; for example, the Chugach will only go out on a sea otter hunt when they are urged, and they shy away from this to give the appearance of being coerced. Moreover the Chugach do not always go to their assigned places to hunt sea otter, but rather go to the closest place. The Kenais, Kuskokwims and Aglegmiuts have no obligations to the Company. If they do something for the Company, it is for money; they do not sell all of their furs to the Company. The Mednovtsy Indians are wholly independent.

APPENDIX 3

INFORMATION ON THE NUMBER OF NATIVES WHO HAVE JOINED THE ORTHODOX GREEK-RUSSIAN CHURCH
AND WHO LIVED IN DEPARTMENTS OF THE RUSSIAN COLONIES IN AMERICA, 1841-1860

1841

	Men	Women	Total
In New Arkhangel: baptized Kolosh	4	–	
In Kodiak parish: Kenai, Katmai and Chugach	99	129	
Total	103	129	232

1842

	Men	Women	Total
In New Arkhangel: Kolosh	38	4	
In Kodiak parish: Kenai, Katmai and Chugach	96	34	
Total	134	38	172

1843

	Men	Women	Total
In New Arkhangel: Kolosh	66	4	
In Kodiak parish: Kenai, Katmai and Chugach	21	23	
In Nushagak mission: Aglegmiut, Kiaten and Kolchan	199	226	
At Kwikpak: Uniagmiut and Inkegmiut	88	75	
Total	374	328	702

1844

	Men	Women	Total
In New Arkhangel: Kolosh	65	30	
In Kodiak parish: Kenai, Katmai and Chugach	20	7	
In Nushagak mission: Aglegmiut, Kiaten and Kolchan	35	28	
At Kwikpak: Uniagmiut and Inkegmiut	48	65	
Total	168	130	298

1845

	Men	Women	Total
In New Arkhangel: Kolosh	4	5	
In Kenai mission: Kenai, Katmai and Chugach	38	52	
In Nushagak mission: Aglegmiut and Kuskokwim	32	44	
At Kwikpak: Kwikpak, Inkegmiut etc.	169	105	
Total	243	206	449

1846

	Men	Women	Total
In New Arkhangel: Kolosh	9	–	
In Kenai mission: Kenai and Chugach	133	178	
In Nushagak mission: Kuskokwim etc.	68	55	
At Kwikpak: Kwikpak etc.	63	25	
Total	273	258	531

1847

	Men	Women	Total
In New Arkhangel: Kolosh	8	19	
In Kenai mission: Kenai	7	6	
In Nushagak mission: Kuskokwim	55	54	
In Kwikpak mission: Kwikpak etc.	172	121	
Total	242	200	442

1848

	Men	Women	Total
In New Arkhangel: Kolosh	12	23	
In Kenai mission: Kenai	18	14	
In Kwikpak mission: Kwikpak etc.	40	30	
Total	70	67	137

144

APPENDIX 3 (continued)

1849

	Men	Women	Total
In New Arkhangel: Kolosh	5	6	
In Kenai mission: Kenai etc.	34	29	
In Kwikpak mission: Kwikpak etc.	36	25	
Total	75	60	135

1850

	Men	Women	Total
In New Arkhangel: Kolosh	33	32	
In Kwikpak mission: Kwikpak etc.	41	28	
In Nushagak mission: Kuskokwim etc.	136	174	
Total	210	234	444

1851

	Men	Women	Total
New Arkhangel: Kolosh	30	31	
Kwikpak mission: Kwikpak etc.	114	84	
Total	144	115	

1852

	Men	Women	Total
New Arkhangel: Kolosh	2	17	
Kenai mission: Ugalen	1	1	
Kwikpak mission: Kwikpak etc.	44	30	
Total	47	48	95

1853

	Men	Women	Total
New Arkhangel: Kolosh	22	19	
Nushagak mission: Kuskokwim	3	2	
Kwikpak mission: Kwikpak, Kuskokwim and Kolchan	157	154	
Total	182	175	357

1854

	Men	Women	Total
New Arkhangel: Kolosh	14	14	
Nushagak mission: Kuskokwim	2	2	
Kenai mission: Ugalen and Kenai	14	14	
Kwikpak mission: Kwikpak etc.	65	47	
Total	95	77	172

1855

	Men	Women	Total
New Arkhangel: Kolosh	1	1	
Nushagak mission: Kuskokwim etc.	8	7	
Kenai mission: Kolchan	1	2	
Kwikpak mission: Kwikpak etc.	10	3	
Total	20	13	33

1856

	Men	Women	Total
New Arkhangel	-	-	
Nushagak mission: Kuskokwim	23	13	
Kwikpak mission: Kwikpak etc.	32	37	
Total	55	50	105

1857

	Men	Women	Total
New Arkhangel: Kolosh	1	2	
Nushagak mission: Kuskokwim	1	2	
Kwikpak mission: Kwikpak etc.	17	15	
Total	19	19	38

1858

	Men	Women	Total
New Arkhangel: Kolosh	-	3	
Nushagak mission: Aglegmiut	2	4	
Kwikpak mission: Kwikpak etc.	10	10	
Total	12	17	29

	Men	Women	Total
1859			
Kwikpak mission: Kwikpak etc.	15	8	
Nushgak mission: Kuskokwim etc.	10	9	
Total	25	17	42

	Men	Women	Total
1860			
New Arkhangel: Kolosh	8	11	
No information has been received from other missions			
TOTALS FOR 20 YEARS	2,508	2,193	4,700

TOTAL WITHIN THE PARISH

	Men	Women	Total
Russians (visiting)	576	208	784
Creoles	853	823	1,676
Aleuts	2,206	2,185	4,391
Aglegmiuts	165	179	344
Kenais	430	507	937
Kuskokwims	755	640	1,395
Chugach	226	230	456
Ugalens	73	75	148
Malegmiuts	18	11	29
Mednovtsy	17	1	18
Uniagliuts	105	101	206
Agelmiuts	19	20	39
Kwikpaks	226	153	379
Inkalits	263	212	475
Kolchans	97	93	190
Kolosh	221	206	427
Kurils	63	48	111
Tungus	1	1	2
Totals	6,314	5,693	12,007

APPENDIX 4

INFORMATION ON COLONIAL SHIPS AS OF JULY 1, 1860

Name of ship	Tonnage	Year purchased or constructed, and of what lumber	Purchase price [in paper rubles]
Nikolai I	595-7/8	Built in New York in 1850; commissioned to be built from white ironwood, oak and yellow pine; copper hull	296,417.07
Tsaritsa	1,089-5/6	Built in 1854 in Portsmouth, America; purchased in Hamburg in 1858; built of oak; copper hull	317,730.87-1/2
Kamchatka	900	Built in 1853 in Hamburg and purchased there that same year; built of oak; copper hull	230,315.33
Tsarevich	529	Built in 1852 in Lubeck for the Company; oak; copper hull	179,732.87-1/2
Kniaz Menshikov (bark)	273	Purchased in 1848 in Sandwich Islands; built in 1845 in Salem, Mass., America; oak; copper hull	100,000.00
Nakhimov (bark)	287	Purchased in 1856 in San Francisco; built in 1848 in Baltimore, Md., America; oak and pine; copper hull	91,649.10
Shelikhov (brig)	270	Built in 1852 in Hamburg; in Ofelgenn near Alton; commissioned; oak and pine; copper hull	84,785.01-1/2
Velikii Kniaz Konstantin (brig)	170	Purchased in 1840 in Valparaiso; American brig built in Boston; oak; copper hull	65,000.00
Tungus (schooner)	65	Built in Port New Arkhangel in 1848; cypress; copper hull	40,000.00

Present value (July 1, 1860)	Armaments	Actual value [in paper rubles]
ship: 192,500 arms: 2,116.24	6 cannon with accessories; 88 cannon balls; 37 cannister shots; 12 guns; 12 sabers	190,000; ship is good and solid, but the value as appraised is high; its real value may be about 180,000
317,730.875	8 12-pound cannon	It is at sea and thus cannot be appraised. It is a good ship but needs repair and may be appraised at 280,000
254,876.86	8 9-pound cannon	This ship was on an around-the-world voyage and therefore I did not inspect her
280,847.735	8 12-pound cannon	There is no information for an appraisal. Also at sea
ship: 19,980 arms: 4,795.44	6 cannon with accessories; 22 pistols; 36 pikes; 24 sabers and bayonets; 200 cannon balls; 132 cannister shots	40,000. Good ship, which is actually worth 40,000
ship: 65,000 arms: 2,954.67	4 brass cannon with accessories; cleaning rods 2; 1 wad; 2 cleaning cloths for cannon; 1 kokor; 20 cannister shots; 30 cannon balls	80,000; waterlogged(?); second-hand ship; poor handling; it may be valued at 70,000
ship: 65,000 arms: 1,310.70	2 guns with accessories; 2 cannon brushes; 1 wad; 3 kokors; 4 cleaning cloths for cannon; 2 copper cleaning rods; 235 cannon balls; 20 cannister shots	70,000; awkward, but quite solid; carries a good deal of freight; may be valued at 60,000
ship: 1,250 arms: none		10,000; it is being completely overhauled, and when finished, may be worth 20,000
ship: 1,750 arms: none		2,000; it is suitable only for storing coal; can be appraised at 1,000

APPENDIX 4 (continued)

Name of ship	Tonnage	Year purchased or constructed, and of what lumber	Purchase price [in paper rubles]
Alexander II (ocean steamer)	500	Purchased in 1856 in New York, where it had been commissioned to be built in 1855; oak; copper hull	285,600.00
Velikii Kniaz Konstantin (steamer)	368	Built in Newcastle for the Company in 1856; iron	282,324.175
Nikolai I (paddlewheel steamer)	60 hp	Built in 1853 in New Arkhangel; unseasoned cypress; copper hull	120,000.00
Baranov (steamer)	30 hp	Built in 1860 in New Arkhangel; unseasoned cypress; copper hull	35,000.00

Present value (July 1, 1860)	Armaments	Actual value [in paper rubles]
ship: 308,000 arms: 2,540.65	6 cannon with accessories; 6 cannon brushes; 4 wads; 1 copper cleaning rod; 1 cleaning cloth; 1 powder box; 120 cannon balls; 30 cannister shots	300,000; needs replacement of sails, which is a small expense; motor is of poor quality; carries small cargo; worth no more than 200,000
282,324.175	6 9-pound cannon; 1 12-pound cannon	Presently in the colonies and therefore cannot be appraised; it is good and can be appraised at 200,000
ship: 68,800 arms: 5,323.03	4 carronades [cannon?]; 5 guns with accessories; 24 shotguns [fuzia]; 6 sabers, 12 broadswords; 12 pikes; 6 bayonets; 8 cannon brushes; 121 cannon balls; 160 cannister shots; 14 cleaning rods; 6 palnik; 2 night lamps; 10 cartridge pouches; 3 powder horns; 6 kokors; 2 copper cleaning rods	70,000; handles badly; low value; may reach up to 50,000
35,000	no armaments	35,000; good, even though she is not beautiful in appearance; may be appraised at 25,000

APPENDIX 5

A LIST OF EXPENDITURES IN THE PORT OF NEW ARKHANGEL
AND IN THE COLONIAL DEPARTMENTS OF THE RUSSIAN AMERICAN COMPANY
FOR 10-1/2 YEARS, JANUARY 1, 1849 TO JULY, 1859
In rubles(paper) and kopecks

		1849	1850	1851	Jan. 1-July 1 1852
1.	Salaries	348,058.02	396,184.35	405,536.87	222,079.70
2.	Bonuses	15,300.00	24,780.00	20,555.00	21,937.50
3.	Provisions for crew	94,305.165	123,208.90	104,026.96	53,601.38
4.	Pensions & assistance	31,926.51	37,811.28	29,499.87	25,388.62
5.	Various expeditions	1,937.61	5,135.19	6,088.26	1,088.70
6.	Entrepreneurial expenses	4,616.94	6,384.61	5,835.02	7,924.20
7.	Repair of immovable property	57,114.11	34,326.08	38,451.62	9,550.06
8.	Repair of seagoing ships	90,000.97	127,317.40	96,154.12	50,961.27
9.	Repair of sailing ships	5,370.45-5/8	8,964.83	6,646.28	4,695.23
10.	Repair in shops	10,592.8375	4,871.41	9,151.12	5,919.81
11.	Heating & lighting	11,384.315	13,299.63	11,017.17	5,985.36
12.	Secretarial & bookkeeping supplies	4,788.1925	3,873.55	5,416.73	2,997.82
13.	Payment for various jobs	20,757.4875	21,279.18	17,919.70	8,467.23
14.	Salvos & signals	1,807.585	2,443.37	2,393.90	1,843.35
15.	Maintenance of clergy	28,921.765	42,062.86	34,176.38	2,431.27
16.	Upkeep of infirmaries & schools	60,345.15	59,304.30	58,461.93	31,889.58
17.	Deduction for uncollectable debts	4,777.94	839.86	739.26	1,020.86
18.	Miscellaneous expenditures	56,248.17-5/8	40,471.38	33,928.87	20,280.31
--	Various losses & disasters	126.19	20,316.12	---	1,515.59
--	Total expenditures in paper rubles	843,579.42	973,734.30	885,993.06	479,527.76
--	Excluding profits made by various departments of the colonies, etc.	---	---	---	2,430.08
--	Total expenditures in paper rubles	843,579.42	973,734.30	885,933.06	477,097.68

July 1852 July 1853	July 1853 July 1854	July 1854 July 1855	July 1855 July 1856	July 1856 July 1857	July 1857 July 1858
405,831.76	407,490.10	461,655.85	445,879.26	459,893.92	476,118.16
16,230.00	26,290.00	15,104.00	17,750.00	13,565.00	14,115.00
98,335.44	406,015.79	117,408.16	102,185.545	119,455.495	137,327.26
24,442.51	28,977.75	32,929.57	26,514.99	39,138.16	32,732.13
1,305.67	1,403.02	---	218.00	---	---
18,506.75	21,082.9725	19,070.75	12,888.64	18,032.225/8	13,478.77
32,356.03	23,739.79	42,312.88	25,237.64	28,605.02	31,227.30
31,277.45	120,294.34	96,529.63	78,733.66	104,270.28	131,476.70
7,152.79	8,725.81	7,892,85	5,944.275	7,337.67	8,766.33
2,791.22	2,361.24	4,620.11	1,800.69	1,687.445	4,524.11
12,860.84	12,835.12	12,677.78	14,850.27	19,941.69	20,181.61
6,290.77	5,147.98	5,959.37	5,636.69	4,846.555	4,721.94
14,651.605	15,764.15	14,469.86	14,414.24	17,632.07	16,663.03
2,948.57	2,371.31	939.88	454.92	637.01	1,187.36
36,334.95	33,264.56	34,032.77	31,133.18	33,378.17	33,631.77
61,369.37	62,096.00	60,650.06	57,405.40	63,597.19	67,157.57
166.30	166.30	5.00	---	13,388.25	---
42,812.15	19,680.1475	49,433.49	25,049.72	77,762.015	81,239.98
---	9,433.7775	11,534.78	18,628.00	273.16	15,231.71
816,661.22	909,170.06	987,447.49	885,025.12	1,023,680.73	1,089,781.50
4,407.43	8,746.26	49,239.28	59,295.28	54,301.20	5,568.46
812,256.79	900,423.80	938,208.21	825,729.84	969,379.53	1,084,213.13

APPENDIX 5   (continued)

		July 1858 July 1859	Total	Average for one year
1.	Salaries	428,162.52	4,461,890.51	424,941.95
2.	Bonuses	25,603.04	211,311.04	20,125.53
3.	Provisions for crew	132,500.90	1,188,701.65	113,263.68
4.	Pensions & assistance	20,977.05	340,288.35	32,408.41
5.	Various expeditions	---	17,236.65	1,661.57
6.	Entrepreneurial expenses	18,123.19	146,564.07	13,958.48
7.	Repair of immovable property	31,225.42	356,546.15	33,936.78
8.	Repair of seagoing ships	118,859.24	1,045,875.16	99,607.16
9.	Repair of sailing ships	8,127.93	80,044.45	7,623.28
10.	Repair in shops	3,200.35	51,520.27	4,906.69
11.	Heating & lighting	21,384.43	136,418.05	14,896.96
12.	Secretarial & bookkeeping supplies	4,992.52	54,672.32	5,206.89
13.	Payment for various jobs	12,614.55	174,633.12	10,621.73
14.	Salvos and signals	920.81	17,968.65	1,709.34
15.	Maintenance of clergy	36,474.70	345,856.38	32,938.70
16.	Upkeep of infirmaries & schools	77,159.18	659,433.73	62,803.40
17.	Deduction for uncollectable debts	---	21,103.77	2,009.88
18.	Miscellaneous expenditures	68,779.24	516,685.48	49,208.14
--	Various losses & disasters	230.70	77,290.03	7,360.96
--	Total expenditures in paper rubles	1,029,424.28	9,924,028.63	945,145.53
--	Excluding profits made by various departments of the colonies, etc.	7,019.03	191,007.02	18,191.15
--	Total expenditures in paper rubles	1,022,405.25	9,733,021.01	926,954.38

APPENDIX 6

INFORMATION ON THE COMPOSITION OF SEA OTTER HUNTING PARTIES
IN THE KODIAK DEPARTMENT
(Population shown as of January 1, 1860)

Name of Settlement	Katmai	Karluk	Three Saints	Orlovsk	Agfognak	Lesnoi	TOTAL
Boys under 18	110	58	121	86	44	35	454
Men from 18 to 40	76	50	107	39	24	43	339
Men over 40	39	31	40	25	12	26	173
Women & girls	215	129	247	163	83	97	934
TOTAL	440	268	515	313	163	201	1,900
Baidarkas*	20	10	30	12	10	10	92
Aleuts from 18 to 40*	42	21	63	25	21	21	193
Remaining men between 18 & 40	34	29	44	14	3	22	146
Men, women & children remaining in settlement	398	247	452	288	142	180	1,707

* Sent out on sea otter hunt in 1861.

Note: Every ten baidarkas comprise a detail which has an elder or a zakashchik [overseer]. The entire hunting party is under the leadership of the chief baidarshchik [hunt leader] and his assistant who have special baidarkas. Often experienced promyshlenniks are sent out with these parties to show them where and how to hunt.

APPENDIX 7

A SUMMARY OF THE ANNUAL TRADE IN FURS IN THE COLONIES
FROM 1842 TO 1861

From Kolosh at the Port

Year	Sea Otter	Beaver	River Otter	Fox	Polar Fox	Bear	Lynx	Sable	Muskrat
1842	99	215	151	117	---	103	13	148	63
1843	136	311	238	93	---	98	---	120	16
1844	74	253	121	---	---	17	3	245	---
1845	91	187	152	63	---	29	---	235	---
1846	62	93	139	60	---	1	---	170	---
1847	158	58	119	29	---	3	---	51	---
1848	44	33	22	---	---	---	---	7	---
1849	75	444	91.50	24	---	4	---	42	---
1850	139	349	81	68	---	13	9	200	---
1851	111	462	65	22	---	1	7	189	---
1852	46.25	143	15	2	---	---	---	24	---
1853	1	79	---	---	---	2	---	---	---
1854	1	23	---	---	---	---	---	21	---
1855	3	9	2	---	---	---	---	---	---
1856	---	15	---	---	---	---	---	---	---
1857	---	---	---	---	---	---	---	---	---
1858	---	---	---	---	---	---	---	---	---
1859	---	32	---	---	---	4	---	---	4
1860	---	73	---	1	---	7	---	3	5
	1,040.25	2,779	1,196.50	481	---	282	32	1,455	90

Minks	Fur Seals	Walrus Teeth	Castoreum (pairs)	Marmot Parkas	Sea Otter Tails	Weasels	Wolverines	Wolves
32	2	---	3	---	84	---	11	4
40	---	---	---	---	130	---	8	7
---	---	---	---	---	76	---	11	1
---	---	---	---	---	118	---	13	9
6	---	---	---	---	64	---	7	2
---	---	---	---	---	141	---	11	1
---	---	---	---	---	29	---	1	---
54	---	---	---	---	96	---	4	1
30	1	---	---	---	135	---	6	---
144	---	---	---	---	114	---	6	---
---	---	---	---	---	58	---	---	---
---	---	---	---	---	7	---	---	---
30	---	---	---	---	1	---	---	---
---	---	---	---	---	---	---	---	---
---	---	---	---	---	---	---	---	---
---	---	---	---	---	---	---	---	---
---	---	---	---	---	---	---	---	---
22	---	---	2	---	3	---	---	---
27	---	---	2	---	---	---	---	---
385	3	---	7	---	1,056	---	78	22

APPENDIX 7 (continued)

From the Kolosh in the Sound

Year	Sea Otter	Beaver	River Otter	Fox	Polar Fox	Bear	Lynx	Sable	Muskrat
1842	32	21	11	12	---	65	1	34	3
1843	62	17	3	8	---	2	---	---	---
1844	7	37	19	3	---	3	---	5	---
1845	53	3	12	15	---	1	---	27	---
1846	80	14	19	18	---	3	---	22	---
1847	---	---	---	---	---	---	---	---	---
1848	51	15	22	7	---	10	6	13	---
1849	89	179	45	9	---	---	1	23	---
1850	121	81	47	37	---	---	2	---	---
1851	---	---	---	---	---	---	---	---	---
1852	---	---	---	---	---	---	---	---	---
1853	---	---	---	---	---	---	---	---	---
1854	---	---	---	---	---	---	---	---	---
1855	---	---	---	---	---	---	---	---	---
1856	---	---	---	---	---	---	---	---	---
1857	---	---	---	---	---	---	---	---	---
1858	---	---	---	---	---	---	---	---	---
1859	---	---	---	---	---	1	---	---	---
1860	---	15	3	---	---	4	---	4	1
	495	382	181	169	---	89	10	128	4

157

Minks	Fur Seals	Walrus Teeth	Castor- eum (pairs)	Marmot Parkas	Sea Otter Tails	Weasels	Wolverines	Wolves
599	---	---	---	---	24	---	---	---
---	---	---	---	---	36	---	1	---
2	---	---	---	---	---	---	---	---
---	---	---	---	---	32	---	1	---
---	---	---	---	---	61	---	3	---
---	---	---	---	---	---	---	---	---
---	---	---	---	---	50	---	1	---
---	---	---	---	---	75	---	1	---
---	---	---	---	---	87	---	3	---
---	---	---	---	---	---	---	---	---
---	---	---	---	---	---	---	---	---
---	---	---	---	---	---	---	---	---
---	---	---	---	---	---	---	---	---
---	---	---	---	---	---	---	---	---
---	---	---	---	---	---	---	---	---
---	---	---	---	---	---	---	---	---
---	---	---	---	---	---	---	---	---
---	---	---	---	---	---	---	---	---
12	---	---	20	---	---	---	---	---
613	---	---	20	---	365	---	10	---

APPENDIX 7 (continued)

Exchanged and Purchased from the English

Year	Sea Otter	Beaver	River Otter	Fox	Polar Fox	Bear	Lynx	Sable	Muskrat
1842	---	---	3,033	331	---	---	251	---	---
1843	27	7	4,403	359	---	19	51	---	1
1844	21	---	3,489	---	---	---	---	---	---
1845	21	---	3,489	---	---	---	---	---	---
1846	33	---	---	---	---	---	---	---	---
1847	4	---	---	---	---	---	---	---	---
1848	---	23	3,012	2	---	---	---	---	---
1849	7	---	3,001	---	---	---	---	---	---
1850	3	---	1,446	---	---	---	---	---	---
1851	---	---	---	---	---	---	---	---	---
1852	---	---	---	---	---	---	---	---	---
1853	---	---	---	---	---	---	---	---	---
1854	---	---	---	---	---	---	---	---	---
1855	---	---	---	---	---	---	---	---	---
1856	---	---	---	---	---	---	---	---	---
1857	---	---	---	---	---	---	---	---	---
1858	---	---	---	---	---	---	---	---	---
1859	---	---	---	---	---	---	---	---	---
1860	---	---	---	---	---	---	---	---	---
	116	30	21,873	692	---	19	302	---	1

Minks	Fur Seals	Walrus Teeth	Castor-eum (pairs)	Marmot Parkas	Sea Otter Tails	Weasels	Wolverines	Wolves
---	---	---	---	---	---	150	---	---
---	---	---	---	---	11	301	---	---
---	---	---	---	---	---	---	---	---
---	---	---	---	---	---	---	---	---
---	---	---	---	---	---	---	---	---
---	---	---	---	---	---	---	---	---
---	---	---	---	---	---	---	---	---
---	---	---	---	---	---	---	---	---
---	---	---	---	---	---	---	---	---
---	---	---	---	---	---	---	---	---
---	---	---	---	---	---	---	---	---
---	---	---	---	---	---	---	---	---
---	---	---	---	---	---	---	---	---
---	---	---	---	---	---	---	---	---
---	---	---	---	---	---	---	---	---
---	---	---	---	---	---	---	---	---
---	---	---	---	---	---	---	---	---
---	---	---	---	---	---	---	---	---
---	---	---	---	---	---	---	---	---
---	---	---	---	---	11	451	---	---

APPENDIX 7 (continued)

Received [from English] as Rent for Stakine

Year	Sea Otter	Beaver	River Otter	Fox	Polar Fox	Bear	Lynx	Sable	Muskrat
1842	---	---	1,854	---	---	---	---	---	---
1843	---	---	2,058	---	---	---	---	---	---
1844	---	---	2,000	---	---	---	---	---	---
1845	---	---	2,000	---	---	---	---	---	---
1846	---	---	2,000	---	---	---	---	---	---
1847	---	---	2,000	---	---	---	---	---	---
1848	---	---	2,000	---	---	---	---	---	---
1849	---	---	2,000	---	---	---	---	---	---
1850	---	---	2,000	---	---	---	---	---	---
1851	---	---	1,475	---	---	---	---	---	---
1852	---	---	1,525	---	---	---	---	---	---
1853	---	---	1,600	---	---	---	---	---	---
1854	---	---	1,025	---	---	---	---	---	---
1855	---	---	---	---	---	---	---	---	---
1856	---	---	---	---	---	---	---	---	---
1857	---	---	---	---	---	---	---	---	---
1858			paid in cash						
1859	---	---	---	---	---	---	---	---	---
1860	---	---	---	---	---	---	---	---	---
	---	---	23,537	---	---	---	---	---	---

Minks	Fur Seals	Walrus Teeth	Castor-eum (pairs)	Marmot Parkas	Sea Otter Tails	Weasels	Wolverines	Wolves
---	---	---	---	---	---	---	---	---
---	---	---	---	---	---	---	---	---
---	---	---	---	---	---	---	---	---
---	---	---	---	---	---	---	---	---
---	---	---	---	---	---	---	---	---
---	---	---	---	---	---	---	---	---
---	---	---	---	---	---	---	---	---
---	---	---	---	---	---	---	---	---
---	---	---	---	---	---	---	---	---
---	---	---	---	---	---	---	---	---
---	---	---	---	---	---	---	---	---
---	---	---	---	---	---	---	---	---
---	---	---	---	---	---	---	---	---
---	---	---	---	---	---	---	---	---
---	---	---	---	---	---	---	---	---
---	---	---	---	---	---	---	---	---
---	---	---	---	---	---	---	---	---
---	---	---	---	---	---	---	---	---
---	---	---	---	---	---	---	---	---
---	---	---	---	---	---	---	---	---

APPENDIX 7 (continued)

Kodiak Department

Year	Sea Otter	Beaver	River Otter	Fox	Polar Fox	Bear	Lynx	Sable	Muskrat
1842	342	6,198	1,018	3,175	---	136	100	---	3,210
1843	294	6,592	1,028	2,022	---	122	111	861	---
1844	191	5,580	727	1,691	---	54	27	346	6
1845	343	4,210	731	1,945	---	88	61	574	145
1846	266	4,853	448	628	---	72	124	1,629	---
1847	251	3,601	361	692	---	69	451	1,585	152
1848	397	5,544	340	1,215	---	169	178	948	60
1849	256	4,333	390	2,151	---	60	298	1,276	146
1850	292	4,679	400	2,145	---	116	267	993	210
1851	416	4,442	253	1,047	---	99	61	173	473
1852	155	3,196	448	1,637	---	65	14	503	---
1853	282	6,179	248	389	---	75	1	232	1,146
1854	390	634	438	1,534	---	22	1	248	167
1855	296	6,837	253	735	---	171	3	990	1,050
1856	251	2,176	506	1,015	---	59	74	886	---
1857	331	4,062	519	1,056	---	97	175	857	2,287
1858	169	3,120	442	1,364	17	76	268	1,002	2,880
1859	491	3,178	557	1,420	---	81	94	675	1,197
1860	396	5,413	421	1,988	12	26	56	527	1,184
	5,809	85,381	9,558	28,049	29	1,597	2,063	14,295	14,313

Minks	Fur Seals	Walrus Teeth	Castoreum (pairs)	Marmot Parkas	Sea Otter Tails	Weasels	Wolverines	Wolves
37	---	*67n 27δ	5,954	60	338	---	35	3
60	---	90n 28δ	3,099	40	284	---	---	1
96	---	103n 18δ	2,513	60	---	---	56	4
78	---	91n	1,856	23	---	---	57	6
154	---	---	1,999	---	---	---	101	6
101	---	---	1,650	60	2	---	56	---
74	---	---	2,533.50	---	2	---	19	4
75	2	250n 02δ	1,836	5	---	---	89	4
69	---	---	1,985	---	---	---	122	6
---	---	---	92	52	---	---	93	---
---	---	---	1,310	---	---	---	80	5
51	---	422n 36δ	2,579	52	---	---	74	6
8	1	---	182	75	---	---	46	1
165	---	157n	---	50	---	---	143	6
3	---	---	3,275	40	---	---	39	---
101	---	---	1,450	55	---	---	70	1
42	---	35n 12δ	1,073	50	---	---	73	4
41	---	---	983	88	---	---	56	1
20	---	78n 19δ	1,727	---	---	---	68	---
1,175	3	1,296n 22δ	36,093.50	712	626	---	1,276	58

*n = pud; δ = funt. Eds.

APPENDIX 7 (continued)

Unalaska Department
Unalaska Island

Year	Sea Otter	Beaver	River Otter	Fox	Polar Fox	Bear	Lynx	Sable	Muskrat
1842	333	---	58	1,691	---	---	---	---	---
1843	281	---	65	1,583	---	---	---	---	---
1844	267	---	97	1,147	---	---	---	---	---
1845	335	---	67	1,134	---	---	---	---	---
1846	255	---	5	1,023	---	---	---	---	---
1847	186	---	5	1,746	---	---	---	---	---
1848	230	---	---	1,180	---	---	---	---	---
1849	195	---	7	423	---	---	---	---	---
1850	239	---	1	680	---	---	---	---	---
1851	270	---	2	943	---	---	---	---	---
1852	203	---	3	1,481	---	---	---	---	---
1853	299	---	3	1,167	---	---	---	---	---
1854	268	---	1	721	---	---	---	---	---
1855	338	---	2	820	---	---	---	---	---
1856	215	---	---	344	---	---	---	---	---
1857	403	---	---	641	---	---	---	---	---
1858	448	---	7	1,102	---	---	---	---	---
1859	443	---	---	1,005	---	---	---	---	---
1860	478	---	6	870	---	---	---	---	---
	5,686	---	329	19,671	---	---	---	---	---

Minks	Fur Seals	Walrus Teeth	Castor-eum (pairs)	Marmot Parkas	Sea Otter Tails	Weasels	Wolverines	Wolves
---	---	11n	---	---	334	---	---	4
2	---	13n 20♂	---	---	280	---	1	3
---	---	---	---	---	117	---	---	4
---	---	512n 09♂	---	---	209	---	---	2
---	---	---	---	---	31	---	---	---
---	---	---	---	---	186	---	---	---
---	---	---	---	---	---	---	---	---
---	---	---	---	---	---	---	1	---
---	---	---	---	---	---	---	---	---
---	---	---	---	---	---	---	---	---
---	---	---	---	---	---	---	---	---
---	---	---	---	---	---	---	---	---
---	---	---	---	---	---	---	---	---
---	---	---	---	---	---	---	---	---
---	---	---	---	---	---	---	---	---
---	---	---	---	---	---	---	---	---
---	---	---	---	---	---	---	---	---
---	---	---	---	---	---	---	---	---
---	---	---	---	---	---	---	---	---
---	---	---	---	---	---	---	---	---
2	---	536n 29♂	---	---	1,157	---	2	13

APPENDIX 7 (continued)

Mednyi Island

Year	Sea Otter	Beaver	River Otter	Fox	Polar Fox	Bear	Lynx	Sable	Muskrat
1842	---	---	---	---	---	---	---	---	---
1843	---	---	---	---	---	---	---	---	---
1844	---	---	---	---	---	---	---	---	---
1845			Furs delivered to the Atkha Office						
1846	---	---	---	---	---	---	---	---	---
1847	---	---	---	---	64	---	---	---	---
1848	---	---	---	---	---	---	---	---	---
1849	---	---	---	---	3	---	---	---	---
1850	---	---	---	---	384	---	---	---	---
1851			Not delivered						
1852	---	---	---	---	516	---	---	---	---
1853	---	---	---	---	261	---	---	---	---
1854	---	---	---	---	220	---	---	---	---
1855	---	---	---	---	133	---	---	---	---
1856	---	---	---	---	180	---	---	---	---
1857	---	---	---	---	2	---	---	---	---
1858	---	---	---	---	---	---	---	---	---
1859	---	---	---	---	776	---	---	---	---
1860	---	---	---	---	488	---	---	---	---
	---	---	---	---	3,027	---	---	---	---

Minks	Fur Seals	Walrus Teeth	Castor-eum (pairs)	Marmot Parkas	Sea Otter Tails	Weasels	Wolverines	Wolves
---	---	---	---	---	---	---	---	---
---	---	---	---	---	---	---	---	---
---	---	---	---	---	---	---	---	---

Furs delivered to the Atkha Office

Minks	Fur Seals	Walrus Teeth	Castor-eum (pairs)	Marmot Parkas	Sea Otter Tails	Weasels	Wolverines	Wolves
---	---	---	---	---	---	---	---	---
---	903	---	---	---	---	---	---	---
---	1,101	---	---	---	---	---	---	---
---	1,377	---	---	---	---	---	---	---
---	727	---	---	---	---	---	---	---

Not delivered

Minks	Fur Seals	Walrus Teeth	Castor-eum (pairs)	Marmot Parkas	Sea Otter Tails	Weasels	Wolverines	Wolves
---	1,819	---	---	---	---	---	---	---
---	300	---	---	---	---	---	---	---
---	500	---	---	---	---	---	---	---
---	1,022	---	---	---	---	---	---	---
---	1,028	---	---	---	---	---	---	---
---	2,118	---	---	---	---	---	---	---
---	2,446	---	---	---	---	---	---	---
---	2,026	---	---	---	---	---	---	---
---	2,088	---	---	---	---	---	---	---
---	17,655	---	---	---	---	---	---	---

APPENDIX 7 (continued)

Atka Island

Year	Sea Otter	Beaver	River Otter	Fox	Polar Fox	Bear	Lynx	Sable	Muskrat
1842	No furs								
1843	281	---	---	---	986	---	---	---	---
1844	387	---	---	237	1,109	---	---	---	---
1845	Because of shipwreck of *Chichagov*, furs were not delivered								
1846	398	---	---	61	1,788	---	---	---	---
1847	87	---	---	27	235	---	---	---	---
1848	113	---	---	19	130	---	---	---	---
1849	148	---	---	---	---	---	---	---	---
1850	33	---	---	---	---	---	---	---	---
1851	25	---	---	90	126	---	---	---	---
1852	91	---	---	34	243	---	---	---	---
1853	4	---	---	285	185	---	---	---	---
1854	9	---	---	125	193	---	---	---	---
1855	36	---	---	---	---	---	---	---	---
1856	86	---	---	74	159	---	---	---	---
1857	3	---	---	11	33	---	---	---	---
1858	32	---	---	223	228	---	---	---	---
1859	106	---	---	195	125	---	---	---	---
1860	49	---	---	42	245	---	---	---	---
	1,883	---	---	1,420	5,785	---	---	---	---

Minks	Fur Seals	Walrus Teeth	Castor-eum (pairs)	Marmot Parkas	Sea Otter Tails	Weasels	Wolverines	Wolves
			No furs					
---	931	---	---	---	272	---	---	---
---	756	---	---	---	233	---	---	---
		Because of shipwreck of *Chichagov* furs were not delivered						
---	---	---	---	---	304	---	---	---
---	---	---	---	---	81	---	---	---
---	---	---	---	---	109	---	---	---
---	---	---	---	---	---	---	---	---
---	---	---	---	---	24	---	---	---
---	---	---	---	---	25	---	---	---
---	---	---	---	---	---	---	---	---
---	---	---	---	---	---	---	---	---
---	---	---	---	---	---	---	---	---
---	---	---	---	---	---	---	---	---
---	---	---	---	---	---	---	---	---
---	---	---	---	---	---	---	---	---
---	---	---	---	---	---	---	---	---
---	---	---	---	---	---	---	---	---
---	---	---	---	---	---	---	---	---
---	1,687	---	---	---	1,048	---	---	---

APPENDIX 7 (continued)

Attu Island

Year	Sea Otter	Beaver	River Otter	Fox	Polar Fox	Bear	Lynx	Sable	Muskrat
1842	---	---	---	---	---	---	---	---	---
1843	---	---	---	---	---	---	---	---	---
1844			Furs delivered to Atkha Office						
1845	---	---	---	---	---	---	---	---	---
1846	91	---	---	---	---	---	---	---	---
1847	4	---	---	---	284	---	---	---	---
1848	91	---	---	---	274	---	---	---	---
1849	238	---	---	---	222	---	---	---	---
1850	298	---	---	---	170	---	---	---	---
1851	21	---	---	---	253	---	---	---	---
1852	123	---	---	---	294	---	---	---	---
1853	193	---	---	---	388	---	---	---	---
1854	74	---	---	---	---	---	---	---	---
1855			Not delivered						
1856	325	---	---	---	280	---	---	---	---
1857	176	---	---	---	180	---	---	---	---
1858	249	---	---	---	94	---	---	---	---
1859	279	---	---	---	5	---	---	---	---
1860	259	---	---	---	59	---	---	---	---
	2,421	---	---	---	2,503	---	---	---	---

Minks	Fur Seals	Walrus Teeth	Castor-eum (pairs)	Marmot Parkas	Sea Otter Tails	Weasels	Wolverines	Wolves
---	---	---	---	---	---	---	---	---
---	---	---	---	---	---	---	---	---

Furs delivered to Atkha Office

Minks	Fur Seals	Walrus Teeth	Castoreum	Marmot Parkas	Sea Otter Tails	Weasels	Wolverines	Wolves
---	---	---	---	---	---	---	---	---
---	---	---	---	---	79	---	---	---
---	---	---	---	---	---	---	---	---
---	---	---	---	---	88	---	---	---
---	---	---	---	---	235	---	---	---
---	---	---	---	---	295	---	---	---
---	---	---	---	---	---	---	---	---
---	---	---	---	---	---	---	---	---
---	---	---	---	---	---	---	---	---
---	---	---	---	---	---	---	---	---

Not delivered

Minks	Fur Seals	Walrus Teeth	Castoreum	Marmot Parkas	Sea Otter Tails	Weasels	Wolverines	Wolves
---	---	---	---	---	---	---	---	---
---	---	---	---	---	---	---	---	---
---	---	---	---	---	---	---	---	---
---	---	---	---	---	---	---	---	---
---	---	---	---	---	---	---	---	---
---	---	---	---	---	697	---	---	---

APPENDIX 7 (continued)

Bering Island

Year	Sea Otter	Beaver	River Otter	Fox	Polar Fox	Bear	Lynx	Sable	Muskrat
1842	---	---	---	---	---	---	---	---	---
1843	---	---	---	---	---	---	---	---	---
1844	Furs delivered to Atkha Office								
1845	---	---	---	---	---	---	---	---	---
1846	---	---	---	---	---	---	---	---	---
1847	---	---	---	---	772	---	---	---	---
1848	---	---	---	---	---	---	---	---	---
1849	---	---	---	---	---	---	---	---	---
1850	---	---	---	---	---	---	---	---	---
1851	No furs								
1852	---	---	---	---	1,900	---	---	---	---
1853	---	---	---	---	547	---	---	---	---
1854	---	---	---	---	435	---	---	---	---
1855	Not delivered								
1856	---	---	---	---	1,025	---	---	---	---
1857	---	---	---	---	---	---	---	---	---
1858	---	---	---	---	---	---	---	---	---
1859	---	---	---	---	1,233	---	---	---	---
1860	---	---	---	---	584	---	---	---	---
	---	---	---	---	6,496	---	---	---	---

Minks	Fur Seals	Walrus Teeth	Castor-eum (pairs)	Marmot Parkas	Sea Otter Tails	Weasels	Wolverines	Wolves
---	---	---	---	---	---	---	---	---
---	---	---	---	---	---	---	---	---

Furs delivered at Athka Office

Minks	Fur Seals	Walrus Teeth	Castor-eum (pairs)	Marmot Parkas	Sea Otter Tails	Weasels	Wolverines	Wolves
---	---	---	---	---	---	---	---	---
---	---	---	---	---	---	---	---	---
---	---	---	---	---	---	---	---	---
---	447	---	---	---	---	---	---	---
---	554	---	---	---	---	---	---	---
---	649	---	---	---	---	---	---	---

No furs

---	1,453	---	---	---	---	---	---	---
---	700	---	---	---	---	---	---	---
---	854	---	---	---	---	---	---	---

Not delivered

---	1,749	---	---	---	---	---	---	---
---	1,050	---	---	---	---	---	---	---
---	1,000	---	---	---	---	---	---	---
---	1,070	---	---	---	---	---	---	---
---	9,526	---	---	---	---	---	---	---

APPENDIX 7 (continued)

Unga Island

Year	Sea Otter	Beaver	River Otter	Fox	Polar Fox	Bear	Lynx	Sable	Muskrat
1842	---	---	---	---	---	---	---	---	---
1843	---	---	---	---	---	---	---	---	---
1844	Furs delivered to Unalaska Office								
1845	---	---	---	---	---	---	---	---	---
1846	64	---	74	511	---	---	---	---	---
1847	214	---	60	121	---	---	---	---	---
1848	109	---	66	634	---	---	---	---	---
1849	185	---	74	358	---	---	---	---	---
1850	236	---	64	439	---	---	---	---	---
1851	209	---	39	514	---	---	---	---	---
1852	232	---	68	468	---	---	---	---	---
1853	242	---	87	317	---	---	---	---	---
1854	Not delivered								
1855	673	---	176	616	---	---	---	---	---
1856	193	---	64	138	---	---	---	---	---
1857	273	---	49	290	---	---	---	---	---
1858	274	---	51	240	---	---	---	---	---
1859	359	---	44	250	---	---	---	---	---
1860	357	---	63	305	---	---	---	---	---
	3,611	---	979	5,731	---	---	---	---	---

Minks	Fur Seals	Walrus Teeth	Castor-eum (pairs)	Marmot Parkas	Sea Otter Tails	Weasels	Wolverines	Wolves
---	---	---	---	---	---	---	---	---
---	---	---	---	---	---	---	---	---

Furs delivered to Unalaska Office

Minks	Fur Seals	Walrus Teeth	Castor-eum (pairs)	Marmot Parkas	Sea Otter Tails	Weasels	Wolverines	Wolves
---	---	---	---	---	---	---	---	---
---	---	---	---	---	---	---	---	---
---	---	---	---	---	214	---	---	---
23	---	---	---	---	---	---	1	---
---	---	---	---	---	---	---	1	---
---	---	---	---	---	---	---	---	1
1	---	---	---	---	---	---	---	---
6	---	---	---	---	---	---	---	---
---	---	---	---	---	---	---	---	---

Not delivered

Minks	Fur Seals	Walrus Teeth	Castor-eum (pairs)	Marmot Parkas	Sea Otter Tails	Weasels	Wolverines	Wolves
---	---	---	---	---	---	---	1	---
---	---	---	---	---	---	---	---	---
---	---	---	---	---	---	---	---	---
---	---	---	---	---	---	---	---	---
---	---	---	---	---	---	---	1	---
---	---	---	---	---	---	---	---	---
30	---	---	---	---	214	---	4	1

APPENDIX 7 (continued)

Mikhailovsk Redoubt

Year	Sea Otter	Beaver	River Otter	Fox	Polar Fox	Bear	Lynx	Sable	Muskrat
1842	---	2,075.5	240.5	453	27	---	36	57	300
1843	---	2,996	274	249	43	---	33	10	64
1844	---	3,169	248	263	35	2	4	5	---
1845	---	2,607	320	504	138	6	27	149	---
1846	---	3,613	226	398	93	3	33	47	---
1847	---	3,401	179	273	78	5	111	---	---
1848	---	2,749	207	457	13	3	110	96	490
1849	---	2,543	269	637	41	2	121	175	---
1850	---	3,505	124	793	15	22	196	64	686
1851	---	3,169	157	259	12	1	106	67	692
1852	---	1,720	116	630	77	5	24	46	1,152
1853	---	3,134	250	434	30.5	3	15	122	568
1854	---	3,855	412	287	4	3	10	254	---
1855	---	1,504	347	470	36	2	4	502	235
1856	---	1,207	248	673	138	19	28	396	220
1857	---	2,683	375	1,059	159	---	33	1,387	52
1858	---	1,449	286	506	150	24	53	1,394	69
1859	---	1,982	333	995	267	37	32	1,946	140
1860	---	1,947	313	856	47	46	28	1,536	---
	---	43,398.5	4,954.5	10,216	1,403.5	183	1,007	8,253	4,668

Minks	Fur Seals	Walrus Teeth	Castor- eum (pairs)	Marmot Parkas	Sea Otter Tails	Weasels	Wolverines	Wolves
73	---	---	---	---	---	---	---	---
---	---	---	60	---	---	---	---	---
---	---	1n	104	---	---	---	---	---
---	---	---	---	---	---	---	---	---
---	---	---	---	---	---	---	---	---
---	---	---	---	---	---	---	---	1
20	---	---	244	---	---	---	---	---
---	---	---	---	---	---	---	---	---
---	---	---	134	---	---	---	---	---
29	---	---	80	---	---	---	---	---
---	---	---	51	---	---	---	---	---
70	---	---	259	---	---	---	---	---
1	---	---	382	---	---	---	---	---
33	---	---	229	---	---	---	---	---
104	---	---	225	---	---	---	---	---
---	---	---	612	---	---	---	52	---
---	---	---	---	---	---	---	---	---
---	---	1n 36ᵭ	508	---	---	---	---	---
---	---	---	397.5	---	---	---	---	---
330	---	2n 36ᵭ	3,315.5	---	---	---	52	1

APPENDIX 7 (continued)

Kalmakovsk Redoubt

Year	Sea Otter	Beaver	River Otter	Fox	Polar Fox	Bear	Lynx	Sable	Muskrat
1842	---	---	---	---	---	---	---	---	---
1843	Furs delivered to Kodiak Office								
1844	---	---	---	---	---	---	---	---	---
1845	---	1,646	76	135	---	3	10	---	---
1846	---	2,091	52	79	---	10	5	---	---
1847	---	2,395	100	236	---	8	49	---	---
1848	---	1,949	75	333	---	14	20	---	---
1849	---	1,436	78	298	---	8	15	---	---
1850	---	1,077	73	285	---	7	28	---	---
1851	---	1,166	45	339	---	---	19	---	---
1852	---	1,732	54	62	---	---	11	---	---
1853	---	2,640	48	163	113	---	---	---	---
1854	---	1,472	42	105	---	---	1	---	---
1855	---	965	67	12	---	---	3	---	---
1856	---	1,161	88	260	99	16	10	450	---
1857	---	---	---	---	---	---	---	---	---
1858	---	1,280	95	128	8	7	95	352	---
1859	---	1,717	193	757	63	10	52	346	---
1860	---	969	79	398	37	10	9	950	---
	---	23,696	1,165	3,590	320	93	327	2,098	---

Minks	Fur Seals	Walrus Teeth	Castor-eum (pairs)	Marmot Parkas	Sea Otter Tails	Weasels	Wolverines	Wolves
---	---	---	---	---	---	---	---	---

Furs delivered to Kodiak Office

Minks	Fur Seals	Walrus Teeth	Castor-eum (pairs)	Marmot Parkas	Sea Otter Tails	Weasels	Wolverines	Wolves
---	---	---	---	---	---	---	---	---
---	---	---	665	---	---	---	---	---
---	---	---	721	---	---	---	---	---
---	---	---	643	---	---	---	---	---
---	---	---	490	---	---	---	---	---
---	---	---	490	---	---	---	---	---
---	---	---	252	---	---	---	---	---
---	---	---	332	---	---	---	---	---
---	---	---	306	---	---	---	---	---
---	---	---	714	---	---	---	---	---
---	---	---	380	---	---	---	---	---
---	---	---	250	---	---	---	---	---
---	---	---	333	---	---	---	---	---
---	---	---	---	---	---	---	---	---
---	---	---	420	---	---	---	---	---
---	---	---	470	---	---	---	---	---
---	---	266	370	---	---	---	---	---
---	---	266	6,836	---	---	---	---	---

APPENDIX 7 (continued)

Bartered from Savages in the North

Year	Sea Otter	Beaver	River Otter	Fox	Polar Fox	Bear	Lynx	Sable	Muskrat
1842	---	13	---	79	522	---	---	1	---
1843	---	8	---	51	381	---	---	1	---
1844	---	11	2	15	139	---	---	24	---
1845				No furs					
1846	---	10	1	10	42	---	---	1	---
1847	---	3	---	20	83	---	---	---	---
1848	---	---	---	12	---	---	---	---	---
1849				No furs					
1850	---	---	---	---	9	---	---	---	---
1851	---	---	---	---	---	---	---	---	---
1852				No furs					
1853	---	---	---	---	---	---	---	---	---
1854	---	---	---	1	---	---	---	---	---
1855	---	---	---	---	---	---	---	---	---
1856	---	---	---	---	---	---	---	---	---
1857				No furs					
1858	---	---	---	---	---	---	---	---	---
1859	---	---	---	---	---	---	---	---	---
1860	---	3	---	39	7	---	---	---	---
	---	48	3	227	1,183	---	---	27	---

Minks	Fur Seals	Walrus Teeth	Castor-eum (pairs)	Marmot Parkas	Sea Otter Tails	Weasels	Wolverines	Wolves
1	---	165n 10♂	---	---	---	---	---	---
---	---	565n 20♂	---	---	---	---	---	---
---	---	148n	---	---	---	---	---	---
			No furs					
---	---	55n	---	---	---	---	---	---
---	---	---	---	---	---	---	---	---
---	---	20n	---	---	---	---	---	---
			No furs					
---	---	30n	---	---	---	---	---	---
---	---	---	---	---	---	---	---	---
			No furs					
---	---	---	---	---	---	---	---	---
---	---	---	---	---	---	---	---	---
---	---	---	---	---	---	---	---	---
---	---	---	---	---	---	---	---	---
			No furs					
---	---	---	---	---	---	---	---	---
---	---	---	---	---	---	---	---	---
---	---	5n 1♂	---	---	---	---	---	---
1	---	988n 31♂	---	---	---	---	---	---

APPENDIX 7 (continued)

St. Paul Island

Year	Sea Otter	Beaver	River Otter	Fox	Polar Fox	Bear	Lynx	Sable	Muskrat
1842	---	---	---	---	505	---	---	---	---
1843	---	---	---	---	515	---	---	---	---
1844	---	---	---	---	394	---	---	---	---
1845	---	---	---	---	363	---	---	---	---
1846	---	---	---	---	528	---	---	---	---
1847	---	---	---	---	515	---	---	---	---
1848	---	---	---	---	461	---	---	---	---
1849	---	---	---	---	519	---	---	---	---
1850	---	---	---	---	519	---	---	---	---
1851	---	---	---	---	517	---	---	---	---
1852	---	---	---	---	645	---	---	---	---
1853	---	---	---	---	641	---	---	---	---
1854	---	---	---	---	624	---	---	---	---
1855	---	---	---	---	---	---	---	---	---
1856	---	---	---	---	341	---	---	---	---
1857	---	---	---	---	1,417	---	---	---	---
1858	---	---	---	---	558	---	---	---	---
1859	---	---	---	---	619	---	---	---	---
1860	---	---	---	---	625	---	---	---	---
	---	---	---	---	10,508	---	---	---	---

Minks	Fur Seals	Walrus Teeth	Castoreum (pairs)	Marmot Parkas	Sea Otter Tails	Weasels	Wolverines	Wolves
---	7,600	---	---	---	---	---	---	---
---	10,236	---	---	---	---	---	---	---
---	11,094	---	---	---	---	---	---	---
---	12,637	---	---	---	---	---	---	---
---	14,053	15n	---	---	---	---	---	---
---	16,703	20n 20♂	---	---	---	---	---	---
---	13,650	---	---	---	---	---	---	---
---	20,450	9n 23♂	---	---	---	---	---	---
---	6,270	---	---	---	---	---	---	---
---	6,064	---	---	---	---	---	---	---
---	6,225	---	---	---	---	---	---	---
---	16,034	25n	---	---	---	---	---	---
---	24,146	19n	---	---	---	---	---	---
---	6,584	---	---	---	---	---	---	---
---	20,550	---	---	---	---	---	---	---
---	18,082	13n	---	---	---	---	---	---
---	29,810	---	---	---	---	---	---	---
---	19,000	---	---	---	---	---	---	---
---	18,590	---	---	---	---	---	---	---
---	277,778	104n 03♂	---	---	---	---	---	---

APPENDIX 7 (continued)

St. George Island

Year	Sea Otter	Beaver	River Otter	Fox	Polar Fox	Bear	Lynx	Sable	Muskrat
1842	---	---	---	---	1,491	---	---	---	---
1843	---	---	---	---	1,377	---	---	---	---
1844	---	---	---	---	1,343	---	---	---	---
1845	---	---	---	---	1,366	---	---	---	---
1846	---	---	---	---	1,418	---	---	---	---
1847	---	---	---	---	1,354	---	---	---	---
1848	---	---	---	---	1,298	---	---	---	---
1849	---	---	---	---	1,069	---	---	---	---
1850	---	---	---	---	1,073	---	---	---	---
1851	---	---	---	---	1,263	---	---	---	---
1852	---	---	---	---	1,477	---	---	---	---
1853	---	---	---	---	1,238	---	---	---	---
1854	---	---	---	---	1,291	---	---	---	---
1855	---	---	---	---	1,123	---	---	---	---
1856	---	---	---	---	1,145	---	---	---	---
1857	---	---	---	---	1,198	---	---	---	---
1858	---	---	---	---	1,555	---	---	---	---
1859	---	---	---	---	1,296	---	---	---	---
1860	---	---	---	---	911	---	---	---	---
	---	---	---	---	24,286	---	---	---	---

Minks	Fur Seals	Walrus Teeth	Castor-eum (pairs)	Marmot Parkas	Sea Otter Tails	Weasels	Wolverines	Wolves
---	2,570	---	---	---	---	---	---	---
---	1,004	---	---	---	---	---	---	---
---	830	---	---	---	---	---	---	---
---	1,000	---	---	---	---	---	---	---
---	1,017	---	---	---	---	---	---	---
---	1,000	---	---	---	---	---	---	---
---	1,000	---	---	---	---	---	---	---
---	1,000	---	---	---	---	---	---	---
---	500	---	---	---	---	---	---	---
---	500	---	---	---	---	---	---	---
---	500	---	---	---	---	---	---	---
---	2,001	---	---	---	---	---	---	---
---	2,000	---	---	---	---	---	---	---
---	2,001	---	---	---	---	---	---	---
---	3,000	---	---	---	---	---	---	---
---	3,000	---	---	---	---	---	---	---
---	3,000	---	---	---	---	---	---	---
---	3,000	---	---	---	---	---	---	---
---	3,000	---	---	---	---	---	---	---
---	31,923	---	---	---	---	---	---	---

APPENDIX 7 (continued)

Shumshu Island

Year	Sea Otter	Beaver	River Otter	Fox	Polar Fox	Bear	Lynx	Sable	Muskrat
1842	---	---	---	---	---	---	---	---	---
1843				No furs					
1844	94	---	---	43	---	---	---	---	---
1845	376	---	---	8	---	---	---	---	---
1846	98	---	---	35	---	---	---	---	---
1847	152	---	---	15	---	---	---	---	---
1848	496	---	---	70	---	---	---	---	---
1849	90	---	---	197	---	---	---	---	---
1850	159	---	---	25	---	---	---	---	---
1851	149	---	---	151	---	---	---	---	---
1852	185	---	---	142	---	---	---	---	---
1853	149	---	---	427	---	---	---	---	---
1854				No furs					
1855	68	---	---	261	---	---	---	---	---
1856	2	---	---	135	---	---	---	---	---
1857	3	---	---	30	---	---	---	---	---
1858	80	---	---	108	---	---	---	---	---
1859	64	---	1	204	---	---	---	---	---
1860	90	---	---	209	---	---	---	---	---
	2,255	---	1	2,051	---	---	---	---	---

Minks	Fur Seals	Walrus Teeth	Castor- eum (pairs)	Marmot Parkas	Sea Otter Tails	Weasels	Wolverines	Wolves
---	---	---	---	---	---	---	---	---
				No furs				
---	---	---	---	---	69	---	---	---
---	---	---	---	---	335	---	---	1
---	---	---	---	---	14	---	---	---
---	---	---	---	---	157	---	---	1
---	---	---	---	---	385	---	---	---
---	---	---	---	---	81	---	---	---
---	---	---	---	---	164	---	---	1
---	---	---	---	---	95	---	---	---
---	---	---	---	---	---	---	---	2
---	---	---	---	---	107	---	---	2
				No furs				
---	---	---	---	---	---	---	---	---
---	---	---	---	---	1	---	---	---
---	---	---	---	---	---	---	---	---
---	---	---	---	---	---	---	---	---
---	---	---	---	---	2	---	---	---
---	---	---	---	---	---	---	---	2
---	---	---	---	---	1,130	---	---	9

APPENDIX 7 (continued)

Urup Island

Year	Sea Otter	Beaver	River Otter	Fox	Polar Fox	Bear	Lynx	Sable	Muskrat
1842	50	---	---	79	---	---	---	---	---
1843	---	---	---	---	---	---	---	---	---
1844	---	---	---	---	---	---	---	---	---
1845	---	---	---	7	---	---	---	---	---
1846	---	---	---	33	---	---	---	---	---
1847	6	---	---	56	---	---	---	---	---
1848	162	---	---	83	---	---	---	---	---
1849	104	---	---	154	---	---	---	---	---
1850	121	---	---	90	---	---	---	---	---
1851	---	---	---	---	---	---	---	---	---
1852	77	---	---	368	---	---	---	---	---
1853	108	---	---	159	---	---	---	---	---
1854	---	---	---	---	---	---	---	---	---
1855	327	---	---	44	---	---	---	---	---
1856	14	---	---	48	---	---	---	---	---
1857	38	---	---	---	---	---	---	---	---
1858	36	---	---	140	---	---	---	---	---
1859	408	---	2	128	---	---	---	---	---
1860	359	---	---	161	---	---	---	---	---
	1,810	---	2	1,550	---	---	---	---	---

Minks	Fur Seals	Walrus Teeth	Castor- eum (pairs)	Marmot Parkas	Sea Otter Tails	Weasels	Wolverines	Wolves
---	---	---	---	---	50	---	---	---
---	---	---	---	---	---	---	---	---
---	---	---	---	---	---	---	---	---
---	---	---	---	---	---	---	---	---
---	---	---	---	---	---	---	---	---
---	---	---	---	---	---	---	---	---
---	---	---	---	---	---	---	---	---
---	---	---	---	---	104	---	---	---
---	---	---	---	---	121	---	---	---
---	---	---	---	---	---	---	---	---
---	---	---	---	---	77	---	---	---
---	---	---	---	---	---	---	---	---
---	---	---	---	---	---	---	---	---
---	---	---	---	---	---	---	---	---
---	---	---	---	---	---	---	---	---
---	---	---	---	---	---	---	---	---
---	---	---	---	---	---	---	---	---
---	---	---	---	---	---	---	---	---
---	---	---	---	---	---	---	---	---
---	---	---	---	---	352	---	---	---

APPENDIX 7 (continued)

Simusir Island

Year	Sea Otter	Beaver	River Otter	Fox	Polar Fox	Bear	Lynx	Sable	Muskrat
1842	34	---	---	12	---	---	---	---	---
1843	---	---	---	---	---	---	---	---	---
1844	64	---	---	19	---	---	---	---	---
1845	229	---	---	19	---	---	---	---	---
1846	98	---	---	---	---	---	---	---	---
1847	---	---	---	---	---	---	---	---	---
1848	---	---	---	---	---	---	---	---	---
1849	---	---	---	---	---	---	---	---	---
1850	---	---	---	---	---	---	---	---	---
1851	---	---	---	---	---	---	---	---	---
1852	---	---	---	---	---	---	---	---	---
1853				No furs					
1854	---	---	---	---	---	---	---	---	---
1855	---	---	---	---	---	---	---	---	---
1856	---	---	---	---	---	---	---	---	---
1857	---	---	---	---	---	---	---	---	---
1858	---	---	---	---	---	---	---	---	---
1859	---	---	---	---	---	---	---	---	---
1860	---	---	---	---	---	---	---	---	---
	445	---	---	50	---	---	---	---	---

Minks	Fur Seals	Walrus Teeth	Castor- eum (pairs)	Marmot Parkas	Sea Otter Tails	Weasels	Wolverines	Wolves
---	---	---	---	---	54	---	---	---
---	---	---	---	---	---	---	---	---
---	---	---	---	---	64	---	---	---
---	---	---	---	---	228	---	---	---
---	29	---	---	---	---	---	---	---
---	---	---	---	---	---	---	---	---
---	---	---	---	---	---	---	---	---
---	---	---	---	---	---	---	---	---
---	---	---	---	---	---	---	---	---
---	---	---	---	---	---	---	---	---
---	---	---	---	---	---	---	---	---

No furs

---	---	---	---	---	---	---	---	---
---	---	---	---	---	---	---	---	---
---	---	---	---	---	---	---	---	---
---	---	---	---	---	---	---	---	---
---	---	---	---	---	---	---	---	---
---	---	---	---	---	---	---	---	---
---	---	---	---	---	---	---	---	---
---	29	---	---	---	346	---	---	---

APPENDIX 7 (continued)

Kenai Mining Camp

Year	Sea Otter	Beaver	River Otter	Fox	Polar Fox	Bear	Lynx	Sable	Muskrat
1860	26	1	5	23	---	16	9	21	---

Lieutenant Zagoskin's Expedition in the North

1844	---	194	42	56	---	---	5	1	---

California Expedition

1845	---	133	---	---	---	---	---	---	---

Kamchatka Commissary

1855	---	---	---	28	---	---	---	106	---

TOTAL NUMBER OF PELTS		AVERAGED PER YEAR	
Sea Otter	25,602.25	Sea Otter	1,347
Beaver	161,042.5	Beaver	8,475
River Otter	63,826	River Otter	3,359
Fox	73,944	Fox	3,891
Polar Fox	55,540	Polar Fox	2,923
Bear	2,283	Bear	120
Lynx	6,443	Lynx	339
Sable	26,384	Sable	1,388
Muskrat	19,076	Muskrat	1,004

Minks	Fur Seals	Walrus Teeth	Castor-eum (pairs)	Marmot Parkas	Sea Otter Tails	Weasels	Wolverines	Wolves
---	---	---	---	---	---	---	10	---
---	---	---	---	---	7	---	---	---
---	---	---	---	---	---	---	---	---
---	---	---	---	---	---	---	---	---

TOTAL NUMBER OF PELTS		AVERAGED PER YEAR	
Minks	2,536	Minks	133
Fur Seals	338,604	Fur Seals	17,821
Walrus Teeth	2,929n 27ᵟ	Walrus Teeth	154n
Castoreum (pairs)	46,274	Castoreum (pairs)	2,435
Marmot Parkas	712	Marmot Parkas	37
Sea Otter Tails	7,309	Sea Otter Tails	384
Weasels	451	Weasels	23
Wolverines	1,432	Wolverines	75
Wolves	104	Wolves	5

APPENDIX 7 (continued)

Sea otters	are sent to Irkutsk office, and from there part are forwarded to Kiakhta; the rest to the Main Governing Board of the Company.
Beavers	are forwarded to Irkutsk, from there 2,000 go to Kiakhta; the rest to Shanghai and to America.
River otters	all go to Irkutsk, and from there to Kiakhta; a part was formerly sent to Shanghai.
Foxes	are sent primarily to Irkutsk; a small number goes to Shanghai.
Arctic Foxes	blue to Irkutsk and Kiakhta; white to America.
Bearskins	go by sea to the Governing Board [St. Petersburg].
Lynx	all go to Irkutsk; a part was formerly sent to Shanghai.
Sables	are sent to Irkutsk, and are sold to service personnel in New Arkhangel. Lately they have also been sent to Shanghai.
Muskrats	are sold in New Arkhangel, but lately they have also been sent to Shanghai.
Minks	are sold in New Arkhangel.
Fur seals	a large part goes by sea to Governing Board; they are also sent to Shanghai and America, and 8,000 every year go to Irkutsk for the Kiakhta trade.
Walrus teeth	go by sea to the Governing Board.
Beavor castors	also are sent the Governing Board.
Marmot parkas	are sold in New Arkhangel and in colonial departments.
Sea otter tails	go to Irkutsk and to Kiakhta.
Wolverines	go to the Mikhailovsk redoubt.
Wolves	go to the Mikhailovsk redoubt.

APPENDIX 8

TAX ON FURS PURCHASED FROM NATIVES IN COLONIES
OF THE RUSSIAN AMERICAN COMPANY [in Rubles and Kopecks]

Animals (per pelt)	Tax on Aleuts' furs		
	before 1836 R/K	from 1836 R/K	from 1852 R/K
MARINE ANIMALS			
Sea otters: prime males and females	20/--	30/--	50/--
yearlings	10/--	15/--	25/--
cubs, *vykhodnoi*	2/--	3/--	3/--
cubs, *nastoiashchii*	1/--	1/--	1/--
prematurely born	--/--	--/--	--/50
Fur seals: prime males and bachelors	--/50	--/75	--/75
gray, 1st & 2nd quality	--/40	--/50	--/50
Sea otter tails	--/--	--/--	--/--
yearling tails	--/--	--/--	--/--
LAND ANIMALS			
Beavers: 1st quality, prime	2/50	4/--	4/--
1st quality, summer	--/--	--/--	1/--
2nd quality, prime	2/--	3/--	3/--
2nd quality, summer	--/--	--/--	1/--
3rd quality, small prime	1/50	2/--	2/--
4th quality, cubs & yearlings	--/--	--/--	1/--
River otters: large, 1st quality, prime	3/20	4/60	6/--
large, summer	--/--	--/--	1/--
medium, prime 2nd quality	2/40	3/20	5/--
medium, summer	--/--	--/--	1/--
prime, 3rd quality	1/--	2/--	3/--
small, prime 4th quality	--/50	1/--	1/--

APPENDIX 8 (continued)

Tax on Kolosh Furs at New Arkhangel		Tax on Kuril Islands	
in 1836	in 1845	Aleuts from 1836	Kurils in 1843
R/K	R/K	(from 1852 pr. beaver)	R/K
140/--	140/--	30/--	70/--
50/--	54/--	15/--	35/--
8/--	9/--	3/--	20/--
4/--	4/--	from 1R to 80K	--/--
1/50	--/--	--/--	--/--
2/--	2/--	--/--	--/--
--/--	--/--	--/--	--/--
6/--	6/--	--/--	5/--
2/--	2/--	--/--	2/50
15/--	18/--	--/--	--/--
--/--	--/--	--/--	--/--
10/--	12/--	--/--	--/--
--/--	--/--	--/--	--/--
7/--	9/--	--/--	--/--
--/--	2/--	--/--	--/--
18/--	18/--	--/--	--/--
--/--	--/--	--/--	--/--
15/--	12/--	--/--	--/--
--/--	--/--	--/--	--/--
7/50	9/--	--/--	--/--
2/50	2/--	--/--	--/--

Tax on Mikhailov & Kolmakov Redoubts			Tax on Chukchis, 1846
from 1836	from 1842	from 1855	
R/K	R/K	R/K	R/K
--/--	--/--	--/--	--/--
--/--	--/--	--/--	--/--
--/--	--/--	--/--	--/--
--/--	--/--	--/--	--/--
--/--	--/--	--/--	--/--
--/--	--/--	--/--	--/--
--/--	--/--	--/--	--/--
--/--	--/--	--/--	--/--
--/--	--/--	--/--	--/--
1/35	2/--	2/50	6/--
--/--	--/50	--/50	1/50
--/95	1/50	2/--	3/--
--/--	--/50	--/50	1/50
--/60	1/--	1/50	3/--
--/20	--/25	--/50	--/50
2/--	2/--	3/50	6/--
--/--	--/50	--/50	1/50
1/12	1/50	2/50	3/--
--/--	--/50	--/50	1/50
--/--	--/--	--/--	--/--
1/75	1/--	1/50	3/--

APPENDIX 8 (continued)

Animals (per pelt)		Tax on Aleuts' furs		
		before 1836 R/K	from 1836 R/K	from 1852 R/K
LAND ANIMALS				
River otters:	young	--/--	--/--	1/--
	cubs	--/--	--/--	1/--
Fox (blackbrown):	finest quality	--/--	9/--	12/--
	prime	6/--	6/--	9/--
	immature	3/--	3/--	3/--
	summer & spring	--/--	--/--	1/--
	damaged & bellies	--/--	--/--	--/--
	cubs	1/50	1/--	1/--
Fox (cross):	prime	3/--	4/--	6/--
	immature	1/50	2/--	2/--
	cubs, summer & spring	--/--	--/--	--/75
	damaged & bellies	--/--	--/--	--/--
	small	--/--	--/--	--/--
	cubs	--/75	--/75	--/75
Fox (red):	prime	2/--	2/--	3/--
	damaged & bellies	--/--	--/--	--/--
	immature	1/--	1/--	1/--
	spring, summer & cubs	--/50	--/50	--/50
Fox (blue):		1/--	1/--	1/50
	immature	--/50	--/50	--/50
Fox (white):		--/20	--/20	--/50
	immature	--/10	--/10	--/10
Sable:	prime	--/50	--/50	1/--
	damaged	--/--	--/--	--/--
	bellies	--/50	--/50	--/50
	summer	--/--	--/--	--/40
Sable bellies:		--/--	--/--	--/--
Wolf:	prime	2/--	2/--	4/--
	summer	1/--	1/--	--/50

Tax on Kolosh Furs at New Arkhangel		Tax on Kuril Islands	
in 1836	in 1845	Aleuts from 1836	Kurils in 1843
R/K	R/K	R/K	R/K
--/--	2/--	--/--	--/--
--/--	--/--	--/--	--/--
35/--	36/--	--/--	--/--
15/--	18/--	6/--	15/--
10/--	9/--	3/--	6/--
--/--	--/--	--/--	--/--
30/--	12/--	--/--	--/--
2/--	3/--	1/--	--/--
15/--	18/--	4/--	10/--
7/50	6/--	2/--	--/--
--/--	--/--	--/75	--/--
12/--	9/--	--/--	--/--
8/--	--/--	--/--	--/--
3/--	--/--	--/--	--/--
10/--	6/--	2/--	5/--
8/--	3/--	--/--	--/--
4 to 5/--	2/50	1/--	2/--
--/50	--/--	--/50	--/--
--/--	--/--	--/--	--/--
--/--	--/--	--/--	--/--
--/--	--/--	--/--	--/--
--/--	--/--	--/--	--/--
3/--	3/--	--/--	--/--
2/--	2/--	--/--	--/--
2/--	2/--	--/--	--/--
1/--	--/50	--/--	--/--
50/--	--/--	--/--	--/--
5/--	5/--	2/--	3/--
2/50	2/50	1/--	--/--

APPENDIX 8 (continued)

Tax on Mikhailov & Kolmakov Redoubts			Tax on Chukchis, 1846
from 1836	from 1842	from 1855	
R/K	R/K	R/K	R/K
--/50	--/50	1/--	1/50
--/25	--/50	--/--	--/--
--/--	--/--	--/--	--/--
--/--	3/--	6/--	10/--
--/--	1/50	1/50	3/--
--/--	--/50	--/50	1/50
--/--	--/--	--/--	--/--
--/--	--/--	--/75	1/50
1/25	2/--	3/50	6/--
--/--	1/--	1/50	3/--
--/--	--/50	--/50	1/50
--/50	--/--	--/--	--/--
--/--	--/--	--/--	--/--
--/25	--/50	--/50	1/50
--/87.5	1/50	2/--	3/50
--/--	--/--	--/--	--/--
--/37.5	--/75	--/50	1/50
--/25	--/50	--/--	1/--
--/87.5	--/--	1/50	3/--
--/--	--/10	--/10	--/--
--/50	--/--	--/50	1/--
--/--	--/--	--/10	--/--
--/30	--/--	--/75	1/--
--/20	--/25	--/50	--/75
--/--	--/--	--/50	--/--
--/--	--/--	--/20	--/--
--/--	--/--	--/--	--/--
--/--	1/50	--/--	3/--
--/--	--/75	--/--	1/50

Animals (per pelt)		Tax on Aleuts' furs		
LAND ANIMALS		before 1836 R/K	from 1836 R/K	from 1852 R/K
Lynx:	prime, large	3/--	3/--	5/--
	medium	2/--	2/--	3/--
	small	1/--	1/--	2/--
Wolverine:	prime, large	2/--	2/--	4/--
	medium	1/--	1/--	3/--
	small	--/--	--/--	2/--
Mink or Muskrat:	prime	--/30	--/25	--/50
	summer	--/15	--/--	--/--
Bears:	1st quality, black prime	--/--	5/--	5/--
	2nd	--/--	4/--	4/--
	3rd	--/--	2/--	2/--
Bear cubs:		--/--	1/--	1/--
ISLAND ANIMALS				
Fox (blackbrown):	prime, 1st quality	4/--	6/--	9/--
	immature, 2nd	2/--	8/--	3/--
	spring & cubs, 3rd	1/--	1/--	1/--
Fox (cross):	prime, 1st quality	3/--	4/--	6/--
	immature, 2nd	1/50	2/--	2/--
	cubs, 3rd	--/75	--/75	--/75
Fox (red):	prime, 1st quality	1/50	2/--	3/--
	immature, 2nd	--/75	1/--	1/--
	cubs, 3rd	--/40	--/50	--/50

APPENDIX 8 (continued)

| Tax on Kolosh Furs at New Arkhangel | | Tax on Kuril Islands | |
in 1836 R/K	in 1845 R/K	Aleuts from 1836 R/K	Kurils in 1843 R/K
8/--	9/--	--/--	--/--
6/--	6/--	--/--	--/--
4/--	3/60	--/--	--/--
5/--	5/--	--/--	--/--
4/--	3/50	--/--	--/--
2/50	2/50	--/--	--/--
--/50	--/45	--/--	--/--
--/--	--/--	--/--	--/--
18/--	18/--	--/--	--/--
15/--	12/--	--/--	--/--
10/--	9/--	--/--	--/--
5/--	6/--	--/--	--/--
--/--	--/--	--/--	--/--
--/--	--/--	--/--	--/--
--/--	--/--	--/--	--/--
--/--	--/--	--/--	--/--
--/--	--/--	--/--	--/--
--/--	--/--	--/--	--/--
--/--	--/--	--/--	--/--
--/--	--/--	--/--	--/--
--/--	--/--	--/--	--/--

Tax on Mikhailov & Kolmakov Redoubts			Tax on Chukchis, 1846
from 1836	from 1842	from 1855	
R/K	R/K	R/K	R/K
1/50	2/--	3/50	6/--
--/75	1/50	2/50	4/--
--/50	--/75	1/50	1/--
--/--	1/50	--/--	3/--
--/--	--/75	--/--	--/--
--/--	--/--	--/--	1/--
--/--	--/20	--/25	--/50
--/--	--/--	--/--	--/--
--/--	from/--	3/50	5/--
1/--	2 to/--	2/50	--/--
--/--	4/--	1/50	--/--
--/--	--/--	--/75	--/--
--/--	--/--	--/--	--/--
--/--	--/--	--/--	--/--
--/--	--/--	--/--	--/--
--/--	--/--	--/--	--/--
--/--	--/--	--/--	--/--
--/--	--/--	--/--	--/--
--/--	--/--	--/--	--/--
--/--	--/--	--/--	--/--
--/--	--/--	--/--	--/--

APPENDIX 8 (continued)

	Tax on Aleuts' furs from 1836 R/K	Tax on Aleuts' furs from 1852 R/K	Tax on Mikhailov & Kilmakov Redoubts from 1842 R/K	Tax on Chukchis, 1846 R/K
BEAVER CASTORS (per pair)				
1st quality	--/--	--/80	--/40	1/--
2nd quality	--/--	--/40	--/30	--/75
3rd quality	--/--	--/30	--/10	--/50
WALRUS TEETH (per pud)				
1st quality		6/--		
2nd quality	3/--	4/--	3/--	5/--
3rd quality		3/--		

Note: figures given in paper rubles

APPENDIX 9

INFORMATION ON ENTERPRISES FINANCIALLY BENEFICIAL
TO THE RUSSIAN AMERICAN COMPANY

Year	Fur Trade Cost to the Company in Rubles*	Ice		Salted Fish	
		Tons	Dollars	Casks	Rubles
From Jan. 1					
1849	273,059/91	---	---	255	6,350
1850	215,427/27	---	---	100	1,500
1851	130,598/65	---	---	158	2,190
1852	179,466/35	250	18,750.00	---	---
1853	150,215/20	1,133	24,030.00	160	2,400
1854	95,207/60	2,869	7,172.50	610	9,156
1855	146,378/30	4,300	16,951.76	399	5,983
1856	65,234/05	830	3,237.00	610	9,150
1857	106,714/45	3,455	13,474.50	700	19,250
1858	163,781/45	4,027	15,794.80	1,070	29,425
1859	144,405/44	3,690	22,575.48	282	7,755
1860	106,390/22			---	---
To July 11	776,878/89	20,555	122,066.04	4,344	93,161

*Note: Figures given in paper rubles

APPENDIX 9 (continued)

Year	Lumber Feet	Rubles	Coal Tons	Rubles
1849	22,974 feet	4,594/80	---	---
	1 shop	} 3,708.75		
	3 homes			
	3 logs	200/--		
1850	3 homes	3,560/25	---	---
	122 logs	1,187/50		
		64/98		
	10 sazh.	115/--		
1851	12,987 feet	259/74	---	---
	35 sazh.	402/50		
1852	4 sazh.	46/90		
	assorted	968/05		
1853	40,708 feet	814/16	---	---
1854	assorted	77/70	---	---
	14,000 feet	820/--		
	80 sazh.	920/--		
1855	216 sazh.	2,484/--	---	---
	46,525 feet	930/52		
	assorted	263/50		
1856	26,891 feet	537/82	---	---
1857	216 sazh.	3,818/20	500	6,250/--
1858	31,250 feet	625/--	---	---
1859	---	---	---	---
1860	---	---	---	---
	assorted	26,399/37	500	6,250/--

APPENDIX 10

INFORMATION ON THE ICE TRADE IN SAN FRANCISCO
FROM ITS INCEPTION TO THE PRESENT

Year	Tons of Ice On Sitka	On Kodiak	Tons Exported From Sitka	From Kodiak	Total Tonnage	Tons sent to Francisco	Sum in Dollars
Jan. 1							
1852	325	---	250	---	250	250	18,750.00
1853	2,000	---	653	---	653	653	22,850.00
	---	---	489	---	480	480	1,200.00
1854	3,000	270	2,869	---	2,869	2,869	7,172.50
1855	4,000	1,000	3,450.5	850	4,300.5	4,300.83	16,951.76
1856	900	---	830	---	830	830	3,237.00
1857	5,735	5,600	2,643	812	3,445	3,445	13,474.50
1858	1,200	5,600	2,276	1,751	4,027	4,027	15,744.80
1859	700	6,730	509	3,990	4,499	3,690	22,575.48
July 1							
1860	17,860	19,200	13,960.5	7,403	21,554.50	20,554.83	121,956.04

In February 1852 a Company ice ship, *Bacchus*, under Captain James Savage came to Sitka; she took on 250 tons of ice at $75 per ton. In October of that year our agent in San Francisco concluded an agreement with the American Russian Trading Company, by terms of which the Russian American Company agreed to deliver up to 1,000 tons of ice per year from its colonies aboard American ships, at $35 per ton, until September, 1855. Meanwhile the former company in 1854 concluded a new agreement in St. Petersburg, with a duration of 20 years, which was to go into effect on 9/21 October, 1855. According to that agreement, ice was to be shipped from the colonies at the same price the Russian American Company paid for it, and the profit was to be divided equally. After the warm winter of 1856 they agreed that ice should be priced at $3.00 per ton, with a markdown of 10%. Additionally they added 75¢ per ton export tax, and a commission of 5%, with the profit to be divided equally as formerly. Freight charge was set at $10 per ton. This agreement was superseded by a new agreement concluded by the Chief Administrator of the colonies with the American Russian Trading Company in San Francisco for a period of three years until January 1, 1863, according to which the American Russian Trading Company pays the Russian American Company $7.00 for each ton of ice exported from the colonies, with a 20% discount for melting. All previous agreements between the companies are terminated, and at the termination of this contract in 1863 the Russian American Company will have free trade in ice.

APPENDIX 10 (continued)

Year	Number of Ice Storage Houses		Tonnage which can be Stored		Current Value of Ice Houses	
	On Sitka	On Kodiak	On Sitka	On Kodiak	On Sitka	On Kodiak
Jan. 1						
1852	3	---	6,000	---	$28,000	---
1853	---	1	---	3,000	---	12,000
	---	1	---	3,000	---	---
1854	---	---	---	---	---	---
1855	---	---	---	---	---	---
1856	---	---	---	---	---	---
1857	---	---	---	---	---	---
1858	---	---	---	---	---	--- *
1859	---	---	---	---	---	---
July 1						
1860	---	---	---	---	---	---

*No information

Who is preparing ice, what payment they receive, from where and by what ships ice was shipped to San Francisco.

Ice is procured on Sitka by service personnel of the Company for 350-500 paper rubles per year, and the Company furnishes their food; also by hired Kolosh for one paper ruble per day and gifts to their toions; on Kodiak it is procured by service personnel of the Company with payment according to agreement, and by hired creoles and Aleuts at one paper ruble per day plus food and vodka from the Company.

Ice has been shipped from Sitka and Kodiak on ships contracted for that purpose by the American Russian Trading Company; at present it is shipped primarily on ships belonging to the Russian American Company. The freight charge has been $10 per ton, and since 28 December 1859/9 January 1860, it is $8.00 per ton according to the agreement.

APPENDIX 11

INFORMATION ON THE AMOUNT OF LUMBER CUT IN NEW ARKHANGEL
FOR PORT FACILITIES AND COLONIAL DEPARTMENTS FROM 1852 TO 1861

Year	1852	1853	1854	1855	1856	1857	1858
Structural timbers	611	2,094	1,378	1,235	656	1,452	515
Rabble [Greochnyi*]	32	73	35	22	---	136	---
Irregular [Krivuli]	134	237	220	84	50	430	241
Supplied by the Kolosh	719	525	---	---	---	---	---
Compass timber [Kokory]	---	50	53	155	67	560	37
Branch wood	---	100	---	---	125	---	250
Debarked trunks	---	78	---	---	---	465	---
Poles	---	---	---	---	---	311	---
Alder	---	14	13	---	---	200	---
Keels and sternposts	1	---	---	1	---	---	---
Staff wood [Klepechnoi*]	---	---	---	---	---	---	---
Apple	---	---	---	---	---	---	100
Sutungi*	---	---	---	---	---	---	---

*Note: The quantity of lumber is indicated in units cut. Logs are usually 13 to 15 sazhens long and 18 to 20 inches thick at the cut. Sutungi are sawed in the mill and are sometimes 32 feet long. Klepechnoi refers to small fir planks from which barrel staves are cut. Lumber from the Kolosh is generally from 4 to 5 sazhens long and from 8 to 10 inches thick. Grebochnyi are 1-1/2 sazhens long and up to 8 inches wide, and are used in the frames of baidarkas.

APPENDIX 12

A SUMMARY OF THE REVENUES OF THE
RUSSIAN AMERICAN COMPANY FOR TEN YEARS

Year	From Tea R/K*	From Furs R/K	From markup in the Colonies		From other commercial Transactions R/K	Total R/K
			For Goods R/K	For Furs R/K		
1850	206,178/78	263,797/73	115,872/13	150,894/91	15,832/98	752,768/63
1851	317,794/71	187,075/49	89,597/32	165,543/55	45,890/45	803,901/52
1852	391,137/90	246,379/85	66,400/20	69,913/42	---/--	773,831/37
1853	421,037/64	38,454/71	68,791/69	138,186/58	4,009/42	670,474/03
1854	434,061/37	134,502/07	68,592/73	188,671/21	1,150/86	826,978/24
1855	360,126/79	204,562/36	51,728/44	216,331/05	---/--	832,748/64
1856	679,006/34	57,189/01	112,749/62	123,173/19	---/--	972,118/16
1857	109,381/25	280,458/69	150,803/48	126,162/10	79,363/15	746,168/67
1858	600,609/88	143,934/01	94,080/27	215,694/91	23,889/81	1,077,208/88
1859	629,535/10	153,795/08	107,568/50	184,547/29	---/--	1,072,445/97
	4,145,869/76	1,709,149/--	926,184/40	1,577,112/21	170,235/76	8,528,551/13

Note: figures are given in silver

*Rubles and Kopecks

APPENDIX 13

A SUMMARY OF EXPENDITURES OF THE
RUSSIAN AMERICAN COMPANY FOR TEN YEARS

Year	Maintenance of the colonies	Maintenance of colonial church	Maintenance of welfare institutions	Maintenance of chief administrator offices, etc.	Payment of duty on tea
	R/K*	R/K	R/K	R/K	R/K
1850	242,912/64	7,722/32	16,132/10	136,657/15	121,569/25
1851	229,286/45	7,722/32	16,132/10	125,665/44	161,717/86
1852	128,955/63	---/--	7,357/99	124,967/40	224,989/11
1853	185,437/39	7,580/--	13,594/88	167,064/32	88,084/96
1854	235,714/52	7,375/74	14,174/18	143,098/58	118,692/72
1855	247,628/32	7,222/--	13,209/17	156,375/17	163,649/99
1856	214,439/89	7,471/16	14,011/76	157,584/99	231,793/58
1857	254,639/75	7,471/16	14,854/67	180,409/95	58,946/80
1858	285,135/61	9,280/98	15,358/59	169,179/93	294,775/51
1859	264,057/--	9,878/--	18,180/79	175,523/56	300,340/67
	2,288,207/20	71,723/18	143,366/23	1,536,436/49	1,764,559/85

Note: figures are given in silver

*Rubles and Kopecks

APPENDIX 13 (continued)

Year	Shipping and packing tea	Shipping and packing furs	Insurance on tea and goods	Wartime losses of ships etc.	Remodeling building in St. Petersburg
	R/K	R/K	R/K	R/K	R/K
1850	68,455/68	20,004/76	15,264/45	---/--	---/--
1851	70,054/95	23,418/84	21,046/80	---/--	---/--
1852	85,626/93	24,086/05	28,991/50	---/--	---/--
1853	25,222/90	5,078/11	29,194/71	---/--	---/--
1854	45,191/59	22,374/65	19,500/--	42,000/00	30,000/--
1855	60,927/23	8,183/73	---/--	26,696/27	---/--
1856	56,396/40	30,463/69	---/--	64,123/93	46,976/--
1857	25,783/28	32,456/30	22,750/--	---/--	---/--
1858	73,047/73	24,912/83	40,121/30	---/--	---/--
1859	76,195/03	22,717/33	40,157/79	---/--	---/--
	586,901/72	213,696/29	217,026/55	132,820/20	76,976/--

Year	Capital set aside for the poor	Reserve funds	Payment of dividends	Total
	R/K	R/K	R/K	R/K
1850	561/30	11,226/--	112,260/--	752,675/65
1851	673/56	13,471/20	134,712/--	803,901/52
1852	673/56	13,471/20	134,712/--	773,831/37
1853	673/56	13,471/20	134,712/--	670,474/03
1854	673/56	13,471/20	134,712/--	826,978/24
1855	673/56	13,471/20	134,712/--	832,748/64
1856	673/56	13,471/20	134,712/--	972,118/16
1857	673/56	13,471/20	134,712/--	746,168/67
1858	748/40	14,968/--	149,680/--	1,077,208/88
1859	748/40	14,968/00	149,680/--	1,072,445/97
	6,773/02	135,460/40	1,354,604/--	8,528,551/13

APPENDIX 14

CHIEF ADMINISTRATORS
OF THE RUSSIAN AMERICAN COMPANY

1790	-- 1818 (January 11)	Aleksandr Baranov
1818 (January 11)	-- 1818 (October 24)	Leontii Hagemeister
1818 (October 24)	-- 1820 (September 15)	Semen Ianovskii (Acting)
1820 (September 15)	-- 1825 (October 22)	Matvei Muraviev
1825 (October 22)	-- 1830 (October 5)	Petr Chistiakov
1830 (October 5)	-- 1835 (October 29)	Ferdinand Wrangell
1835 (October 29)	-- 1840 (June 1)	Ivan Kupreianov
1840 (June 1)	-- 1845 (July 6)	Adolf Etolin
1845 (July 6)	-- 1850 (October 14)	Mikhail Tebenkov
1850 (October 14)	-- 1853 (March 31)	Nikolai Rosenberg
1853 (March 31)	-- 1854 (April 22)	Aleksandr Rudakov
1854 (April 22)	-- 1859 (June 22)	Stepan Voevodskii
1859 (June 22)	-- 1864 (May 17)	Ivan Furuhelm
1864 (May 17)	-- 1867 (October 18)	Dmitrii Maksutov

APPENDIX 15

RUSSO-AMERICAN CONVENTION CONCERNING THE PACIFIC OCEAN
AND NORTHWEST COAST OF AMERICA, APRIL 17, 1824

In the name of the Most Holy and Indivisible Trinity.

The President of the United States of America and His Majesty the Emperor
of all the Russias, wishing to cement the bonds of amity which unite them, and
to secure between them the invariable maintenance of a perfect concord, by
means of the present convention, have named as their Plenipotentiaries to this
effect, to wit:

The President of the United States of America, Henry Middleton, a citizen
of said States, and their Envoy Extraordinary and Minister Plenipotentiary near
his Imperial Majesty; and His Majesty the Emperor of all the Russias, his
beloved and faithful Charles Robert Count of Nesselrode, actual Privy Counsellor
Privy Counsellor, Member of the Council of State, Secretary of State directing
the administration of Foreign Affairs, actual Chamberlain, Knight of the Order
of St. Alexander Nevsky, Grand Cross of the Order of St. Wladimir of the first
class, Knight of that of the White Eagle of Poland, Grand Cross of the Order of
St. Stephen of Hungary, Knight of the Orders of the Holy Ghost and St. Michael,
and Grand Cross of the Legion of Honor of France, Knight Grand Cross of the
Orders of the Black and of the Red Eagle of Prussia, of the Annunciation of
Sardinia, of Charles III of Spain, of St. Ferdinand and of Merit of Naples, of
the Elephant of Denmark, of the Polar Star of Sweden, of the Crown of Wurtem-
berg, of the Guelphs of Hanover, of the Belgic Lion, of Fidelity of Baden, and
of St. Constantine of Parma; and Pierre de Poletica, actual Counsellor of State,
Knight of the Order of St. Anne of the first class, and Grand Cross of the
Order of St. Wladimir of the second;

Who, after having exchanged their full powers, found in good and due form
have agreed upon and signed the following stipulations:

ARTICLE I.

It is agreed that, in any part of the Great Ocean, commonly called the
Pacific Ocean or South Sea, the respective citizens or subjects of the high
contracting Powers shall be neither disturbed or restrained, either in navigation or in fishing, or in the power of resorting to the coasts, upon points
which may not have already been occupied, for the purpose of trading with the
natives, saving always the restrictions and conditions determined by the
following articles.

Source: Mallory, William M. comp. *Treaties, Conventions, International Acts,
Protocols and Agreements Between the United States of America and
Other Powers, 1776-1909* (Washington: Government Printing Office, 1910)
II, pp. 1,512-14.

ARTICLE II.

With a view of preventing the rights of navigation and of fishing exercised upon the Great Ocean by the citizens and subjects of the high contracting Powers from becoming the pretext for an illicit trade, it is agreed that the citizens of the United States shall not resort to any point where there is a Russian extablishment, without the permission of the governor or the commander; and that, reciprocally, the subjects of Russia shall not resort, without permission, to any establishment of the United States upon the Northwest coast.

ARTICLE III.

It is moreover agreed that, hereafter, there shall not be formed by the citizens of the United States, or under the authority of the said States, any establishment upon the Northwest coast of America, nor in any of the islands adjacent, to the north of fifty-four degrees and forty minutes of north latitude; and that, in the same manner, there shall be none formed by Russian subjects, or under the authority of Russia, south of the same parallel.

ARTICLE IV.

It is, nevertheless, understood that during a term of ten years, counting from the signature of the present convention, the ships of both Powers, or which belong to their citizens of subjects respectively, may be reciprocally frequent, without any hindrance whatever, the interior seas, gulfs, harbors, and creeks, upon the coast mentioned in the preceding article, for the purpose of fishing and trading with the natives of the country.

ARTICLE V.

All spirituous liquors, fire-arms, other arms, powder, and munitions of war of every kind, are always excepted from this same commerce permitted by the preceding article; and the two Powers engage, reciprocally, neither to sell, nor suffer them to be sold, to the natives by their respective citizens and subjects, nor by any perdon who may be under their authority. It is likewise stipulated that this restriction shall never afford a pretext, nor be advanced, in any case, to authorize either search or detention of the vessels, seizure of the merchandize, or, in fine, any measures of constraint whatever towards the merchants or the crews who may carry on this commerce; the high contracting Powers reciprocally reserving to themselves to determine upon the penalties to be incurred, and to inflict the punishments in case of the contravention of this article by their respective citizens or subjects.

ARTICLE VI.

When this convention shall have been duly ratified by the President of the United States, with the advice and consent of the Senate, on the one part, and on the other, by His Majesty the Emperor of all the Russias the ratifications shall be exchanged at Washington in the space of ten months from the date below, or sooner if possible.

In faith whereof the respective Plenipotentiaries have signed this convention and thereto affixed the seals of their arms.

Done at St. Petersburg the 17-5 of April, of the year of Grace one thousand eight hundred and twenty-four.

HENRY MIDDLETON.
le Comte CHARLES DE NESSELRODE.
PIERRE DE POLETICA.

APPENDIX 16

TREATY OF COMMERCE AND NAVIGATION
BETWEEN RUSSIA AND THE UNITED STATES, DECEMBER 18, 1832

In the name of the Most Holy and indivisible Trinity.

The United States of America and His Majesty the Emperor of all the Russias, equally animated with the desire of maintaining the relations of good understanding, which have hitherto so happily subsisted between their respective States, and of extending and consolidating the commercial intercourse between them, have agreed to enter into negotiations for the conclusion of a Treaty of navigation and commerce, For which purpose the President of the United States has conferred full powers on James Buchanan their Envoy Extraordinary and Minister Plenipotentiary near his Imperial Majesty; and His Majesty the Emperor of all the Russias has conferred like powers on the Sieur Charles Robert Comte de Nesselrode, His Vice-Chancellor, Knight of the Orders of Russia, and of, many others &c; and the said Plenipotentiaries having exchanged their full powers, found in good and due form, having concluded and signed the following Articles:

ARTICLE I.

There shall be between the territories of the high contracting parties, a reciprocal liberty of commerce and navigation. The inhabitants of their respective States shall, mutually have liberty to enter the ports, places and rivers of the territories of each party, wherever foreign commerce is permitted. They shall be at liberty to sojourn and reside in all parts whatsoever of said territories, in order to attend to their affairs, and they shall enjoy, to that effect, the same security and protection as natives of the country wherin they reside, on condition of their submitting to the laws and ordinances there prevailing, and particularly to the regulations in force concerning commerce.

ARTICLE II.

Russian vessels arriving laden or in ballast, in the ports of the United States of America; and reciprocally in the ports of the Empire of Russia, shall be treated, on their entrance, during their stay, and at their departure, upon the same footing as national vessels, coming from the same place, with respect to the duties of tonnage. In regard to light house duties pilotage, and port charges, as well as to the fees and perquisites of public officers,

---

Source: Mallory, William M. comp. *Treaties, Conventions, International Acts, Protocols and Agreements Between the United States of America and Other Powers, 1776-1909* (Washington: Government Printing Office, 1910) II, pp. 1,514-19.

and all other duties and charges, of whatever kind or denomination, levied upon vessels of commerce, in the name or to the profit of the Government, the local authorities, or any of the private establishments whatsoever, the high contracting parties shall reciprocally treat each other, upon the footing of the most favored nations, with whom they have not Treaties now actually in force, regulating the said duties and charges on the basis of an entire reciprocity.

ARTICLE III.

All kinds of merchandise and articles of commerce, which may be lawfully imported into the ports of the Empire of Russia, in Russian vessels, may, also be so imported in vessels of the United States of America, without paying other or higher duties or charges, of whatever kind or denomination, levied in the name, or to the profit of the Government, the local authorities, or of any private establishments whatsoever, than if the same merchandise or articles or commerce had been imported in Russian vessels. And, reciprocally, all kinds of merchandise and articles of commerce, which may be lawfully imported into the ports of the United States of America, in vessels of the said States, may also be imported in Russian vessels, without paying other or higher duties or charges, of whatever kind or denomination, levied in the name or to the profit of the Government, the local authorities, or any private establishments whatsoever, than if the same merchandise or articles of commerce had been imported in vessels of the United States of America.

ARTICLE IV.

It is understood that the stipulations contained in the two preceding Articles, are, to their full extent, applicable to Russian vessels, and their cargoes arriving in the ports of the Empire of Russia, whether the said vessels clear directly from the ports of the country to which they respectively belong, or from the ports of any other foreign country.

ARTICLE V.

All kinds of merchandise and articles of commerce, which may be lawfully exported from the ports of the United States of America in national vessels may, also, be exported therefrom in Russian vessels, without paying other or higher duties or charges, of whatever kind or denomination, levied in the name, or to the profit of the Government, the local authorities, or of any private establishments whatsoever, than if the same merchandise or articles of commerce had been exported in vessels of the United States of America. And, reciprocally, all kinds of merchandise and articles of commerce, which may be lawfully exported therefrom in vessels of the United States of America, without paying other or higher duties or charges of whatever kind or denomination, levied in the name, or to the profit of the Government, the local authorities, or of any private establishment whatsoever, than if the same merchandise or articles of commerce had been exported in Russian vessels.

ARTICLE VI.

No higher or other duties shall be imposed on the importation into the United States, of any article, the produce or manufacture of Russia; and no higher or other duties shall be imposed on the importation into the Empire of Russia, of any article, the produce or manufacture of the United States, than are, or shall be, payable on the like article, being the produce or manufacture of the United States, or of Russia, to, or from the ports of the United States, or to, or from the ports of the Russian Empire, which shall not equally extend to all other nations.

ARTICLE VII.

It is expressly understood that the preceding Articles II, III, IV, V, and VI, shall not be applicable to the coastwise navigation of either of the two countries, which each of the high contracting parties reserves exclusively to itself.

ARTICLE VIII.

The two contracting parties shall have the liberty of having, in their respective ports, Consuls, Vice-Consuls, Agents and commissaries of their own appointment, who shall enjoy the same privileges and powers, as those of the most favored nations; but if any such Consul shall exercise commerce they shall be submitted to the same laws and usages to which the private individuals of their Nation are submitted, in the same laws and usages to which the private individuals of their Nation are submitted, in the same place.

The Consuls, Vice-Consuls, and Commercial Agents shall have the right, as such, to sit as judges and arbitrators in such differences as may arise between the Captains and crews of the vessels belonging to the nation whose interests are committed to their charge, without the interference of the local authorities, unless the conduct of the crews, or of the captain should disturb the order of the tranquillity of the country; or the said Consuls, Vice-Consuls, or Commercial Agents should require their assistance to cause their decisions to be carried into effect or supported. It is, however, understood, that this species of judgement or arbitration shall not deprive the contending parties of the right they have to resort, on their return, to the judicial authority of their Country.

ARTICLE IX.

The said Consuls, Vice-Consuls, and Commercial Agents, are authorized to require the assistance of the local authorities, for the search, arrest, detention and imprisonment of the deserters from ships of war and merchant vessels of their country. For this purpose they shall apply to the competent tribunals, judges, and officer, and shall in writing demand said deserters, proving by the exhibition of the registers of the vessels, the rolls of the crews, or by other official documents that such individuals formed part of the crews; and, this reclamation being thus substantiated, the surrender shall not be refused.

Such deserters, when arrested, shall be placed at the disposal of the said Consuls, Vice-Consuls, or Commercial Agents, and may be confined in the public prisons, at the request and cost of those who shall claim them, in order to be detained until the time when they shall be restored to the vessels to which they belonged, or sent back to their own country by a vessel of the same nation or any other vessel whatsoever. But if not sent back within four months, from the day of their arrest, they shall be set at liberty, and shall not be again arrested for the same cause.

However, if the deserter should be found to have committed any crime or offense, his surrender may be delayed until the tribunal before which his case shall be depending shall have pronounced it's sentence, and such sentence shall have been carried into effect.

ARTICLE X.

The citizens and subjects of each of the high contracting parties shall have power to dispose of their personal goods within the jurisdiction of the other, be testament, donation, or otherwise, and their representatives, being citizens or subjects of the other party shall succeed to their said personal goods, whether by testament or ab intestato, and may take posession thereof, either by themselves, or by other acting for them, and dispose of the same, at will, paying to the profit of the respective Governments such as dues only as the inhabitants of the country wherein the said goods are, shall be subject to pay in like cases. And in case of the absence of the representative, such care shall be taken of the said goods, as would be taken of the goods of a native of the same country, in like case, until the lawful owner may take measures for receiving them. And if a question should arise among several claimants, as to which of them said goods belong, the same shall be decided finally by the laws and judges of the land wherein the said goods are. And where, on the death of any person holding real estate, within the territories of one of the high con-tracting parties, such real estate would by the laws of the land, descend on a citizen or subject of the other party, who by reason of alienage may be in-capable of holding it, he shall be allowed the time fixed by the laws of the country, and in case the laws of the country, actually in force may not have fixed any such time, he shall then be allowed a reasonable time to sell such real estate and to withdraw and export proceed without molestation, and paying to the profit of the respective Governments, any other dues than those to which the inhabitants of the country wherein said real estate is situated, shall be subject to pay, in like cases. But this Article shall not derogate, in any manner, from the force of the laws already published, or which may hereafter be published by His Majesty the Emperor of all the Russias: to prevent the emigration of his subjects.

ARTICLE XI.

If either party shall, hereafter, grant to any other nation, any particular favor in navigation or commerce, it shall, immediately, become common to the other party, freely, where it is freely granted to such other nation, or on yielding the same compensation, when the grant is conditional.

ARTICLE XII.

The present treaty, of which the effect shall extend, in like manner, to the Kingdom of Poland, so far as the same may be applicable thereto, shall continue in force until the first day of January, in the year of our Lord one thousand Eight hundred and Thirty nine, and if, one year before that day, one of the high contracting parties, shall not have announced to the other, by an official notification, it's intention to arrest the operation thereof, this treaty shall remain obligatory one year beyond that day, and so on until the expiration of the year which shall commence after the date of a similar notification.

ARTICLE XIII.

The present Treaty shall be approved and ratified by the President of the United States of America, by and with the advice and consent of the Senate of the said States, and by His Majesty the Emperor of all the Russias; and the ratifications shall be exchanged in the City of Washington within the space of one year, or sooner if possible. In faith whereof, the respective Plenipotentiaries have signed the present treaty in duplicate and affixed thereto the seal of their arms.

Done at St. Petersburg eighteenth <u>sixth</u> December, in the year of Grace, One thousand Eight hundred and thirty two.

JAMES BUCHANAN.   (SEAL.)
(SEAL.)   CHARLES COMTE DE NESSELRODE.

SEPARATE ARTICLE

Certain relations of proximity and anterior engagements, having rendered it necessary for the Imperial Government to regulate the commercial relations of Russia with Prussia and the Kingdoms of Sweden and Norway by special stipulations are, in no manner connected with the existing regulations for foreign commerce in general; the two high contracting parties, wishing to remove from their commercial relations every kind of ambiguity or subject of discussion, have agreed, that the special stipulations granted to the commerce of Prussia, and of Sweden and Norway, in consideration of equivalent advantages granted in these countries, by the one to the commerce of the Kingdome of Poland, and by the other to that of the Grand Ducy of Finland, shall not, in any case, be invoked in favor of the relations of commerce and navigation, sanctioned between the two high contracting parties by the present Treaty.

The present Separate Article shall have the same force and value as if it were inserted, word for word, in the Treaty signed this day, and shall be ratified at the same time.

In faith whereof, we, the undersigned, by virtue of our respective full powers, have signed the present Separate Article, and affixed thereto the seals of our arms.

Done at St. Petersburg, the $\frac{6}{18}$ of December, in the year of Grace, one Thousand Eight hundred & thirty two.

JAMES BUCHANAN,
CHARLES COMTE DE NESSELRODE.

APPENDIX 17

RUSSO-AMERICAN CONVENTION CONCERNING
RIGHTS OF NEUTRALS AT SEA, JULY 22, 1854

The United States of America and His Majesty the Emperor of all the Russias, equally animated with a desire to maintain, and to preserve all from harm, the relations of good understanding which have at all times so happily subsisted between themselves, as also between the inhabitants of their respective States, have mutually agreed to perpetuate, by means of a formal convention, the principles of the rights of neutrals at sea, which they recognize as indispensable conditions of all freedom of navigation and maritime trade. For this purpose, the President of the United States has conferred full powers on William L. Marcy, Secretary of State of the United States; and his Majesty the Emperor of all the Russias has conferred like powers on Mr. Edward de Stoeckl, Counsellor of State, Knight of the Orders of St. Anne of the 2nd Class, of St. Stanislas, of the 4th Class, and of the Iron Crown of Austria, of the 3rd Class, His Majesty's Charge d'Affaires near the Government of the United States of America: and said Plenipotentiaries, having exchanged their full powers found in good and due form, have concluded and signed the following Articles:

ARTICLE I.

The two High and Contracting Parties recognize as permanent and immutable the following principles, to wit:

1st That free ships make free goods that is to say, that the effects or goods belonging to subjects or citizens of a Power or State at war are free from capture and confiscation when found on board of neutral vessels, with the exception of articles contraband of war.

2nd That the property of neutrals on board an enemy's vessel is not subject to confiscation, the same contraband be of war. They engage to apply these principles to the commerce and navigation of all such Powers and States as shall consent to adopt them on their part as permanent and immutable.

ARTICLE II.

The two High Contracting Parties reserve themselves to come to an ulterior understanding as circumstances may require, with regard to the application and extension to be given, if there be any cause for it, to the principles laid down in the 1st Article. But they declare from this time that they will take the stipulations contained in said Article I., as a rule, whenever it shall become a question, to judge of the rights of neutrality.

Source: Mallory, William M. comp. *Treaties, Conventions, International Acts, Protocols and Agreements Between the United States of America and Other Powers, 1776-1909* (Washington: Government Printing Office, 1910) II, pp. 1,519-21.

ARTICLE III.

It is agreed by the High Contracting Parties that all Nations which shall or may consent to accede the rules of the first Article of this convention, by a formal declaration stipulating to observe them, shall enjoy the rights resulting from such accession as they shall be enjoyed and observed by the two Powers signing this convention. They shall mutually communicate to each other the results of the steps which may be taken on the subject.

ARTICLE IV.

The present convention shall be approved and ratified by the President of the United States of America, by and with the advice and consent of the Senate of said States, and by His Majesty the Emperor of all the Russias, and the ratification of the same shall be exchanged at Washington within the period of ten months, counting from this day, or sooner, if possible.

In faith whereof, the respective Plenipotentiaries have signed the present convention, in duplicate, and thereto affixed the seal of their arms.

Done at Washington the twenty second day of July, the year of grace 1854.

W. L . MARCY

EDOUARD STOECKL.

APPENDIX 18

CONVENTION CEDING ALASKA, MARCH 30, 1867

The United States of America and His Majesty the Emperor of all the Russias, being desirous of strengthening, if possible, the good understanding which exists between them, have, for that purpose, appointed as their Plenipotentiaries: the President of the United States, William H. Seward, Secretary of State; and His Majesty the Emperor of all the Russias, the Privy Counsellor Edward de Stoeckl, his Envoy Extraordinary and Minister Plenipotentiary to the United States.

And the said Plenipotentiaries, having exchanged their full powers, which were found to be in due form, have agreed upon and signed the following articles:

ARTICLE I.

His Majesty the Emperor of all the Russias agrees to cede to the United States by this convention, immediately upon the exchange of the ratifications thereof, all the territory and dominion now possessed by his said Majesty on the continent of America and in the adjacent islands, the same being contained within the geographical limits herein set forth, to wit: The eastern limit is the line of demarcation between the Russian and the British possessions in North America, as established by the convention between Russia and Great Britain, of February 28-16, 1825 and described in Articles III and IV of said convention, in the following terms:

"Commencing from the southernmost point of the island called Prince of Wales Island, which point lies in the parallel of 54 degrees 40 minutes latitude, and between the 131st and 133rd degree of west longitude, (meridian of Greenwich) the said line shall ascend to the north along the channel called Portland channel, as far as the point of the continent where it strikes the 56th degree of north latitude; from this last mentioned point, the line of demarcation shall follow the summit of the mountains situated parallel to the coast as far as the point of intersection of the 141st degree of west longitude, (of the same meridian); and finally, from the said point of intersection, the said meridian line of the 141st degree, in its prolongation as far as the Frozen ocean.

"IV. With reference to the line of demarcation laid down in the preceding article, it is understood--

---

Source: Mallory, William M. comp. *Treaties, Conventions, International Acts, Protocols and Agreements Between the United States of America and Other Powers, 1776-1909* (Washington: Government Printing Office, 1910) II, pp. 1,521-24.

"1st That the island called Prince of Wales Island shall belong wholly to Russia," (now, by this cession, to the United States.)

"2nd That whenever the summit of the mountains which extend in a direction parallel to the coast from the 56th degree of north latitude to the point of intersection of the 141st degree of west longitude shall prove to be at the distance of more than ten marine leagues from the ocean, the limit between the British possessions and the line of coast which is to belong to Russia as above mentioned (that is to say, the limit to the possessions ceded by this convention) shall be formed by a line parallel to the winding of the coast, and which shall never exceed the distance of ten marine leagues therefrom."

The western limit within which the territories and dominion conveyed, are contained, passes through a point in Behring's straits on the parallel of sixty-five degrees thirty minutes north latitude, at its intersection by the meridian which passes midway between the island of Ratmanoff, or Noonarbook, and proceeds thence in a course nearly southwest, through Behring's straits and Behring's sea, so as to pass midway between the northwest point of the island of St. Lawrence and the southeast point of Cape Choukotski, to the meridian of one hundred and seventy-two west longitude; thence, from the intersection of that meridian, in a southwesterly direction, so as to pass midway between the island of Attou and the Copper island of the Kormandorski couplet or group, in the degrees of west longitude, so as to include in the territory conveyed the whole of the Aleutian islands east of that meridian.

ARTICLE II.

In the cession of territory and dominion made by the preceding article, are included the right of property in all public lots and squares, vacant lands, and all public buildings, fortifications, barracks, and other edifices which are not private individual property. It is, however, understood and agreed, that the churches which have been built in the ceded territory by the Russian government, shall remain the property of such members of the Greek Oriental Church resident in the territory, as may choose to workship therein. Any Government archives, papers and documents relative to the territory and dominion aforesaid, which may now be existing there, will be left in the possession of the agent of the United States; but an authenticated copy of such of them as may be required, will be, at all times, given by the United States to the Russian government, or to such Russian officers or subjects as they may apply for.

ARTICLE III.

The inhabitants of the ceded territory, according to their choice, reserving their natural allegiance, may return to Russia within three years; but if they should prefer to remain in the ceded territory, they, with the exception of uncivilized native tribes, shall be admitted to the enjoyment of all the rights, advantages, and immunities of citizens of the United States, and shall be maintained and protected in the free enjoyment of their liberty, property, and religion. The uncivilized tribes will be subject to such laws and regulations as the United States, may from time to time, adopt in regard to aboriginal tribes of that country.

ARTICLE IV.

His Majesty, the Emperor of all the Russias shall appoint, with convenient dispatch, an agent or agents for the purpose of formally delivering to a similar agent or agents appointed on behalf of the United States, the territory, dominion, property, dependencies and appurtenances which are ceded as above, and for doing any other act which may be necessary in regard thereto. But the cession, with the right of immediate possession, is nevertheless to be deemed complete and absolute on the exchange of ratifications, without waiting for such formal delivery.

ARTICLE V.

Immediately after the exchange of the ratifications of this convention, any fortifications or military posts which may be in the ceded territory, shall be delivered to the agent of the United States, and any Russian troops which may be in the Territory shall be withdrawn as soon as may be reasonably and conveniently practicable.

ARTICLE VI.

In consideration of the cession aforesaid, the United States agree to pay at the Treasury in Washington, within ten months after the exchange of the ratifications of this convention, to the diplomatic representative or other agent of his Majesty the Emperor of all the Russias, duly authorized to receive the same, seven million two hundred thousand dollars in gold. The cession of territory and dominion herein made is hereby declared to be free and unincumbered by any associated companies, whether corporate or incorporate, Russian or any other, or by any parties, except merely private individual property-holders; and the cession hereby made, conveys all the rights, franchises, and privileges now belonging to Russia in the said territory or dominion, and appurtenances thereto.

ARTICLE VII.

When this convention shall have been duly ratified by the President of the United States, by and with the advice and consent of the Senate, on the one part, and on the other by His Majesty the Emperor of all the Russias, the ratifications shall be exchanged at Washington within three months from the date hereof, or sooner, if possible.

In faith whereof, the respective plenipotentiaries have signed this convention, and thereto affixed the seals of their arms.

Done at Washington, the thirtieth day of March in the year of our Lord one thousand eight hundred and sixty-seven.

EDOUARD DE STOECKL.
WILLIAM H. SEWARD.

GLOSSARIES

GLOSSARY OF TERMS*

Baidara. Open boat made of seal or walrus hide (lavtak) stretched over a light wooden framework.

Baidarka. A kayak. Smaller than a baidara; enclosed, with open hatches for one, two or three persons.

Baidarshchik. Owner or skilled steersman of a baidara; overseer of a crew or group of baidaras.

Charka. Liquid measure; 10 charkas = 2.16 pints.

Chetvert. Dry measure; 1 chetvert of wheat = 49 pounds.

Chief Manager. Glavnyi pravitel.

Creole. Term used by Russians to refer to a person of mixed Russian and native blood. (The Russian American Company made great efforts to educate, train and employ creoles.)

Feldsher. Physician's assistant; in Alaska feldshers were often the only medical personnel.

Governing Board. Glavnoe pravlenie.

Iasak. A tax paid in furs.

Inorodtsy. Independent, "foreign" natives, usually hostile in Russian America.

Iukola. Fish, generally salmon, which has been split, cleaned and dried for food; a staple in native diet in Siberia and Alaska.

Kalga. Kolosh (Tlingit) term for a native slave.

Kolosh. Tlingit Indians.

Lavtak. Cured seal or walrus hide used to make baidaras and baidarkas.

Marki. Colonial scrip paid to service personnel.

---

*Other foreign and Russian words that occur only once are explained in the text.

Mednovtsy. Copper Indians.

Odinochka. A small administrative post used to arrange barter with natives; can refer to a single log cabin manned by an overseer with two or three assistants.

Ostrog. Fort.

Otdel. Department.

Prikashchik. In Russia originally an official of the prikaz or administrative department; in Alaska a minor official, a special agent employed by the Russian American Company, or the supercargo on a ship.

Promyshlennik. Fur trapper and trader.

Pud. Measure of weight; 1 pud = 36.11 pounds.

R. A. K. Rossiisko-Amerikanskaia Kompaniia (Russian American Company).

Sazhen. Linear measure; 1 sazhen = 7 feet.

Toion. A Yakut word meaning "leader," applied by the Russians to tribal elders of large tribes in both Siberia and Alaska.

Tuzemtsy. Subjugated natives.

Vedro. Measure for liquids or grain; 1 vedro = 2.70 gallons; 12 vedros = 1 barrel (approx.).

Zol. A dry measure; 1 zol = 4.25 grains.

PLACE NAME GLOSSARY

Translations directly from Golovin are given first; current names are then supplied.

Aleksandrovsk = at English Bay

Arkhangel Michael = Saint Michael

Bering Bay = Yakutat Bay

Borka Island = Sedanka Island

Chugach Sound = Prince William Sound

Dobraia Pogoda Mountains = Fairweather Range

Elovka Island = Spruce Island

Elovoi Island = Spruce Island

Georgievsk = Kasilof

Gvosdev Islands = Diomede Islands

Iablonnyi Islands = Apple Islands (Middle Islands)

Kakhna River = Kenai River

Kirinsk River = Sawmill Creek

Klokachev Sound = Salisbury Sound

Koloshenko Archipelago = Alexander Archipelago

Komandorskie Islands = Commander Islands

Konstantin and Elena (Constantine and Helena) = Constantine Harbor

Konstantin redoubt = at Constantine Harbor

Kuskovym River = Kuskokwim River

Kwikhpak River = Yukon River

Lebiazhe Lake = Swan Lake

Lesnoi Island = Woody Island

Mikhailovsk redoubt = Saint Michael

New Albion = California

New Arkhangel = Sitka

Nikolaevsk = Kenai

Ozersk redoubt = The Redoubt

Pavlovsk = Kodiak

Pavlovsk Harbor = Saint Paul Harbor

Plavezhnoi Lake = Tazlina Lake

St. Dionysius = Wrangell

Serebriannikov Bay = Silver Bay

Shumshu Island = Shumushu Island

Simeonovsk = (Cape Suckling-Yakataga area)

Sinnakh Islands = Sanak Islands

Sitak Island = Baranof Island

Slava Rossii = Glory of Russia

Tlieshitna River = Tazlina River

Ugiiak Island = Fairway Rock

Ukamok Island = Chirikof Island

Ukibok Island = King Island

Uziak Island = Sledge Island

Voskresensk = Resurrection Bay (Seward?)

BIBLIOGRAPHY

BIBLIOGRAPHY

BIBLIOGRAPHIES

Fuller, Grace H. *ALASKA: A LIST OF SELECTED REFERENCES*. Washington, D.C., 1943.
------. *ALEUTIAN ISLANDS: A LIST OF REFERENCES*. Washington, D.C., 1943.
Kerner, Robert J. *NORTHEASTERN ASIA: A SELECTED BIBLIOGRAPHY*. 2 vols. Berkeley, 1939.
Lada-Mocarski, Valerian. *BIBLIOGRAPHY OF BOOKS ON ALASKA PUBLISHED BEFORE 1868*. New Haven, Conn., 1969.
Phillips, Philip L. *ALASKA AND THE NORTHWEST PART OF NORTH AMERICA, 1588-1898: MAPS IN THE LIBRARY OF CONGRESS*. Washington, D.C., 1898.
U.S., Coast and Geodetic Survey. *PACIFIC COAST PILOT: COAST AND ISLANDS OF ALASKA*. Second Series. Washington, D.C., 1879 [Bibliography (pp.225-375) compiled by W.H. Dall and Marcus Baker].
Wickersham, James. *A BIBLIOGRAPHY OF ALASKAN LITERATURE, 1724-1924*. Cordova, Alaska, 1927.

BOOKS

(Afonsky, George) Gregory, Bishop of Sitka and Alaska. *A HISTORY OF THE ORTHO-DOX CHURCH IN ALASKA, 1794-1917*. Kodiak, 1977.
------. *SITKA AND ST. MICHAEL'S CATHEDRAL*. Kodiak, 1974.
Alekseev, Aleksandr I. *ILIA GAVRILOVICH VOZNESENSKII, 1816-1871*. Moscow, 1977.
------. *RUSSKIE GEOGRAFICHESKIE ISSLEDOVANIIA NA DALNEM VOSTOKE I V SEVERNOI AMERIKE XIX-NACHALO XX* v. Moscow, 1976
------. *SUDBA RUSSKOI AMERIKI* [The Fate of Russian America]. Magadan, U.S.S.R. 1975.
Andreev, Aleksandr K., ed. *RUSSKIE OTKRYTIIA V TIKHOM OKEANE I SEVERNOI AMER-IKE V XVIII VEKE*. Moscow-Leningrad, 1948. [Translated by Carl Ginsburg. *Russian Discoveries in the Pacific and in North America in the Eighteenth and Nineteenth Centuries*. Ann Arbor, 1952]
Andrews, Clarence L. *SITKA: THE CHIEF FACTORY OF THE RUSSIAN AMERICAN COMPANY*. Caldwell, Idaho, 1945.
------. *THE STORY OF ALASKA*. Caldwell, Idaho, 1938.
------. *THE STORY OF SITKA*. Seattle, [1922].

Bancroft, Hubert H. *HISTORY OF ALASKA, 1730-1855.* San Francisco, 1886.
------. *HISTORY OF BRITISH COLUMBIA, 1792-1887.* San Francisco, 1887.
------. *HISTORY OF CALIFORNIA.* 7 vols. San Francisco, 1886-90.
------. *HISTORY OF THE NORTHWEST COAST.* 2 vols. San Francisco, 1884-86.
Beechey, Frederick W. *NARRATIVE OF A VOYAGE TO THE PACIFIC AND BEERING'S STRAIT.* 2 vols. London, 1831.
Belcher, *Sir* Edward. *NARRATIVE OF A VOYAGE ROUND THE WORLD, PERFORMED IN HER MAJESTY'S SHIP* SULPHUR, *DURING THE YEARS 1836-1842.* London, 1843.
Beretti, N.N. *NA KRAINEM SEVERO-VOSTOKE* [*In the Northeastern Regions*]. Vladivostok, 1929.
Black, James J. *NOTES ON THE RUSSIAN-AMERICAN COMPANY'S TRADING POSTS.* [San Francisco, 1867].
Bolkhovitinov, Nikolai N. *RUSSKO-AMERICANSKIE OTNOSHENIIA, 1815-1832* [*Russian-American Relations, 1815-1832*]. Moscow, 1975.
------. *STANOVLENIE RUSSKO-AMERIKANSKIKH OTNOSHENII, 1775-1815.* Moscow, 1966. [Translated by Elena Levin. *The Beginnings of Russian-American Relations, 1775-1815.* Cambridge, Mass., 1975.]
Brooks, Alfred H. *THE GEOGRAPHY AND GEOLOGY OF ALASKA.* U.S. Geological Survey Paper 45, House Document 201, 59th Cong., 1st Sess., vol. 66. Washington, D.C., 1906.
Chevigny, Hector. *RUSSIAN AMERICA: THE GREAT ALASKAN VENTURE, 1741-1867.* New York, 1965.
Dall, William H. *ALASKA AND ITS RESOURCES.* Boston, 1897.
DOKLAD KOMITETA OB USTROISTVYE RUSSKIKH AMERIKANSKIKH KOLONII [*Report of the Committee on the Organization of the Russian American Colonies*]. St. Petersburg, 1863. [First English translation in prepartion by Oregon Historical Society for *North Pacific Studies Series*.]
Duflot de Mofras, Eugene. *EXPLORATION DU TERRITOIRE DE L'OREGON, DES CALIFORNIES ET DE LA MER VERMEILLE.* 2 vols. & atlas. Paris, 1844.
Fedorova, Svetlana G. *RUSSKOE NASELENIE ALIASKI I KALIFORNII.* Moscow, 1971. [Translated by Richard Pierce and Alton Donnelly. *The Russian Population in Alaska and California, Late 18th Century-1867.* Kingston, Ontario, 1973.
Fisher, Raymond H. *RECORDS OF THE RUSSIAN-AMERICAN COMPANY, 1802, 1817-1867.* Washington, 1971.
Gibson, James R. *IMPERIAL RUSSIA IN FRONTIER AMERICA: THE CHANGING GEOGRAPHY OF SUPPLY OF RUSSIAN AMERICA, 1784-1867.* New York, 1976.
Golder, Frank A. *RUSSIAN EXPANSION ON THE PACIFIC, 1641-1850.* Cleveland, 1914.
Holmberg, Heinrich J. *ETNOGRAPISCHE SKIZZEN UBER DE VÖLKER DES RUSSISCHEN AMERIKA* [*Ethnographic Outlines of the People of Russian America*]. [n.p.], [1854].
ISTORII ROSSIISKO-AMERIKANSKOI KOMPANII (SBORNIK DOCUMENTALNYKH MATERIALOV). Krasnoiarsk, U.S.S.R., 1957. [Translated by Marina Ramsay. *Documents on the History of the Russian-American Company.* Kingston, Ontario, 1976.]
Khlebnikov, Kyrill T. *COLONIAL RUSSIAN AMERICA: KYRILL T. KHLEBNIKOV'S REPORTS, 1817-1832.* Translated by Basil Dmytryshyn and E.A.P. Crownhart-Vaughan. Portland, 1976. [Translation from: "*ZAPISKI K. KHLEBNIKOVA, O AMERIKE,*" Supplement to *MORSKOI SBORNIK,* St. Petersburg, 1861.]
Kinzhalov, Rostislav V., ed. *KULTURA I BYT NARODOV AMERIKI* [*Culture and Life of the Natives of America*]. Leningrad, 1967.

Kittlitz, Friedrich Heinrich von. *DENKWÜRDIGKEITEN EINER REISE NACH DEM RUS-SISCHEN AMERIKA* [*Memorable Occurances on a Journey to Russian America*]. Gotha, 1858.

Kushner, Howard I. *CONFLICT ON THE NORTHWEST COAST: AMERICAN-RUSSIAN RIVALRY IN THE PACIFIC NORTHWEST, 1790-1867.* Westport, Conn., 1975.

Liapunova, Roza G. *OCHERKI PO ETNOGRAFII ALEUTOV, KONETS XVIII-PERVAIA POLO-VINA XIX v* [*Essays on the Ethnography of the Aleuts from the Late 18th Century to the First Half of the 19th*]. Leningrad, 1975.

Lütke, Fedor P. *PUTESHESTVIE VOKRUG SVETA. . .NA VOENNOM SHLIUPE* SENIAVINE [*Voyage Around the World. . .on the Sloop* Seniavin]. St. Petersburg, 1835.

Markov, Aleksandr I. *RUSSKIE NA VOSTOCHNOM OKEANE.* Moscow, 1849. [Trans-lated by Ivan Petroff. *The Russians on the Pacific Ocean*, Los Angeles, 1955.]

MATERIALY DLIA ISTORII EKSPEDITSII AKADEMII NAUK V XVIII I XIX vv [*Materials Pertaining to the History of the Expeditions of the Academy of Sciences in the 18th and 19th Centuries*]. Moscow-Leningrad, 1940.

MATERIALY DLIA ISTORII RUSSKIKH ZASELENII PO BEREGAM VOSTOCHNAGO OKEANA [*Mate-rials Pertaining to the History of Russian Settlements Along the Shores of the Pacific Ocean*]. Supplement to *MORSKOI SBORNIK*. St. Petersburg, 1861.

Ministerstvo Oborony SSSR. Voenno-Morskoi Flot. *BOLSHOI ATLAS OKEANOV: TIKHII OKEAN* [*The Great Atlas of the Oceans: The Pacific Ocean*]. Moscow, 1974.

Ogden, Adele. *THE CALIFORNIA SEA OTTER TRADE, 1784-1848.* Berkeley and Los Angeles, 1941.

Okladnikov, Aleksei P. *PO ALIASKE I ALEUTSKIM OSTROVAM* [*Through Alaska and the Aleutian Islands*]. Novosibirsk, 1976.

Okun, Semen B. *ROSSIISKO-AMERIKANSKAIA KOMPANIIA.* Moscow-Leningrad, 1939. [Translated by Carl Ginsburg. *The Russian American Company.* Cambridge, Mass., 1951.]

OTCHETY ROSSIISKO-AMERIKANSKOI KOMPANII [*Reports of the Russian American Com-pany*]. St. Petersburg, 1843-65.

THE PACIFIC: RUSSIAN SCIENTIFIC INVESTIGATIONS. Leningrad, 1926.

PEOPLE AND PELTS: SELECTED PAPERS OF THE SECOND NORTH AMERICAN FUR TRADE CON-FERENCE. Edited by Malvina Bolus. Winnipeg, 1972.

Pilder, Hans. *DIE RUSSISCH-AMERIKANISCHE HANDELS-KOMPANIE BIS 1825* [*The Rus-sian-American Trading Company to 1825*]. Berlin, 1914.

[Politovskii, V.G.]. *KRATKOE ISTORICHESKOE OBOZRENIE OBRAZOVANII I DEISTVII ROSSIISKO-AMERIKANSKOI KOMPANII S SAMOGO NACHALA UCHREZHDENIIA ONOI DO NASTOIASHCHEGO VREMENI* [*A Brief Historical Survey of the Founding and Activities of the Russian American Company from the very Beginning of Its Establishment to the Present Time*]. St. Petersburg, 1861.

Ray, Dorothy J. *THE ESKIMOS OF BERING STRAIT, 1650-1898.* Seattle, 1975.

Sachot, Octave. *LA SIBERIE ORIENTALE, L'AMERIQUE RUSSE ET LES REGIONS PO-LAIRES: RECITS DES VOYAGES.* Paris, 1875.

Sarafian, Winston L. "*RUSSIAN-AMERICAN COMPANY EMPLOYEE POLICIES AND PRAC-TICES, 1799-1867.*" Ph.D. dissertation, UCLA, 1970.

Sherwood, Morgan B. *EXPLORATION OF ALASKA 1865-1900.* New Haven, Conn., 1965.

Shur, Leonid A.K. *BEREGAM NOVOGO SVETA* [*To the Shores of the New World*]. Moscow, 1971.

Simpson, *Sir* George. *NARRATIVE OF A JOURNEY ROUND THE WORLD DURING THE YEARS 1841 AND 1842.* 2 vols. London, 1847.

Smith, Barbara. *PRELIMINARY SURVEY OF DOCUMENTS IN THE ARCHIVES OF THE RUSSIAN ORTHODOX CHURCH IN ALASKA.* Boulder, Colo., 1974.

Tebenkov, Mikhail D. *ATLAS SEVEROZAPADNYKH BEREGOV AMERIKI.* [St. Petersburg], 1852.

Tikhmenev, Petr A. *ISTORICHESKOE OBOZRENIE OBRAZOVANIIA ROSSIISKO-AMERIKANSKOI KOMPANII.* 2 vols. St. Petersburg, 1861, 1863. [Translated by Dmitri Krenov. *"Historical Review of the Formation of the Russian-American Company."* Typescript. Seattle, 1939.]

U.S., Department of State. *GEOGRAPHICAL NOTES UPON RUSSIAN AMERICA.* Washington, D.C., 1868.

VanStone, James W., ed. *A.F. KASHEVAROV'S COASTAL EXPLORATIONS IN NORTHWEST ALASKA, 1838.* Translated by David Kraus. Vol. 69. Fieldiana: Anthropology. Chicago, 1977.

Vilar, E. Vila. *LOS RUSOS EN AMERICA.* Seville, 1966.

Volkov, F.K. and S.I. Rudenko. *ETNOGRAFICHESKIE KOLLEKTSII IZ BYVSHYKH ROSSIISKO-AMERIKANSKIKH VLADENII* [*The Ethnographic Collections from the Former Russian American Possessions*]. St. Petersburg, 1910.

Wrangell, Ferdinand P. *STATISTISCHE UND ETNOGRAPFISCHE NACHRICHTEN UBER DIE RUSSISCHEN BESITZUNGEN AN DER NORDWESTKUSTE VON AMERIKA* [*Statistical and Ethnographic Reports About the Russian Occupation of the Northwest Coast of America*]. St. Petersburg, 1839.

Zagoskin, Lavrentii A. *PESHEKHODNAIA OPIS CHASTI RUSSKIKH VLADENII V AMERIKE.* St. Petersburg, 1847-48. [Translated by Penelope Rainey. *Lieutenant Zagoskin's Travels in Russian America, 1842-1844.* edited by Henry M. Michael. Toronto, 1967.]

[Zavalishin, Dmitrii I.] *RUSSIISKO-AMERIKANSKAIA KOMPANIIA.* Moscow, 1865.

ARTICLES

Allen, Robert V. *"Alaska Before 1867 in Soviet Literature,"* QUARTERLY JOURNAL OF THE LIBRARY OF CONGRESS 23:3 (1966): 243-50.

Basanoff, V. *"Archives of the Russian Church in Alaska in the Library of Congress,"* PACIFIC HISTORICAL REVIEW 2:1(1933): 72-84.

Blomkvist, E.E. *"Risunki I.B. Voznesenskogo (ekspeditsiia 1839-1849 godov),"* SBORNIK MUZEIA ANTROPOLOGII I ETNOGRAFII, t. 13 (1951). [Translated by Basil Dmytryshyn and E.A.P. Crownhart-Vaughan. *"A Russian Scientific Expedition to California and Alaska, 1839-1849,"* OREGON HISTORICAL QUARTERLY 73:2(1972): 101-170.]

Doroshin, P.P. *"Is zapisok vedennykh v Russkoi Amerike,"* GORNYI ZHURNAL No.3 (1866): 365-401.

Gibson, James R. *"Bostonians and Muscovites on the Northwest Coast, 1788-1841,"* in THE WESTERN SHORE: OREGON COUNTRY ESSAYS HONORING THE AMERICAN REVOLUTION, edited by Thomas Vaughan. Portland, 1975.

Gilbert, Benjamin F. *"Arts and Sciences in Alaska: 1784-1910,"* JOURNAL OF THE WEST 1:2(1962): 135-48.

Golder, F.A. *"Mining in Alaska before 1867,"* WASHINGTON HISTORICAL QUARTERLY 7:3(1916): 233-38.

Golovin, Pavel N. *"Ueber die russischen Colonien an der Nordwestküste von Amerika,"* ARCHIV FUR WISSENSCHAFTLICHE KUNDE VON RUSSLAND 22(1866): 47-70.

Kennicott, Robert. *"Russian America,"* ATLANTIC MONTHLY (1867): 731-50.

Lain, Bobby D. *"The Decline of Russian America's Colonial Society,"* WESTERN HISTORICAL QUARTERLY 7:2(1976): 143-53.

McPherson, Hallie M. *"The Interest of William McKendree Gwin in the Purchase of Alaska, 1854-1861,"* PACIFIC HISTORICAL REVIEW 3:1(1934): 28-38.

Ostenstad, James W. *"A Lucrative Contract: The HBC and the Pacific Ice Trade,"* THE BEAVER (1977): 36-40.

Saul, Norman E. *"Beverley C. Sanders and the Expansion of American Trade with Russia, 1853-1855,"* MARYLAND HISTORICAL MAGAZINE 67:2(1972): 156-70.

Sherwood, Morgan B. *"Science in Russian America, 1741 to 1865,"* PACIFIC NORTHWEST QUARTERLY 58:1(1967): 33-39.

Stepanova, M.V. *"I.G. Voznesenskii i etnograficheskoe izuchenie Severo-Zapadna Ameriki,"* IZVESTIIA VSESOIUZNOGO GEOGRAFICHESKOGO OBSHCHESTVA 76:5(1944): 277-81.

VanStone, James W. *"Russian Exploration in Interior Alaska: An Extract from the Journal of Andrei Glazunov,"* PACIFIC NORTHWEST QUARTERLY 50:2(1959): 37-47.

INDEX

INDEX

THE END OF RUSSIAN AMERICA
was printed by offset from typescripts
produced by
Wendy Willa Won
in 12 pt. IBM Adjutant and *Courier Italic*
The titling was set in Goudy Oldstyle
by Harrison Typesetting, Inc.
The book was printed on 70# Mountie Matte
text paper by Glass-Dahlstrom Graphic Press
and bound in Crown Linen by
Lincoln & Allen
Designed by
Bruce Taylor Hamilton